W9-BNO-385

AND
STILL
I RISE

Choreographer Bill T. Jones's *We Set Out Early . . . Visibility Was Poor* premieres at the Brooklyn Academy of Music in 1997. Here, it is performed in London.

ALSO BY HENRY LOUIS GATES, JR.

Finding Your Roots:
The Official Companion to the PBS Series

The African Americans:
Many Rivers to Cross, *with Donald Yacavone*

The Henry Louis Gates, Jr. Reader

Life Upon These Shores:
Looking at African American History, 1513–2008

Black in Latin America

Tradition and the Black Atlantic:
Critical Theory in the African Diaspora

Faces of America:
How 12 Extraordinary Americans Reclaimed Their Pasts

In Search of Our Roots:
How 19 Extraordinary African Americans Reclaimed Their Past

Finding Oprah's Roots:
Finding Your Own

The Trials of Phillis Wheatley:
America's First Black Poet and Her Encounters
with the Founding Fathers

The African American Century:
How Black Americans Have Shaped Our Century

Wonders of the African World

Thirteen Ways of Looking at a Black Man

The Norton Anthology of African American Literature,
with Nellie Y. McKay

The Future of the Race, *with Cornel West*

Colored People: A Memoir

Loose Canons: Notes on the Culture Wars

The Signifying Monkey

Figures in Black: Words, Signs, and the "Racial" Self

ecco

An Imprint of HarperCollins*Publishers*

AND
STILL
I RISE

BLACK AMERICA SINCE ML

HENRY LOUIS GATES, JR
AND KEVIN M. BURKE

For Larry Bobo and Marcyliena Morgan
and
Brian and Sharon Burke

AND STILL I RISE. Copyright © 2015 by Henry Louis Gates, Jr., and Kevin M. Burke. All rights reserved. Printed in the United States of America. No part of this book may be used or reproduced in any manner whatsoever without written permission except in the case of brief quotations embodied in critical articles and reviews. For information address HarperCollins Publishers, 195 Broadway, New York, NY 10007.

HarperCollins books may be purchased for educational, business, or sales promotional use. For information please e-mail the Special Markets Department at SPsales@harpercollins.com.

FIRST EDITION

Designed by Suet Yee Chong

Library of Congress Cataloging-in-Publication Data has been applied for.

ISBN 978-0-06-242700-7

15 16 17 18 19   OV/RRD   10 9 8 7 6 5 4 3 2 1

Grant Park, Chicago, IL: President-elect Barack Obama walks across the stage with his family on election night 2008.

(on previous page) A profile view of the Martin Luther King, Jr., Memorial on the National Mall in Washington, DC.

CONTENTS

Martin Luther King, Jr., at home with his wife, Coretta, and their children Yolanda and Martin Luther King III in 1960.

INTRODUCTION

. . . I'm a black ocean, leaping and wide,
Welling and swelling I bear in the tide.

Leaving behind nights of terror and fear
   I rise
Into a daybreak that's wondrously clear
   I rise
Bringing the gifts that my ancestors gave,
I am the dream and the hope of the slave.
   I rise
   I rise
   I rise.

—Maya Angelou, "Still I Rise" from *And Still I Rise* (1978)

A companion book to the PBS series of the same name, *And Still I Rise: Black America Since MLK*, is an illustrated chronology of the last fifty years in African American history and culture, bookended by the climactic moments of the civil rights movement—including the passage of the Voting Rights Act of 1965 and the assassinations of Malcolm X and Martin Luther King, Jr.—and the once unimaginable, and now nearly complete, two-term presidency of Barack H. Obama. More broadly, it is a record of a people whose numbers have nearly doubled since 1970, from twenty-two million to forty-two million, such that if they constituted their own country, its population would be ranked thirty-second in the world. It also is a record of a people whose history-defying rise from bondage to the highest rungs of society, amassing accolades and power, wealth and land, genius and achievement, provides the nation with some of the most heroic strokes of its broader narrative.

At the same time, *And Still I Rise* is the record of divergence—of a childhood poverty rate that remains stubbornly close to what it was the day MLK was assassinated, even as the ranks of the middle and upper classes have swelled; of an unemployment rate that runs nearly double that of the national average; and, as alarming, of a society where the harassment of and distrust between impoverished communities and the police that once galvanized the formation of the Black Panthers in 1966 continue to plague us, with an ever greater number of place names in America seared into memory for the lives there cut short. It is also the record of a people who, in the government's shift from battling poverty to crime over these decades, now comprise more than a third of the US prison population, even if only 13 percent of the larger population. *And*

Still I Rise is a record of a people who have made astonishing progress since the King years but who also continue to confront questions that have persisted in this country since the first slave ships arrived: of whether black lives matter at all.

At the root of this book is a seemingly simple question: What binds African Americans together? Is it the inheritance of memories and experiences from one generation to another? Is it the legacy of a system of laws that, for the majority of American history, drew a color line based on drops of blood? Is it the common cause that has come from fighting for so long for freedom and equality, or the cultural ties that unite a people through the poems, sermons, and songs that speak to their epic struggles? Or, given the sheer diversity and divergence in evidence within black America, especially since 1965, is it still even possible to think of forty-two million people as a unified cultural or social entity at all?

While the documentary series *And Still I Rise* wrestles with these tensions through big and small stories, and through the expertise of some of the finest thinkers in our country, our motivation in fashioning this companion book was to establish the basic plot points of this fifty-year period in a year-by-year chronology of what happened when and where and how events remembered distinctly actually happened alongside others that sometimes sync and at other times clash. Our chronology is in no way exhaustive. It is intended to start a conversation, within generations and between generations.

Put another way, it is a book that illuminates the world that the Civil Rights Movement birthed and enabled, and that its legacy sustained—from affirmative action to the integration of our nation's universities, from the ascent of numerous black mayors in numerous cities to the development of black capitalism and the phenomenal growth of the black middle class, from the domination of popular culture by black artists and performers to the rise of black access to and leadership in any number of fields once closed to the many millions of descendants of slaves.

This is also a chronology of voices. The half century that follows the passage of the Voting Rights Act and the deaths of Malcolm and Martin really was the first period in American history when the country as a whole began to see and hear black people as themselves—because black people insisted upon being seen and heard as themselves. With that unmasking came an evolution at hyperspeed of what we might call "styles of blackness," styles signified not only by dashikis and Afros but also by business suits and designer gowns.

To be sure, these voices are anything but a single chorus singing from the same page. In this same period, the "double consciousness" that W. E. B. Du Bois introduced in *The Souls of Black Folk* (1903) as the defining concept of African American existence began to reveal itself to have fragmented into myriad black identities that refute the very idea of a monolithic "black identity" or of a single entity that we can call "Black America." African Americans may have voted for Barack Obama in overwhelming numbers—twice—but in many real ways, that's where the unified identity ends: African Americans today are as riven by class distinctions just as profoundly (and just as jaggedly) as Americans as a whole are: there is a "1 percent" of African Americans, too.

Of course, these multiple class affiliations have long been in place. In his 1899 field-defining work of sociology, *The Philadelphia Negro*, Du Bois defined four classes in the black community, placing the "well-to-do and educated Negroes" ("the talented tenth") at the top and the "criminals and prostitutes of Seventh and Lombard streets" at the bottom. Du Bois claimed that divisions among these groups was both "natural" and "justified," but that they had remained largely hidden outside of the black community because of the unifying, indeed evil, force of de jure segregation. But once the cataclysmic events of the 1960s happened, and affirmative action enabled the integration of American society in ways scarcely imaginable before the culmination of the Civil Rights Movement, the proverbial cat was out of the bag. The class divisions that Jim Crow (both by law and by tradition) had contained within the race began to emerge, enabled by the pronounced class stratification resulting from affirmative action.

We needn't subscribe to the language of "natural" or "justified" to understand the potency of Du Bois's stratifications. Look at it this way: while Martin Luther King has been sanctified and popularized as the eloquent prophet of racial equality between blacks and whites, he was at least as committed to righting the economic wrongs of the poor. Remember that he was killed the morning after he delivered a speech to striking sanitation workers in Memphis, Tennessee. Race was of great significance, of course—too often still race and poverty are partners—but it wasn't of *singular* significance. MLK understood that the elevation of some blacks to positions of strength and prominence did not mean that all blacks would share in the spoils.

At the same time that we document the last half century of African American history in all of its glory, irony, triumph, and pain and show the ways in which a segment of the black community has enjoyed unparalleled success and opportunity at precisely the same time that the class divide within the black community seems to have become permanent and irrevocable, we look at a concomitant development: how "black" American culture itself has become. The culture with which so many grew up and love so much has been transformed from a largely underground existence, to become both aboveground and inextricably intertwined with mainstream, or "white," culture. One way to think about this is that black culture has become the lingua franca of white American culture. Black culture, back in the day, was something celebrated privately: in barbershops, on black radio programs, awaiting Redd Foxx albums mailed in brown paper bags (seriously!). Now we have hip-hop infusing the language of all teens in this country, black hair products readily available at Target and Walmart, and the trend-setting technology giant Apple snatching up Beats Electronics, founded by none other than Dr. Dre and his partner Jimmy Iovine, for a whopping $3 billion.

The book's chronology begins in the second half of the 1960s with the origins and expansion of the Black Power Movement, which develops in the rural South in the immediate wake of the Voting Rights Act of 1965. In addition to the emergence of this radical political movement, we see the birth of artistic movements such as the Black Arts Movement and blaxploitation, the dramatic realignments wrought by affirmative action, and also eruptions of violence in the Watts Riots (1965) and the revolt in Attica prison (1971), all of which send powerful signals to white America and the world beyond that a new black consciousness is characterized by the empowerment of black people to express their creativity, their intellectual and professional capabilities, and their frustrations at the inequalities that still prevail, and that will continue to do so for decades.

We then move into the 1970s and '80s, a period in which we see an increasing diversity of experience and self-representation. The black middle class booms. Black entertainment becomes more complex and varied. Black athletes come to dominate multiple sporting arenas with both their physical prowess and their intellectual forthrightness (think Muhammad Ali). Black women and feminists move to the fore in the arts and the academy. Black elected officials ascend to the leadership of major US cities (and a handful of black women are even elected to national office). Black political allegiance becomes less reliably Democratic as Ronald Reagan woos some black conservatives with his philosophy of "self-determination." At the same time that these significant moves ahead are being made, once-thriving black neighborhoods are falling apart, devastated by the middle class (both white and black) lighting out for the suburbs, manufacturing leaving the cities, and the severe decline in property values and a tax base. Unbroken, young black (and brown) people of diverse origins create a vibrant new culture in these crumbling inner cities: hip-hop, which begins as a musical language of the city, will grow to become the vernacular for youth culture everywhere. And during this period, Jesse Jackson changes our national political scene, energizing the black electorate and articulating to the country as a whole that the rights and lives of all citizens are at stake in presidential elections.

The 1990s can be characterized as a period in which "cultural wars" erupted in a variety of arenas, even as blacks climbed to heights of success previously unimagined. We see the global adoration of icons such as Oprah Winfrey and Michael Jackson and the emergence of hip-hop as the powerful and contested language of pop culture. We also see the circuslike coverage of the Los Angeles riots, the O.J. Simpson murder trial, and the Senate confirmation hearings for Clarence Thomas's nomination to the US Supreme Court, all of which expose seismic rifts within American society. Other ascents point to how high and how quickly blacks have risen. Black media entrepreneurs, epitomized by Robert Johnson of Black Entertainment Television, begin to take charge of the management of a field that has long profited from the creative talents of blacks. African American Studies, an academic field born out of the struggles and protests of the 1960s, emerges as a force of undeniable intellectual heft and influence as Harvard University (where the authors of this book first met) assembles a "dream team" including Kwame Anthony Appiah, Evelyn Brooks Higginbotham, Cornel West, and William Julius Wilson, and the field as a whole gains prominence in elite research institutions throughout the American academy. The pattern is clear: black success in business, the arts, sports, and academia skyrockets even as millions of black people suffer in bad schools, bad jobs, bad housing, and, increasingly, in the confines of our nation's increasingly plentiful jails and prisons. Racial profiling takes on a new life in the War on Terror, and the calls for social justice and police reform that would serve many in the black community become muffled in the race for homeland security.

In the new millennium, we see the US grappling with gross and increasingly destructive inequalities of income and opportunity, not limited to but certainly felt profoundly, and often in extremis, by African Americans. Hurricane Katrina in 2005 reveals the desperate situation of the nation's poorest and most marginalized citizens, as well as the political disregard in which they are held. Following the 2008 economic crash, African Americans discover that despite odds-defying progress and upward mobility over the last five decades, the wealth disparity between white and black Americans has remained constant since the 1960s. Inner-city schools continue to crumble, though bright spots emerge in organizations like Geoffrey Canada's Harlem Children's Zone, where local solutions take aim at the historic problems that have brought the education of disadvantaged children of color to this low point. African Americans quickly adapt to new technologies and social media, turning Black Twitter into a powerful cultural force that can be employed for entertainment (to catch up on the latest twists of Shonda Rhimes's *Scandal*, for instance) but also for serious causes (to raise voices against an alarming rash of killings of unarmed black people). African American creativity also is on the rise and dominant, as films like *Twelve Years a Slave* and *Selma* and television shows like *Scandal* and *Empire* receive widespread accolades and draw huge black audiences—and cut across class in their appeal.

And almost all of this happened after the historic election in 2008 of Barack Obama as the first African American president of the United States. Obama's election throws the word—the misnomer—*post-racial* into common parlance and is the most dramatic, meaningful lens through which to ask the question that runs throughout this book: What has happened to black America in the wake of the massive societal, political, and cultural changes that have

transpired in the last half century? Has the country moved beyond race, or does race continue to define us, to direct our national narrative, to shape our lives? If "We Shall Overcome" was a refrain of the civil rights movement, "Black Lives Matter" has become a refrain of today's searchers for justice and equality.

As this book brings together pieces of our collective past, every question it answers in terms of dates, names, and places raises more about where we, as a country, are going from here, and how. Maya Angelou, the poet of the people and of presidents, died in 2014, but her words continue to give lyrical voice to the triumphs and defeats, the rises and the falls, that have characterized the story of African Americans in these last fifty years. It is her poem "Still I Rise" that gives this book its name.

Just like moons and like suns,
With the certainty of tides,
Just like hopes springing high,
    Still I'll rise.

Did you want to see me broken?
Bowed head and lowered eyes?
Shoulders falling down like teardrops.
Weakened by my soulful cries . . .

    I rise
    I rise
    I rise.

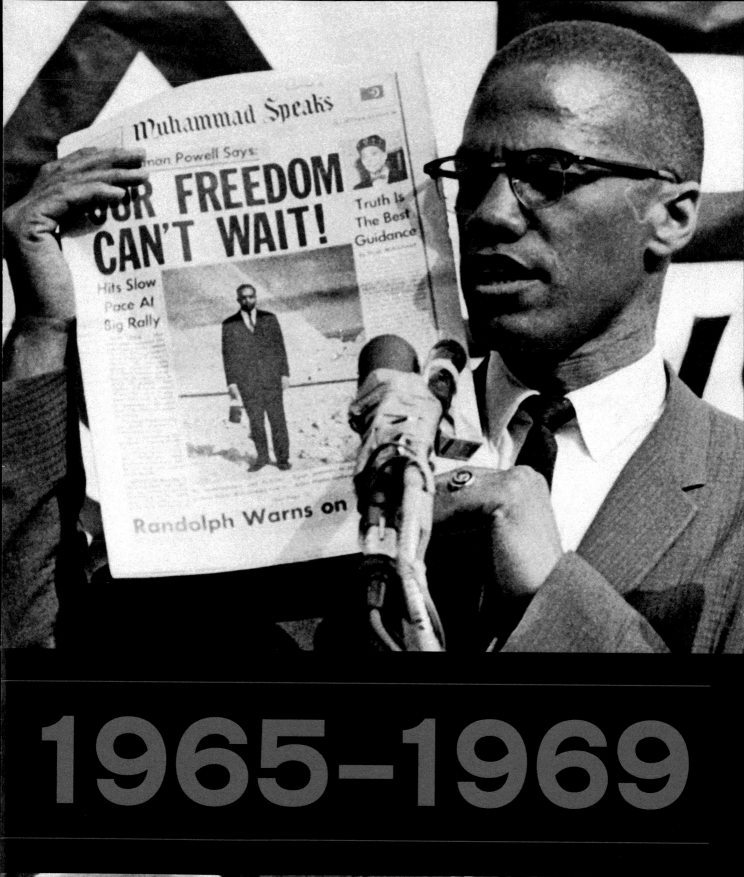

1965–1969

Malcolm X holds up a newspaper during a Black Muslim rally in New York.

1965

JANUARY 2, 1965 At the invitation of local civil rights activists, Rev. Dr. Martin Luther King, Jr., president of the Southern Christian Leadership Conference (SCLC), makes his first visit to Selma, Alabama, where he announces a nonviolent campaign for voting rights to appeal to the state's segregationist governor, George Wallace, and to "arouse the federal government" to action under President Lyndon B. Johnson, who, having signed the Civil Rights Act of 1964 the previous July, is about to begin his first full term in the White House. Drawn up by movement leaders Diane Nash and James Bevel in the wake of the Birmingham church bombing in 1963, Selma will be King's first direct-action campaign since receiving the Nobel Peace Prize in December

President Lyndon B. Johnson at the White House in 1964 with civil rights leaders Rev. Dr. Martin Luther King, Jr., Whitney Young, Jr., and James Farmer.

1964. Returning on January 18, King and John Lewis, chair of the Student Nonviolent Coordinating Committee (SNCC), already engaged in Selma for two years, lead their first coordinated march to the Dallas County courthouse, where they are met by the imposing—and easily provoked—sheriff, Jim Clark. Afterward, while registering at Selma's Hotel Albert, King is punched by a local white supremacist, James Robinson. In a campaign that witnesses thousands of arrests, King himself spends February 1–5 in jail, during which time the former Nation of Islam leader Malcolm X visits Selma to lend his support in a speech at Brown Chapel, where he is joined by King's wife, Coretta Scott King.[1]

FEBRUARY 15, 1965 World War II veteran Morrie Turner, a police-department clerk in Oakland, California, publishes his first *Wee Pals* comic strip. With his integrated cast of characters, Turner becomes the first African American artist to have a comic strip syndicated in newspapers nationwide. "I couldn't participate in the civil rights marches in the South, and I felt I should," Turner reflects later. "I was working and had a wife and kid. So I decided I would have my say with my pen."[2]

FEBRUARY 18, 1965 The Selma campaign takes a violent turn when night marchers in Marion, Alabama, are attacked by state troopers after the streetlights go out. Indoors at Mack's Café, a twenty-six-year-old army veteran and church deacon named Jimmie Lee Jackson is shot twice in the stomach trying to protect his mother, Viola. At Jackson's funeral on March 3, Martin Luther King announces a fifty-four-mile march for voting rights, from Selma to Montgomery, the state capital, starting the following Sunday,

March 7. In his eulogy, King preaches, "Jimmie Lee Jackson is speaking to us from the casket and he is saying to us that we must substitute courage for caution. . . . His death says to us that we must work passionately and unrelentingly to make the American dream a reality."[3]

FEBRUARY 21, 1965 Malcolm X, the thirty-nine-year-old founder of the Organization of Afro-American Unity, is shot and killed moments into his speech before a crowd of between four hundred and five hundred at the Audubon Ballroom in the Washington Heights section of New York City. A week before, Malcolm X's house was bombed after his return from Europe, and now what he suspected would happen following his rift with the Nation of Islam the year before comes to pass in a violent, chaotic scene clouded in mystery. Three men linked to the Nation of Islam are sentenced for the crime, though only one confesses. "Malcolm X died broke, without even an insurance policy," Percy Sutton, a black New York State assemblyman and attorney for the family, is quoted in the press the next day. "Every penny that he received from books, magazine articles, and so on was assigned to the Black Muslims before he broke with them, and after that to the Muslim Mosque, Inc." Martin Luther King, "appalled" at the news out of New York, issues his own statement: "We have not learned to disagree without being violently disagreeable. This vicious assassination should cause our whole society to see that violence and hatred are evil forces that must be cast into unending limbo." At the Harlem funeral for Malcolm X on February 27, with more than 1,500 people assembled—including prominent civil rights leaders like John Lewis—the actor Ossie Davis eulogizes the man born as Malcolm Little as "our

Mourners line the funeral route as the body of Malcolm X leaves the Faith Temple, New York City.

own black shining Prince!" Following the assassination, *The Autobiography of Malcolm X*, written with Alex Haley, becomes a canonical text for the Black Power movement, selling more than six million copies worldwide by 1977. In the obituary he drafts for the *New York Times* on February 22, 1965, Philip Benjamin closes with Malcolm X's own words: "I dream that one day history will look upon me as having been one of the voices that helped to save America from a grave, even possibly fatal catastrophe."[4]

MARCH 7, 1965 On the day forever after known as Bloody Sunday, John Lewis and the SCLC leader Hosea Williams lead more than five hundred civil rights marchers to Selma's Edmund Pettus Bridge, with Montgomery their destination. At the bridge, they confront a wall of state troopers who, in a flash after an order to disperse is given, drive the marchers back violently with clubs and tear gas. According to Roy Reed, the *New York Times* reporter on the scene, some eighty-five marchers are injured, with seventeen

sent to the hospital. Among those beaten, his skull cracked, is John Lewis. "I fought in World War II," Hosea Williams is quoted as saying by Reed, "and I once was captured by the German army, and I want to tell you that the Germans never were as inhuman as the state troopers of Alabama." The next day, Martin Luther King, in Atlanta—where he was preaching to his home congregation at Ebenezer Baptist Church—calls for volunteers from around the country, including white and black clergy, to join him in Selma. Two nights later, after King leads a second march to the Edmund Pettus Bridge only to turn back to avoid violating a court order (a decision that infuriates SNCC), James Reeb, a white minister from Boston, is beaten outside a Selma diner by white supremacists. With the eyes of the nation now on Selma, President Johnson, at a joint session of Congress on Monday evening, March 15, announces that he is submitting a federal voting-rights bill for passage. "What happened in Selma is part of a far larger movement which reaches into every section and State of America," John-

Bloody Sunday SNCC leader John Lewis is attacked by state troopers in Selma, Alabama.

son declares in his nationally televised address. "It is the effort of American Negroes to secure for themselves the full blessings of American life. Their cause must be our cause, too, because it is not just Negroes, but really it is all of us, who must overcome the crippling legacy of bigotry and injustice. And we shall overcome." King watches the speech from a friend's home in Alabama, where John Lewis observes him wiping away tears.[5]

MARCH 17, 1965 After Federal District Court Judge Frank Johnson issues a ruling allowing King's Selma-to-Montgomery march to proceed, President Johnson accedes to Governor Wallace's request to send in the National Guard. The long walk commences on March 21 and culminates on March 25 on the steps of the state capitol in Montgomery (the Confederacy's first capital during the Civil War), where King declares to a throng of thousands: "They told us we wouldn't get here. And there were those who said that we would get here only over their dead bodies, but all the world today

Revs. Ralph Abernathy and Martin Luther King, Jr., lead a sea of marchers from Selma to Montgomery, Alabama, in pursuit of voting rights.

knows that we are standing before the forces of power in the state of Alabama saying, 'We ain't goin' let nobody turn us around.'" Tragically, that night, Victoria Liuzzo, a white volunteer from Detroit, Michigan, is shot by Klansmen as she drives marchers back to Selma.[6]

MARCH 1965 As part of President Johnson's War on Poverty, Daniel Patrick Moynihan, assistant secretary for policy planning and research in the US Department of Labor, authors *The Negro Family: The Case for National Action.* The Moynihan Report, as it becomes known, argues that black poverty is not caused by economic factors or racism, but instead is rooted in the harmful legacy of slavery, which has weakened the black family through an alarming out-of-wedlock birth rate. To address it, the report states, "A national effort is required that will give a unity of purpose to the many activities of the Federal government in this area, directed to a new kind of national goal: the establishment of a stable Negro family structure." When a link is drawn between its findings and other social factors, such as crime and racial uprisings in the urban North, the Moynihan Report provokes an intense scholarly debate on the origins of poverty, the black family, and social policy. "People got very upset. I mean, it was rejected," Moynihan, who would go on to serve as a US senator from New York, recalled in an interview with PBS years later. Whatever its intentions, he added, "In the popular press it was regarded as something that was anti-black."[7]

JUNE 4, 1965 In a commencement speech at Howard University in Washington, DC, President Johnson commits the federal government to affirmative action policies designed to rem-

Audience members respond to President Lyndon B. Johnson's commencement address at Howard University calling for affirmative action.

edy past racial discrimination. "Unemployment strikes most swiftly and broadly at the Negro, and this burden erodes hope," Johnson declares in cap and gown. "Blighted hope breeds despair. Despair brings indifferences to the learning which offers a way out. And despair, coupled with indifferences, is often the source of destructive rebellion against the fabric of society. There is also the lacerating hurt of early collision with white hatred or prejudice, distaste or condescension. Other groups have felt similar intolerance. But success and achievement could wipe it away. They do not change the color of a

President Lyndon B. Johnson signs the Immigration and Nationality Act on Liberty Island, with the New York City skyline in the background.

man's skin." Specific measures follow. Executive Order 11246 prohibits federal contractors from discriminating "against any employee or applicant for employment because of race, color, religion, or national origin," laying the groundwork for affirmative action. In 1968, Executive Order 11375 extends affirmative action rights on the basis of gender.[8]

JUNE 30, 1965 Congress passes the Immigration and Nationality Act of 1965, sponsored by Senator Philip Hart (D-Mich.) and Representative Emanuel Celler (D-N.Y.). The act ends the long-standing US policy of favoring immigrants from primarily white, Northern European nations. Its passage significantly increases the number of black immigrants to the US from Latin America, the Caribbean, and Africa itself.

AUGUST 6, 1965 President Johnson signs the Voting Rights Act of 1965 in the Capitol Rotunda, with Martin Luther King, Jr., looking on. "Today is a triumph for freedom as huge as any victory that has ever been won on any battlefield," Johnson says in his remarks. Five days later, an altercation between a white policeman and an African American motorist in the Watts section of Los Angeles leads to widespread confrontations between black youths and the authorities. Eleven hundred people are injured and thirty-four people are killed, twenty-five of them black. Fifteen thousand National Guardsmen, police, and state troopers restore order after six days of violence in which the ravaged city incurs $40 million in property damage. When King arrives in Los Angeles on August 17, he is met with boos and insults. "Get out of here,

Dr. King. We don't need you!" one black factory laborer shouts. "I believe what has happened in Los Angeles is of grave national significance," King writes in an August 28 editorial, "Feeling Alone in the Struggle," printed in the *New York Amsterdam News*. "What we witnessed in the Watts area is the beginning of a stirring of a deprived people in a society who have been by-passed by the progress of the past decade. For this reason, I would minimize the racial significance and point to the fact that these were the rumblings of discontent from the 'have nots' within the midst of an affluent society."[9]

SEPTEMBER 15, 1965 Bill Cosby and Robert Culp play Pentagon agents on *I Spy*, the first television show to feature a black actor as a major and equal

Bill Cosby (foreground) as Alexander Scott, with Robert Culp as Kelly Robinson, in the TV series *I Spy*.

National Guardsmen respond to the uprising in the Watts section of Los Angeles.

Dancer Judith Jamison in costume for the Broadway musical *Sophisticated Ladies*.

decades, she will become one of the world's leading dancers and choreographers. Before his death in 1989, Ailey invites Jamison to replace him as AADT director; she retires as artistic director emerita in 2011.[10]

1965 IN MUSIC Curtis Mayfield and the Impressions' indelible gospel crossover hit, "People Get Ready," is directly inspired by the 1963 March on Washington and, in turn, becomes an anthem for the civil rights movement. The song will be covered by numerous artists in the coming decades. Also this year, Otis Redding's *Otis Blue* captures the Memphis Stax sound at its tightest and the South's finest soul vocalist at his sweetest. In jazz, the saxophonist John Coltrane's *A Love Supreme*, released as a four-part suite, from "Acknowledgement" to "Resolution," "Pursuance," and "Psalm," is regarded as one of the finest jazz albums ever recorded.[11]

costar. Cosby wins three Emmy Awards in the three-year run of the series, breaking the mold of stereotypical roles for African Americans in television drama.

OCTOBER 30, 1965 Judith Jamison makes her debut with the Alvin Ailey American Dance Theater. Over the next four

John Coltrane in concert.

1966

JANUARY 7, 1966 The SCLC, under the leadership of Martin Luther King, shifts its focus to the urban North in what becomes known as the Chicago Freedom Movement (CFM). Devoted primarily to ending discrimination in the city's housing market, the CFM exposes the depth and intensity of white northern hostility to civil rights. King is so committed that he relocates his family to the city for a long-term stay. On August 5, a march through southwest Chicago is met by a hail of bottles and bricks. A white teenager is knifed, and King is struck on the side of the head while exiting his car at Marquette Park. A group of 250 white youths waves Confederate and American flags out in front of the marchers. "I have to do this—to expose myself—to bring this hate into the open," King is quoted in the *Washington Post* on August 6. "I have never seen such hate—not in Mississippi or Alabama—as I see here in Chicago." A deal brokered with the Chicago Housing Authority and Mortgage Bankers Association on August 26 eases the immediate crisis ahead of a rally in Cicero, Illinois, though King remains active in Chicago into 1967.[12]

JANUARY 13, 1966 President Johnson nominates Robert C. Weaver to head his newly created Department of Housing and Urban Development, making him the nation's first African American cabinet member. Other notable Johnson appointments in 1966 include Constance Baker Motley and Spottswood Robinson, both of whom are appointed to federal court judgeships. In electoral politics, Edward Brooke (R-Mass.) becomes the first African American in the Senate since Blanche K. Bruce (R-Miss.)

Edward Brooke of Massachusetts celebrates after winning the Republican nomination for the US Senate.

served during Reconstruction. Southern legislatures keenly feel the impact of the Voting Rights Act, including in Texas, where Barbara Jordan becomes the first black woman to serve in the state senate.

APRIL 18, 1966 The Boston Celtics' Bill Russell becomes the NBA's first African American head coach following the retirement of his coach, Red Auerbach, and a new era of opportunities for black sports figures is ushered in. In football, the Cleveland Browns' legendary running back Jim Brown chooses to retire after nine seasons to pursue a career in acting. Brown's first role is as Robert Jefferson in the World War II action classic *The Dirty Dozen*, released in 1967.

MAY 1, 1966 George Wiley, a black chemist and associate national director of the Congress of Racial Equality (CORE), draws up his Prospectus for the Establishment of an Anti-Poverty/Civil

Celtics great Bill Russell elevates to the basket over Leroy Ellis of the Lakers in the 1966 NBA Finals.

Football legend Jim Brown (third from left) as Robert Jefferson in *The Dirty Dozen*.

Rights Action Center, with the goal of building an interracial coalition of the poor. In 1967, along with the black welfare activists Beulah Sanders and Johnnie Tillmon, Wiley establishes the National Welfare Rights Organization (NWRO), dedicated to securing dignity and justice for welfare recipients, many of whom are women. At its peak, the NWRO has more than thirty thousand members and three hundred local affiliates.[13]

JUNE 6, 1966 James Meredith, who integrated the University of Mississippi under federal protection in 1962, commences his March Against Fear from Memphis, Tennessee, to Jackson, Mississippi, to protest whites' continued economic and physical intimidation of African Americans seeking to exercise their rights under the Civil Rights and Voting Rights Acts. When Meredith is shot, his cause is taken up by SNCC and SCLC, who continue the march and register more than

Dick Gregory and James Meredith walk with Martin Luther King, Jr., in the March Against Fear.

Floyd McKissick, Martin Luther King, Jr., Stokely Carmichael, and James Lawson speak with law enforcement during a voter registration march in Mississippi.

four thousand black voters. Tensions emerge regarding future strategy, however, as SCLC's demands for "Freedom Now" are eclipsed by SNCC's chants of "Black Power," articulated most forcefully by Trinidad-born Stokely Carmichael (later known as Kwame Ture). "We are oppressed because we are black. And in order to get out of that oppression one must wield the group power that one has, not the individual power which this country then sets the criteria under which a man may come into it," Carmichael says in a landmark address on October 29 in Berkeley, California. "This country knows what power is," he adds. "It knows it very well. And it knows what Black Power is, because it deprived black people of it for four hundred years."[14]

JULY 1966 Stan Lee and his team at the Marvel Comics Group unveil a new superhero as part of their *Fantastic Four* series: the Black Panther (aka T'Challa). Dressed all in black, with pointy ears, a cape, claws, and glowing-light eyes, the Black Panther is out to avenge the murder of his father, the African king T'Chaka of the Wakanda nation. The Panther also happens to have a PhD in physics from Oxford. The source of his powers is a magical herb shaped in the form of a heart. "It is not for nothing that I am called the Black Panther!" he declares, and among his quests, he battles the Ku Klux Klan.[15]

AUGUST 25, 1966 A Chicago chapter of Operation Breadbasket, directed by the twenty-five-year-old theology student Jesse L. Jackson, reaches agreement with the Coca-Cola Bottling Company of Chicago to hire thirty African American employees. Modeled on the efforts of Rev. Leon Sullivan in Philadelphia, Breadbasket lobbies white businesses in black commu-

nities to hire black workers, using the threat of community-wide boycotts as leverage. During Jackson's first fifteen months as director, Coke, Pepsi, and several supermarkets hire two thousand new black workers to jobs that pay a total $15 million in wages. Operation Breadbasket's weekly workshops draw large crowds to hear the charismatic Jackson, who will become the Second City's leading civil rights activist in the 1970s and '80s. "Coca-Cola has made a decision to join the ministers in the revolution for human dignity and increased expectation," Jackson says following the announcement at the H and H Café in Chicago.[16]

OCTOBER 15, 1966 Oakland students Bobby Seale and Huey Newton establish the Black

Actor and singer Harry Belafonte speaking out for Operation Breadbasket.

Celebrating Kwanzaa.

Panther Party for Self-Defense (BPP), inspired by Stokely Carmichael's party of the same name in Lowndes County, Alabama. Seale and Newton's Ten Point Program demands full employment, decent housing, and an end to the military draft and police brutality, a manifesto that proves popular with young urban African Americans, as does the party's free breakfast program. The Oakland BPP chapter also initiates a new style of radicalism, gaining national and global attention in 1967 when armed members in black militaristic uniforms protest at the California state capitol in Sacramento. The Panthers' revolutionary rhetoric places the black American struggle in a broader anticolonial context, inspired by radicals like Frantz Fanon, the Martinican author of *The Wretched of the Earth* (1961), and Che Guevara, the Argentine hero of the Cuban revolution. The Black Panther movement goes into decline in the 1970s, the result of internecine divisions, many fostered by the FBI's counterintelligence program of surveillance, known as COINTELPRO. While Seale continues a career in politics, teaching, and business, Newton is shot and killed in 1989 outside an Oakland crack house. His fellow Panther leader Kathleen Cleaver will recall, "Newton's flamboyance, vision, and passion came to symbolize an entire era, yet in the end, the same demons that ravaged the community he had sought to transform destroyed him as well."[17]

DECEMBER 26, 1966 Maulana Karenga, a young Black Nationalist student, creates Kwanzaa, a winter holiday designed for African Americans and celebrated from December 26 to January 2. It is based on seven communitarian Swahili principles: *umoja* (unity), *kujichagulia* (self-determination), *ujima* (collective work and responsibility), *ujamaa* (cooperative economics), *nia* (purpose), *kuumba* (creativity), and *imani* (faith).[18]

1966 IN THE ARTS The race-conscious works of several black poets, writers, and artists come to be seen as part of a broadly unified Black Arts Movement (BAM) in which, according to the writer Larry Neal, the primary duty of the black artist is to "speak to the spiritual and cultural needs of Black people." Amiri Baraka's poem "Black Art" (1966) highlights the radical aesthetic of the movement in its demand for " 'poems that kill.' / Assassin poems, Poems that shoot / guns. Poems that wrestle cops into alleys / and take their weapons leaving them dead / with tongues pulled out and sent to Ireland."[19] Although some

Elizabeth Catlett. *Malcolm X Speaks for Us*. 1969. Linoleum cut.

BAM works are tainted by homophobia and anti-Semitism, the movement opens space for innovative African American women writers, notably Sonia Sanchez and Nikki Giovanni.[20]

1966 IN MUSIC The year's No. 1 singles on the rhythm and blues charts bear witness to the ascendance of soul in its many regional forms, with Detroit's Motown label spending thirty weeks in the top position with singles by the Temptations (sixteen weeks), the Supremes (six weeks), and Stevie Wonder (six weeks). Mem-

phis's Stax Records claims the top spot with Eddie Floyd's "Knock on Wood," while the magic of its sound can be heard on Wilson Pickett's "634-5789 (Soulsville, U.S.A.)" (recorded at Stax and released on the Atlantic label) and Sam and Dave's "Hold On! I'm a Comin'." The quintessential Stax artist, though, is the Georgia native Otis Redding, whose powerful renditions of "Satisfaction" and "My Lover's Prayer" both crack the top ten. Among other hits in 1966 are James Brown's "I Got You (I Feel Good)" and "It's a Man's Man's Man's World"; Slim Harpo's Louisiana swamp blues "Baby Scratch My Back"; and Ray Charles's "Let's Go Get Stoned," written by a young Nicholas Ashford and Valerie Simpson, prior to their move to Motown. Last but not least, soaring to the top of *Billboard*'s Hot 100 in 1966 are the Supremes' "You Keep Me Hangin' On" and Percy Sledge's romantic ballad "When a Man Loves a Woman," which is recorded for Atlantic at the legendary Muscle Shoals studio in Alabama.

Florence Ballard, Mary Wilson, and Diana Ross—the Supremes.

1967

MARCH 9, 1967 The dramatic increase in African Americans serving in Vietnam results in twenty black GIs earning the Medal of Honor, the nation's highest military award. Specialist Lawrence Joel of the 173rd Airborne Brigade, whose actions under heavy fire near Saigon saved the lives of many of his fellow soldiers, is the first of his peers to receive the coveted award, presented by President Johnson at a White House ceremony. "I'm just a soldier, and a soldier does his job," Joel tells reporters. Out of some 275,000 black troops serving in Vietnam, 7,214 are killed.[21]

APRIL 4, 1967 Growing opposition to Vietnam in the black community receives vivid expression in Martin Luther King's sermon at Riverside Church in New York City. In it, King breaks with his partner on civil rights, President Johnson, for moral reasons and because he is concerned that the conflict is undermining Johnson's Great Society reforms at home. "If America's soul becomes totally poisoned, part of the autopsy must read Vietnam," King says from the pulpit. "[A] nation that continues year after year to spend more money on military defense than on programs of social uplift is approaching spiritual death."

In calling for a boycott of the war, King is also spirited by the racial disparity he sees in combat assignments in Vietnam; how else to make sense of the fact, he asks, that "twice as many Negroes as whites are in combat" than that it is "a reflection of the Negro's position in America"?[22]

Dr. Benjamin Spock, Martin Luther King, Jr., Father Frederick Reed, and Cleveland Robinson lead an antiwar rally in New York City.

APRIL 28, 1967 As divisions widen over the Vietnam War, the twenty-five-year-old world heavyweight boxing champion Muhammad Ali (who changed his name from Cassius Clay after defeating Sonny Liston for the title in 1964) is stripped of his title following his refusal to be drafted into the military. "I have searched my conscience and I find I cannot be true to my belief in my religion by accepting such a call," Ali says in a press statement. "In my view, the deposed champion has demonstrated that he is fighting for a principle," baseball great Jackie Robinson writes in an editorial on October 10. "While I cannot agree with him, I respect him sincerely." Ali is not reinstated into boxing until 1970.[23]

JUNE 12, 1967 The Supreme Court's unanimous 9–0 verdict in the case of *Loving v. Virginia* strikes down laws in sixteen states that prohibit marriages between white and black men and women. In 1958, Richard Loving, a white man, and Mildred Jeter Loving, a black woman, who had married in nearby Washington, DC, were arrested in their Virginia home and convicted for violating Virginia's 1924 Racial Integrity Act. They were given a one-year suspended sentence, with the proviso that they not return to Virginia for twenty-five years. "The Fourteenth Amendment requires that the freedom of choice to marry not be restricted by invidious racial discriminations," Chief Justice Earl Warren writes for the Court. "Under our Constitution, the freedom to marry, or not marry, a person of another race resides with the individual, and cannot be infringed by the State."[24]

JULY 12, 1967 The arrest and beating of a black cab driver by police in Newark, New Jersey, escalates into a violent stand-off between law

Mildred and Richard Loving after the Supreme Court rules in their favor, rejecting Virginia's anti-miscegenation law.

enforcement and African American youth. In this majority-black city, which is challenged by poor housing, unemployment, high infant mortality, and violent crime, only one in nine officers on the police force is black. When the dust settles five days later, twenty-six people, mostly African American, are dead, 750 are injured, and more than a thousand are in jail, while looting and arson result in property damage in excess of $10 million. A week after the uprising, one thousand activists, including Ossie Davis and James Farmer of CORE, converge on Newark for the nation's first National Black Power Conference.

JULY 23, 1967 Six days after the violence in Newark subsides, a police raid on an unlicensed bar in a black

neighborhood of Detroit, Michigan, precipitates an even greater loss of life and property. By July 30, forty-three people have been killed, thirty-three of them black; 1,180 injured; and 7,200 arrested. Property damage registers at $32 million. As in Newark, the rebellion encourages a new radical politics. In the city's auto plants, the League of Revolutionary Black Workers tries to reconcile and infuse black liberation ideas with Marxist-Leninist ideology.[25]

AUGUST 1, 1967 In Chicago, Albert William Johnson becomes the first African American to be awarded his own General Motors (Oldsmobile) dealership. Three years later, he helps establish the National Black Automobile Dealer

Newark uprising: one man expresses where he stands to a National Guardsman on the scene.

Association. Johnson remains in the business until 1995.[26]

AUGUST 15, 1967 Following the June publication of his book *Where Do We Go from Here: Chaos or Community?*, Martin Luther King reflects on this question in his address to the eleventh annual SCLC convention in Atlanta, in which he calls for massive "disruptions" in big cities across the country in an effort to repurpose African American anger from rioting to effective action for economic justice. In his speech, King can be heard adjusting his message to the militancy of Black Power without surrendering his inviolable commitment to nonviolence. "The slums are the handiwork of a vicious system of the white society," King argues, while cautioning, "We reject both armed insurrection, either for shock value or conquest, along with pleas to insensitive government. . . . Mass civil disobedience can use rage as a constructive and creative force." Reviews of King's book are mixed, signaling a shift in leadership and mood. In an especially biting review in the *New York Review of Books* on August 24, the critic Andrew Kopkind writes, "Martin Luther King once had the ability to talk to people, the power to change them by evoking images of revolution. But the duty of a revolutionary is to make revolutions (say those who have done it), and King made none."[27]

AUGUST 30, 1967 Solicitor General Thurgood Marshall becomes the first African American appointed to the US Supreme Court when the Senate confirms President Johnson's nomination of him by a vote of 69–11. The former head of the NAACP Legal Defense Fund during its historic crusade to desegregate the nation's public schools in *Brown v. Board of Education* (1954),

Thurgood Marshall prior to being sworn in as the first black US Supreme Court justice.

Marshall will be a resolutely liberal voice on the Court for nearly a quarter of a century. "Let me take this opportunity to affirm my deep faith in this Nation and its people, and to pledge that I shall be ever mindful of my obligation to the Constitution and to the goal of equal justice under law," Marshall says in a statement following the vote.[28]

OCTOBER 23, 1967 Stokely Carmichael publishes his manifesto, *Black Power: The Politics of Liberation*, with coauthor Charles V. Hamilton, a political scientist at Roosevelt University in Chicago. In it they argue: "The adoption of the concept of Black Power is one of the most legitimate and healthy developments in American politics and race relations in our time. The concept of Black Power . . . is a call for black people in this country to unite, to recognize their heritage, to build a sense of community. It is a call for black people to begin to define their own goals,

Carl Stokes, mayor of Cleveland, speaks at Temple Buell College, Cleveland.

to lead their own organizations and to support those organizations. It is a call to reject the racist institutions and values of this society." The book is less sanguine about the potential for interracial coalition building, except among the poor. Instead, it advocates blacks controlling and supporting their own businesses, employment, education, and political institutions. In his review for the *New York Times* on December 10, "A Slogan, a Chant, a Threat," Fred Powledge writes: "In the absence of more detailed political frameworks and ideologies for black Americans, some students of the struggle are likely to conclude, after reading this book, that Black Power is not much more than an organizing vehicle and a scant phrase."[29]

NOVEMBER 7, 1967 Democrat Carl Stokes is elected the first black mayor of a major city, Cleveland, Ohio, while Democrat Richard Hatcher wins election as mayor of Gary, Indiana. (Earlier in the year, President Johnson appointed Walter Washington as Washington, DC's first black mayor-commissioner.)

DECEMBER 10, 1967 Otis Redding, along with six others, including the pilot and a group of young back-up musicians on tour with him, dies in a private plane crash on the way from Cleve-

Otis Redding.

Sidney Poitier and Rod Steiger, the stars of the 1967 film *In the Heat of the Night.*

land, Ohio, to Madison, Wisconsin. Two months earlier, Redding replaced Elvis Presley as the world's top male vocalist according to a poll by the London-based publishing company Melody Maker and he had only recently recorded the song that would become his signature, "Sittin' on the Dock of the Bay." The Georgia-born Redding, known variously as "the King of Soul Singers" and "the Crown Prince of Soul," was twenty-six years old.[30]

1967 IN FILM Among the year's top movies are three with Sidney Poitier in a leading role. In *In the Heat of the Night,* Poitier stars as a black detective from Philadelphia investigating a murder in Mississippi alongside a white police chief played by Rod Steiger. In it, Poitier's character, Virgil Tibbs, is seen slapping back a white Southern gentleman who slaps him for his questions, and when the police chief refers to him as "nigger" and asks him what "they" call him back home, Poitier's character famously

answers, "They call me *Mister* Tibbs." The film's soundtrack earns its composer, Quincy Jones, a Grammy Award, flowing out of the first of his record-breaking seventy-nine Grammy nominations (as of 2014). In the same year Poitier also stars in *Guess Who's Coming to Dinner,* which confronts the theme of interracial marriage, and *To Sir with Love,* in which he plays a Guyanese teacher in a tough inner-city school in London.

1967 IN MUSIC In a banner year for African American women vocalists, Aretha Franklin tops the R&B and *Billboard* Top 100 charts with her cover of Otis Redding's "Respect," to which she adds the classic "R-E-S-P-E-C-T" refrain. Other female hit makers include Gladys Knight, Bettye Swann, and Martha Reeves and the Vandellas. In other music news, Louis Armstrong's "What a Wonderful World" tops the charts in several European countries and becomes Satchmo's final US hit in a career spanning fifty years.

— 1968 —

FEBRUARY 8, 1968 Police officers kill three unarmed students and wound twenty-eight others on the campus of the historically black South Carolina State College in Orangeburg. Martin Luther King demands that the government "act now to bring to justice the perpetrators of the largest armed assault undertaken under color of law in recent American history." Despite the efforts of the historians Jack Bass and Cleveland Sellers, a SNCC activist injured that day, the massacre remains one of the least well-known events of the civil rights era.[31]

FEBRUARY 17, 1968 The Oakland Black Panther Party becomes a national and global cause célè-

Orangeburg, South Carolina: the aftermath.

bre after a major publicity campaign and series of rallies are staged to "Free Huey Newton." The cofounder of the BPP had been imprisoned since October 1967 following a shoot-out with police in which he was wounded and an officer was killed. At a rally in Oakland on this day, Newton's birthday, Stokely Carmichael and H. Rap Brown dedicate SNCC to an alliance with the Panthers.

FEBRUARY 29, 1968 In what becomes known as the Kerner Report, Illinois governor Otto Kerner, appointed by President Johnson to head the National Advisory Commission of Civil Disorders, formed in response to the urban rebellions in Newark and Detroit the previous summer, warns that America is becoming "two societies—one black, one white—separate and unequal." Citing white racism as a cause of the recent urban unrest while warning against black separatism, Kerner recommends immediate federal action to remedy racial discrimination in housing, education, and employment. The president, however, refrains from taking action. With the conflict in Vietnam dividing the country, Johnson, in a televised address from the Oval Office on March 31,

Eldridge Cleaver addressing a rally at American University.

announces that he will not run for a second term as president.[32]

MARCH 25, 1968 The Black Panther leader Eldridge Cleaver releases his book of essays, *Soul on Ice*. Written largely while serving a sentence in Folsom Prison after being convicted of assault with intent to kill in 1958, *Soul on Ice* is chosen as one of the *New York Times*' best books of the year. In her prescient review for the *Times* on March 24, "Mr. and Mrs. Yesterday," Charlayne Hunter concludes, "'Soul on Ice' is not a book about the prison life of a black man, although a very good picture of prison life does emerge secondarily. The book is about the imprisonment of men's souls by society. This, of course, can happen outside prison walls, too, but if you're a black man in this country, you stand an excellent chance of having as your ultimate frame of reference a jail cell." That same year, Cleaver jumps bail for Cuba, then Algeria, to avoid trial for an Oakland shoot-out with police that resulted in the death of the Black Panther Bobby Hutton.[33]

APRIL 4, 1968 The day after delivering his famous "To the Mountaintop" speech, in which he weighed his desire for "a long life" against the urgency of his calling as a civil rights leader, Rev. Dr. Martin Luther King, Jr., is assassi-

The open window used by James Earl Ray to assassinate Rev. Dr. Martin Luther King, Jr., in Memphis, Tennessee.

nated on the balcony of the Lorraine Motel in Memphis, Tennessee. He is only thirty-nine years old, the same age Malcolm X was when he was assassinated three years earlier. King was in Memphis in support of striking sanitation workers, part of the SCLC's Poor People's Campaign launched in 1967. News of the assassination sparks disbelief, anger, and violence in the black neighborhoods of several cities, including Washington, DC, Baltimore, and Chicago, which witness several deaths and millions of dollars in property damage. In Indianapolis, Senator Robert Kennedy (D-N.Y.), who will suffer the same fate as King two months later, plays a central role in persuading outraged protesters to follow King's example of nonviolence; the singer James Brown makes a similar plea at a concert at the Boston Garden in Massachusetts. One immediate consequence of the assassina-

Residents of Resurrection City, Washington, DC, learn of Ray's capture.

tion and the riots is Congress's passage on April 11 of the 1968 Civil Rights Act, better known as the Fair Housing Act, which enshrines in law protections against racial discrimination in housing. Coretta Scott King, at a press confer-

The Poor People's Campaign.

Aretha Franklin, the Queen of Soul, on *Soul Train*.

ence held at Ebenezer Baptist Church in Atlanta just two days after her husband's death, says to the gathered audience: "He knew that this was a sick society, totally infested with racism and violence that questioned his integrity, maligned his motives and distorted his views which would ultimately lead to his death, and he struggled with every ounce of his energy to save society from itself."[34]

JUNE 28, 1968 A preacher's daughter from Detroit, Michigan, Aretha Franklin graces the cover of *Time* magazine under the banner "The Sound of Soul" and tops that year's R&B charts with "Chain of Fools," "Think!," and "(Sweet Sweet Baby) Since You've Been Gone." She is, and will remain, the undisputed Queen of Soul.

AUGUST 7, 1968 James Brown records "Say It Loud—I'm Black and I'm Proud" in Los Angeles. The song quickly becomes a Black Power anthem, topping the R&B charts for six weeks and reaching No. 10 on the *Billboard* 100 in October. Brown later regrets that "many white people didn't understand it" and instead misconstrued the song's sentiment as an attack on them. "But really," he adds, "if you listen to it, it sounds like a children's song. That's why I had children in it,

James Brown, the Godfather of Soul.

Dick Gregory for president "Cannot be bought, sold, or traded."

What might have been: 1968 campaign buttons, including Dick Gregory and Benjamin Spock on the Peace and Freedom ticket and, while he lived, Martin Luther King, Jr., and Spock.

so children who heard it could grow up feeling pride."[35]

AUGUST 26–29, 1968 At a fractious Democratic National Convention in Chicago, the SNCC cofounder Julian Bond becomes the first black vice presidential candidate to be nominated from the floor. In the general election, Democrat Hubert Humphrey wins the vast majority of black votes but loses to Republican Richard Nixon in a three-way race that includes Alabama's segregationist governor, George Wallace. Nixon's emphasis on "law and order" signals the politics of the 1970s, dominated by appeals to a "silent majority" of white conservatives in both the North and South. Although they pool few votes, among those seeking the Democratic nomination in 1968 are three African Americans: Eldridge Cleaver (like Bond, he is under thirty-five and thus constitutionally ineligible for the office) for the Peace and Freedom Party; the comedian Dick Gregory, for the alternative Freedom and Peace Party; and the Communist Party's Charlene Mitchell, the first black woman to run for the presidency.[36]

Diahann Carroll in *Julia*.

A student during the Harvard strike.

SEPTEMBER 8, 1968 The tennis legend Arthur Ashe wins the inaugural US Open, the first in which professionals can compete. Still an amateur, and serving as an officer in the US Army, Ashe forgoes the $14,000 prize but ends the year as the world's top-ranked player.

SEPTEMBER 17, 1968 With the debut of *Julia*, the actress Diahann Carroll becomes the first black star of a television situation comedy to have a non-domestic role (that ground was broken in 1950 by Ethel Waters, starring as the titular housekeeper of the sitcom *Beulah*). Carroll's role as nurse Julia Baker reflects the emergence of professional African American women. The same year sees Clotilde Dent Bowen become the first African American woman to be promoted to the rank of colonel in the US Army. Also in 1968, twenty-one-year-old Nancy Hicks becomes the first African American woman reporter hired by the *New York Times*. Among Hicks's first assignments is covering the growing tensions between black and Jewish Brooklyn residents over school integration in the Ocean Hill–Brownsville neighborhood. A year later, WAGA-TV in Atlanta hires Xernona Clayton, the first black woman to host a television show in the South.

SEPTEMBER 18, 1968 The first department of black studies opens at San Francisco State University, chaired by Professor Nathan Hare, a sociologist fired by Howard University the year before for his Black Power activism. Despite the opposition of faculty skeptical that black studies is a serious academic discipline, student protests lead to the founding of programs at Howard, Cornell, Harvard, and the University of California campuses in Los Angeles, Berkeley, and Santa Barbara by the end of 1969. In September 1970, the scholars Molefi Asante and Robert Singleton launch the *Journal of Black Studies* at the University of California, Los Angeles. In its formative years, black studies, with its blend of activism and academics, is seen as a way of helping the first generation of affirmative action students adjust to life at historically white colleges and universities.

SEPTEMBER 26, 1968 The Studio Museum of Harlem opens in a loft at 125th Street and Fifth Avenue with an inaugural program by Tom Lloyd called *Electronic Refractions II*. Over the decades the museum will play a leading role in developing and promoting the work of black artists from across the African diaspora.[37]

OCTOBER 16, 1968 Arguably the most iconic image of the Black Power era is captured at the

Gold medalist Tommie Smith and bronze medalist John Carlos raise their fists in a Black Power salute at the 1968 Mexico City Olympics.

alumna of Howard University and the University of Michigan, wins the Walden Trust Award at the Metropolitan Opera National Council Regional Auditions National Finals in New York. She picked up other prizes earlier in the year, including first prize at the Seventeenth International Music Competition held in Munich, Germany. Paul Hume, in a review in the *Washington Post* on December 30, writes: "Jessye Norman has a prodigious voice and, at the relatively early age of 23, gives every indication of presenting it to the world with the taste, the sensitivity, the discriminating style of the truly distinguished artist." Norman will go on to enjoy one of the most celebrated careers in contemporary opera, winning five Grammys, the Kennedy Center Honors, and more than thirty honorary degrees, including one from Harvard.[38]

medal ceremony for the men's 200-meter sprint at the Summer Olympics in Mexico City, when Tommie Smith, who sets a world-record time of 19.83 seconds, and third-place finisher John Carlos bow their heads and raise their fists in a Black Power salute. An instant headline, the defiant act polarizes Americans watching back home: some see it as an embarrassment and an outrage with the country at war in Vietnam, while others view it as a noble gesture in solidarity with the growing Black Power movement. The US Olympic Committee sends both San Jose State sprinters home, although they are not officially stripped of their medals, as has often been reported.

NOVEMBER 17, 1968 The twenty-three-year-old soprano Jessye Norman, an African American

NOVEMBER 22, 1968 In the *Star Trek* episode "Plato's Stepchildren," Nichelle Nichols, portraying the African American chief communications officer Lieutenant Uhura, shares a kiss with Captain Kirk, played by the white actor William Shatner, in what becomes the first interracial kiss on a television drama.

Star Trek's William Shatner and Nichelle Nichols engage in TV's first interracial kiss.

1969

JANUARY 2, 1969 Following the election of nine black members of Congress in 1968, Representative Charles Diggs (D-Mich.) founds the Democratic Select Committee. Stern critics of the Nixon administration's appointment of conservative judges, all of the committee members find themselves on the Nixon White House's notorious Enemies List. In 1971, with thirteen members, the committee is formally renamed the Congressional Black Caucus, with Diggs as its first chairperson.[39]

JANUARY 17, 1969 Inside UCLA's Campbell Hall, a twenty-one-year-old African American, Claude Hubert, shoots and kills a pair of Black Panther Party members, twenty-three-year-old John J. Huggins and twenty-six-year-old Alprentice "Bunchy" Carter, in the middle of a student meeting over the direction of black studies on campus. The killings are seen as part of a larger power struggle over the meaning and control of Black Power.[40]

FEBRUARY 14, 1969 As part of a yearlong boycott of the Hyde County, North Carolina, public schools by African American parents, teachers, and students, more than a thousand demonstrators converge on the state capitol in Raleigh to protest the closing of the county's historically black schools while its historically white schools remain open. As the work of desegration continues, the Hyde County boycott demonstrates blacks' growing demands, especially in the rural South, that integration should be a two-way

Holding a Black Power sign, attorney Floyd B. McKissick, former director of CORE, emphasizes black economic empowerment and goes on to press for the creation of a black-controlled town in his native North Carolina, known as Soul City. Before his death in 1991, McKissick is appointed a district judge in North Carolina.

street that preserves the historic role of black schools and black teachers in local communities.

MARCH 1969 An *Ebony* cover story examines the rise of radical black theology and the rejection by some black Christian ministers of a "honky Christ." Among those featured is the Detroit minister Albert B. Cleage, Jr., whose book *The Black Messiah* (1968) depicts Jesus as a black revolutionary of African descent. Rev. Cleage, who later renames himself Jaramogi Abebe Agyeman, is perhaps the most radical voice in demanding a separate black church as the "unifying center for the totality of the black man's life and struggle." More-mainstream ministers like Jesse Jackson argue for the inclusion of black imagery and customs at Easter and Christmas, and for the recognition of Jesus as "dark complexioned" with "some African blood."[41]

MARCH 1969 After its final screening of *2001: A Space Odyssey*, Loew's Theatre, an opulent 1930 art deco building on 175th Street in Manhattan, closes its doors and is purchased soon after by the black evangelist minister Frederick J. Eikerenkoetter II, better known as Reverend Ike. Describing the building as "fantabulous," Reverend Ike renames it the Palace Theatre, and it serves as the venue for his radio show, which is nationally syndicated to more than 1,700 stations. The show has several million listeners at its peak. At the forefront of a wave of television evangelists who would emerge in the 1970s, Reverend Ike preaches the Science of Life, a doctrine that highlights the power and responsibility of the individual to shape his or her life chances. In 1972, he becomes the first black speaker to sell out New York's Madison Square Garden since Marcus Garvey did it fifty years before.[42]

APRIL 20, 1969 Long before he is known as the voice of Darth Vader, the actor James Earl Jones wins his first Tony Award for his performance as Jack Johnson, the first black heavyweight boxing champion of the world, in Howard Sackler's Broadway hit *The Great White Hope*. Jones reprises the role in Martin Ritt's 1970 screen adaptation.

MAY 16, 1969 Howard Lee is elected mayor of Chapel Hill, North Carolina, becoming the first African American mayor of a majority-white city in the South since Reconstruction.

20th Century-Fox Presents
A Lawrence Turman-Martin Ritt Production.
The Great White Hope
PANAVISION® Color by DE LUXE®

Movie theater lobby card for *The Great White Hope*, starring James Earl Jones and Jane Alexander.

Martha P. Johnson at New York City's Gay Pride Parade in 1973.

Power movement and his friend, the "Godfather of Soul," James Brown, Powell produces stamps bearing Brown's image that are an example of black capitalism in action. A book of fifty pages of stamps buys three dollars' worth of merchandise. At their peak, the stamps are accepted by a thousand merchants across California, generating more than $1 million in business.[44]

AUGUST 2, 1969 Jackie "Moms" Mabley, a seventy-five-year-old veteran of the chitlin circuit and the original Queen of Black Comedy, enjoys a surprise US Top 40 hit with her poignant version of "Abraham, Martin and John," a cover of Dion's tribute to the assassinated figures of Abraham Lincoln, Martin Luther King, John Kennedy, and Bobby Kennedy. In the same week that Mabley's Mercury recording lands at No. 18 on the *Billboard* chart, another version of the song by Smokey Robinson and the Miracles registers two spots higher

JUNE 28, 1969 Gay and transgender African Americans play a central role in riots against police harassment at the Stonewall Inn, a gay bar in New York City's Greenwich Village. Marsha P. Johnson, a black transgender activist, is among the first to fight back against the police that night in what becomes the catalyst for the modern US gay rights movement. Another participant is Miss Major Griffin-Gracy, a black transgender woman who later takes part in the 1971 Attica prison riot.[43]

JULY 11, 1969 *Time* magazine features the Black and Brown Trading Stamp Corporation, founded in Oakland, California, by former Raiders wide receiver Art Powell. Influenced by the Black

Veteran stage and screen performer Moms Mabley.

at No. 16. Mabley, who records her next album live at Sing Sing Prison in New York, says, "If there was ever a time in history when people needed to laugh, then now is the time."[45]

AUGUST 6, 1969 Gordon Parks, Sr., one of his generation's most influential photographers, becomes the first African American director of a major studio-backed Hollywood film. *The Learning Tree,* which Parks also writes, is based on his 1963 coming-of-age novel of the same title. "We deliberately planted some militants at a screening in New York," Parks tells Gene Robertson of the *Sun-Reporter.* "They did laugh a few times at the wrong places, but at the end they came up to me and said: 'You did it, baby, you did it!' "[46]

Jimi Hendrix at Woodstock.

AUGUST 15–18, 1969 Although most of the audience is white, African American performers star at the three-day Woodstock music festival in upstate New York. The event begins with a three-hour set by the black folk singer Richie Havens, including his memorable, improvised "Freedom." Other performers include Sly and the Family Stone, a large, interracial and mixed-gender group that fuses soul, funk, gospel, and psychedelic rock, famously on "I Want to Take You Higher." The guitarist Jimi Hendrix closes the festival with a set largely regarded as one of his greatest ever, including his feedback-fueled rendition of "The Star-Spangled Banner."[47]

SEPTEMBER 23, 1969 The black keyboardist, vocalist, and producer Isaac Hayes previews the future of soul music in the early 1970s with the release of his pioneering album *Hot Buttered Soul.* The LP features just four songs, each showcasing lush orchestration and Hayes's deep baritone, and includes a twelve-minute reworking of Burt Bacharach and Hal David's "Walk On By" and an extended stream-of-consciousness rap on the eighteen-minute "By the Time I Get to Phoenix," a hit penned for the white country artist Glen Campbell by the songwriter Jimmy Webb in 1967.

DECEMBER 4, 1969 The Federal Bureau of Investigation's COINTELPRO policy of surveillance and intimidation of the Black Panther Party comes to a head in the FBI's raid on the home of Chicago BPP leader Fred Hampton; the twenty-one-year-old is assassinated by two bullets to the back of his head, and others are injured. "Have the lynch mob of my youth been replaced by the platoons of police?" Louis E. Martin, a black newspaperman and political adviser to President

Isaac Hayes.

says jazz's elder statesman Dizzy Gillespie in a *Los Angeles Times* article in 1970, but he adds, "I won't put him down." On the flip side is Quincy Jones, who, in the same article, credits Davis for his experimentation with the form: "A whole lot of cats who were hesitating will be running into that bag now that Miles has done it. With every change of direction he's always arrived at a valid musical conclusion. Anyhow, I'd rather hear him do it than the Doors." In 2006, Davis is inducted posthumously into the Rock and Roll Hall of Fame, with a bio that quotes his own thoughts on the subject: "The way you change and help music is by tryin' to invent new ways to play."[49]

Johnson on civil rights, wonders in an editorial in the *Chicago Daily Defender* on December 13. Martin adds, "While I am convinced that the struggle of black men for respect and power, for life and dignity, can not be won in this society at the point of a gun, I am also convinced that guns will not stop the struggle." *The Murder of Fred Hampton*, a documentary film by Howard Alk, is released two years later.[48]

DECEMBER 13, 1969 The legendary jazz trumpeter Miles Davis, who has been recording since the 1940s, appears at age forty-four on the cover of *Rolling Stone* in a year that witnesses the release of his double album *Bitches Brew*, a tour de force in the emergence of what becomes known as jazz-rock fusion. The album's cover art, created by Abdul Mati Klarwein, "capture[s] the zeitgeist of free love and flower power, depicting a naked black couple looking expectantly at an ocean, a huge vibrant, red flower beside them," writes Paul Tingen in *JazzTimes*. "I still don't understand,"

Bullet-riddled bedroom of Fred Hampton following Chicago police raid.

1970–1974

Cicely Tyson in a still from the 1972 film *Sounder.*

1970

JANUARY 12, 1970 With encouragement from her friend and fellow writer James Baldwin, Maya Angelou (born Marguerite Johnson), a forty-one-year-old poet and dancer from Stamps, Arkansas, publishes her first book, *I Know Why the Caged Bird Sings*. In a review for the *Washington Post*, Ward Just writes: "This is a memoir of a black girl-hood, or childhood, and it is written from the center of blackness." Nominated for the National Book Award, *I Know Why the Caged Bird Sings* becomes a standard on college campuses in the coming decades. It also signals the emergence of critically acclaimed popular fiction by African American women. The same year witnesses the publication of Toni Morrison's debut novel, *The Bluest Eye*; Alice Walker's *The Third Life of Grange Copeland*; and Toni Cade Bambara's *The Black*

Woman: An Anthology, which includes writing by Walker, Nikki Giovanni, Paule Marshall, and Audre Lorde. "The woman is a butt of the nation's sneer and the black is the butt of the nation's joke," Angelou tells Hollie West of the *Washington Post* on April 3, 1970. "Black women feel the joke and the sneer."[1]

JANUARY 31, 1970 "I Want You Back" by Motown's newest sensation, the Jackson Five—brothers Jackie, Tito, Jermaine, Marlon, and

The Jackson Five performing on *The Flip Wilson Show*.

Michael—reaches No. 1 on the *Billboard* 100. By the end of the year, they become the first group to top the US charts for eleven weeks with their first four singles, a mark of their crossover appeal. Jacksonmania keeps the Gary, Indiana, siblings on top of the Hot Soul Singles chart for twenty-one weeks.

MARCH 9, 1970 Two SNCC workers, Ralph Featherstone and William "Che" Payne, are killed when a bomb explodes in their car on US Route 1 South in Bel Air, Maryland. Local and federal authorities claim that the SNCC members were planning to use the bomb to assist the organization's leader, H. Rap Brown, in an escape from a Cambridge, Maryland, courthouse, where he was on trial. Others believe the two men were targeted by the FBI's COINTELPRO program.

APRIL 16, 1970 A *Time* magazine survey of "The Black Mood" finds it "More Militant" in its support of black cultural distinctiveness; "More Hopeful" when it comes to seizing greater economic opportunities; and "More Determined" to build on the gains of the civil rights struggles of the prior decade.[2]

APRIL 19, 1970 Tony Awards for Cleavon Little and Melba Moore in the musical comedy *Purlie* usher in a decade of standout performances by African American actors on Broadway. *Purlie*, based on the Ossie Day play *Purlie Victorious*, also features actor Sherman Hemsley and the orchestral conductor Joyce Brown, the first black conductor to open a Broadway show. "Black theatergoers particularly are coming to The Broadway Theater in large numbers to see this great show," Roland Forte writes in his rave review for the Cleveland *Call and Post* on June 27. *Purlie*

enjoys a nearly seven-hundred-show run on Broadway before closing in November 1971.[3]

MAY 1970 The first edition of *Essence* magazine is published, a testament to the growing purchasing power of African American women. The importance of African Americans in corporate America is also recognized in August 1970, when Earl Graves publishes the first edition of *Black Enterprise* magazine, with sponsorships from Coca-Cola, American Airlines, Ford, and Philip Morris.

MAY 1, 1970 Some fifteen thousand students at Yale University in New Haven, Connecticut, attend a series of rallies on campus to protest the jailing and trial of the Black Panther leaders Ericka Huggins and Bobby Seale. A year before, following the May 20, 1969, murder of a nineteen-year-old Black Panther named Alex Rackley in New Haven, the federal government, as part of its crackdown on the group's growing media presence and popularity, arrested Huggins and Seale (in addition to the three actual killers, also Panthers). Between the escalating war in Vietnam and fury over the unfair prosecution of Huggins and Seale, tensions on campus are at a fever pitch. Authorities fear the worst from the promised May Day protest of the Panthers' trial in New Haven, particularly after a mass meeting at Yale University's Ingalls Rink on April 21, 1970, during which the Panther David Hilliard challenges a packed audience of students to "off the pigs." In an effort to minimize injuries and bloodshed during the coming mass demonstration, Yale's president, Kingman Brewster, agrees to keep the university's gates open over the objections of faculty and alumni. Despite the presence of four thousand National Guardsmen

A protestor participates in a rally held for Bobby Seale and other members of the New Haven Nine on the campus of Yale University, 1970.

on the scene, with tanks, tear gas, and bombs intensifying the confusion, there are no major injuries suffered, and only twenty-one people are arrested, largely thanks to the behind-the-scenes coordination of President Brewster, his special assistant Henry "Sam" Chauncey, and three black student leaders, Glenn DeChabert, William F. Farley, Jr., and Kurt Schmoke, the future mayor of Baltimore. The May Day rally proves that as challenging as the transition is, African American students integrating Yale—

ninety-six black students had entered in 1969, as a result of affirmative action policies, as opposed to only twenty-three in 1965—had developed a stake in protecting peace at their alma mater. Reflecting on his experiences as a member of the class of 1973 at Yale, Henry Louis Gates, Jr., writes in his book *The Future of the Race*, coauthored with Cornel West: "It should be said that the adjustment was a two-way street: we were as strange to the institutions in which we found ourselves as those institutions were to us. In short, we were part of a grand social experiment—a blind date, of sorts. We weren't a tenth, of course; and whatever talent we had wasn't necessarily greater than our compeers who were passed over, or who opted out; but we were here. You might call us the crossover generation."[4]

MAY 13, 1970 Beulah Sanders and 150 mainly black female members of the National Welfare Rights Organization (NWRO) occupy the US Department of Health, Education, and Welfare offices in Washington, DC, for nine hours, until they are forcibly removed by several hundred police officers. The protest helps the NWRO defeat President Nixon's Family Assistance Plan (FAP), which proposes mandatory workfare and a national minimum income of $1,600 for a family of four.

MAY 15, 1970 At Jackson State College in Mississippi, a student protest against the Vietnam War results in police firing more than 150 rounds of ammunition into a student dormitory, killing two black students, twenty-one-year-old Phillip J. Gibbs and seventeen-year-old James Earl Green. The shootings fail to generate the same national attention seen ten days earlier when National Guardsmen killed four white students in a crowd of demonstrators at Kent State University in Ohio.

JUNE 7, 1970 At the twenty-second Emmy Awards celebration, Gail Fisher, starring as secretary Peggy Fair opposite actor Mike Connors in the hit detective drama *Mannix*, becomes the first African American woman to win an Emmy when her name is called for outstanding performance by an actress in a supporting role in a drama. (Harry Belafonte, the King of Calypso, was the first black performer to win an Emmy Award for his 1960 special *Tonight with Harry Belafonte*.) Fisher is quoted in the *Philadelphia Tribune* on June 30: "There's a whole new era coming in and actresses who've been around for years will most probably get a chance to show themselves. Take me, for example. Before 'Mannix' nobody knew me from a hole in the wall. . . . But I've had ten years of acting experience behind me."[5]

SEPTEMBER 5, 1970 Edwin Starr's "War," with its driving refrain, reaches No. 1 on the *Billboard* charts, capturing the prevailing mood of opposition to the Vietnam War, especially among African Americans. The song reflects a more radical political edge at Motown and proves to be an enduring antiwar anthem. It will be three more years before the troops return home.

SEPTEMBER 17, 1970 *The Flip Wilson Show* debuts on NBC. While Hazel Scott, in 1950, and Nat King Cole, in 1956, were the first black artists to host their own musical or variety TV shows, this is the first major comedy variety hour to be hosted by an African American. It becomes the nation's second-most-watched television show in its first season thanks to Wilson's comic cre-

Flip Wilson.

ations, including (in drag) the sassy southern Geraldine; the Reverend Leroy of the Church of What's Happenin' Now; and Sonny, the White House janitor who is more knowledgeable than the president. Wilson wins a Grammy in 1971 for his comedy album *The Devil Made Me Buy This Dress* (one of Geraldine's enduring catchphrases, along with "What you see is what you get") and two Emmys in 1973 for his television show, which ends after ninety-four episodes in June 1974.

OCTOBER 13, 1970 Angela Davis, a twenty-six-year-old former UCLA instructor, now a fugitive on the FBI's Ten Most Wanted list, is captured at a New York City motel and eventually extradited to California, where she will face trial for her alleged role in supplying guns to Jonathan Jackson, a seventeen-year-old who, on August 7, barged into a Marin County, California, courtroom to liberate three prisoners and take hostages. In all, four men were killed, including

Jackson and Judge Harold Haley. On Wednesday, October 14, members of the Northern California District of the Communist Party declare their solidarity with Davis: "Angela's record of defense of the Black community is a heroic one. She joined herself openly with the cause of all oppressed people. As a result of her good work, her job was taken from her, her life was threatened many times, her sister and brother-in-law were shot at and the houses of her friends were raided." Acquitted in 1972, Davis goes on to a distinguished teaching career at San Francisco State University and UC Santa Cruz and twice runs for vice president on the Communist Party USA ticket.[6]

1970 IN LETTERS The cultural critic and essayist Albert Murray publishes his controversial book *The Omni-Americans*. Where the Black Arts Movement (BAM) sees "the black experience" as separate and distinct from white American culture, Murray argues that "American" and "black American" culture are inseparable. They define one another, such that there is no so-called American culture without the African American formal element and content in its marvelous blend, and no black American culture without its white American influences and forms. Murray's *The Omni-Americans* spells the beginning of the end of BAM's dominance in the late 1960s and early '70s and helps give rise to the modernist and postmodernist artistic practices of writers such as Toni Morrison, Alice Walker, Maya Angelou, Leon Forrest, Ishmael Reed, Ernest Gaines, James Alan McPherson, Rita Dove, Elizabeth Alexander, and Colson Whitehead, who understand the task of the artist as finding the universal in African American history and culture. "There are white Americans so to speak and black Americans. But any fool can see that the white people are not really white and that black people are not black," Murray writes. "They are all interrelated one way or another."[7]

A supporter holds up a sign demanding the release of Angela Davis following her arrest.

1970 IN MUSIC The twenty-one-year-old musician and spoken-word performer Gil Scott-Heron's *A New Black Poet: Small Talk at 125th and Lenox* includes "The Revolution Will Not Be Televised" and "Whitey on the Moon." His experimental fusion of poetry, jazz, soul, and Black Nationalist politics enjoys only a small,

Gil Scott-Heron.

if dedicated, audience; in the decades to come, however, he will go on to be regarded as a godfather of rap. In a 2011 essay, "Prophetic Genius," the former NAACP president Benjamin Chavis will write on the death of his friend: "After you listen to Heron's music, it will make you want to join the movement for change where ever you are located. Gil Scott-Heron once told me, 'Hey man, each one of us has to play a role in making the revolution for freedom real. If someone merely gives you what you might think is your freedom, then it is not really freedom; it is just an illusion of freedom. . . . But, if you fight for your freedom, no one can ever take it away from you, can you dig it?' "[8]

1971

JANUARY 4, 1971 General Motors appoints Leon Sullivan to its board of directors. A Baptist minister whose efforts at organizing black-consumer boycotts of white businesses that refused to employ African Americans served as the inspiration for Martin Luther King's and Jesse Jackson's Operation Breadbasket, Sullivan is the first African American in the automobile industry to be so appointed.[9] Also in 1971, Johnson Products Company, Inc., becomes the first black-owned company listed on the American Stock Exchange.[9]

MARCH 8, 1971 After returning to professional boxing in 1970, Muhammad Ali (31–0 since 1960) is stunned when he loses a fifteen-round title fight to Joe Frazier at a sold-out Madison Square Garden in New York. "Defying an anonymous 'lose or else' death threat," Dave Marsh of the *New York Times* writes in his column the next day, "Frazier settled the controversy over the world heavyweight championship by handing Ali his first defeat with a savage attack that culminated in a thudding knockdown of the deposed titleholder from a hammerlike left hook in the final round." Frazier, notching his twenty-

seventh win, says afterward, "I always knew who the champion was." "In his failure," Marsh concludes, "Ali not only lost, but more embarrassing, he was silenced." What is known simply as "the Fight" is considered one of the most riveting—and most watched—boxing matches in history. It is not the last time the two heavyweights will square off in the ring.[10]

MARCH 11, 1971 Whitney M. Young, Jr., executive director of the National Urban League and one of the most prominent civil rights leaders of his generation, dies tragically while swimming in the waters off Lagos, Nigeria, where he is attending a conference on African and African American relations sponsored by the Ford Foundation. Young is only forty-nine years old, and his death is felt as a shock, especially by those who look to the Urban League for leadership on job creation in the black community. Young's funeral at Riverside Church in New York City is attended by throngs of mourners, including former US president Lyndon B. Johnson, while the sitting president, Richard M. Nixon, delivers remarks at Young's burial in Kentucky the following day. To fill the void, the Urban League in June names

Margaret Young walks toward the plane bearing the body of her husband, Whitney Young, following his sudden death in Lagos, Nigeria, in 1971. Young headed the National Urban League and acted as a trusted adviser to US president Lyndon Johnson.

Vernon Jordan, civil rights activist and influential consultant to national policy makers, serves as head of the National Urban League following the death of Whitney Young.

Vernon E. Jordan, Jr., a thirty-six year-old attorney who formerly headed the United Negro College Fund, as Young's successor. Jordan will take up his mantle in January 1972 and serve as executive director and later president of the Urban League until 1981.[11]

MARCH 25, 1971 The renowned black artist Romare Bearden launches his exhibition *The Prevalence of Ritual* at New York's esteemed Museum of Modern Art. Among the fifty-six works he displays is *The Block,* a collage of black life in Harlem enhanced by a recording of street sounds. A founder of the Spiral Group in 1963, with its focus on nurturing black artists, Bearden two years earlier joined with other creatives in protesting the dearth of African American visual arts at New York City's art museums. Out of that demonstration emerged the Black Emergency Cultural Coalition, which, among other achievements, brought an arts-exchange program to

Leading lights of the Black Arts Movement (standing from left to right): Bob Rogers, Ishmael Reed, Jayne Cortez, Léon-Gontran Damas, Romare Bearden, Larry Neal; (sitting) Nikki Giovanni, Evelyn Neal.

the prison system. "Art celebrates a victory," Bearden says in the press release for his breakthrough MOMA launch. "I look for all those elements in which life expresses that victory."[12]

APRIL 20, 1971 The US Supreme Court's unanimous 9–0 decision in *Swann v. Charlotte-Mecklenburg County Board of Education* is a major victory for the NAACP Legal Defense Fund's (LDF) strategy of promoting school integration through court-ordered busing. The case marks the high-water mark of the LDF's long crusade in the courts to secure equality in public education. As a result of the ruling, by 1972 46 percent of black children in the South will attend public schools in which whites are a majority. The equivalent figure for blacks in northern schools is only 28 percent.[13] In the same Court term, however, another ruling, *Palmer v. Thompson*, signals a shift away from integration, with the majority

Romare Bearden, *The Prevalence of Ritual-Baptism.*

holding that a decision by Jackson, Mississippi, to close its public swimming pools, rather than integrate them, did not conflict with the Equal Protection Clause of the Fourteenth Amendment. In his dissent, Justice Thurgood Marshall argues: "By effectively removing publicly owned swimming pools from the protection of the Fourteenth Amendment—at least if the pools are outside school buildings—the majority and concurring opinions turn the clock back 17 years. After losing a hard-fought legal battle to maintain segregation in public facilities, the Jackson, Mississippi, authorities now seek to pick and choose which of the existing facilities will be kept open. Their choice is rationalized on the basis of economic need, and is even more transparent than putting the matter to a referendum vote."[14]

APRIL 22, 1971   The Third Circuit US Court of Appeals in Philadelphia upholds the revised Philadelphia Plan formulated in 1969 by Arthur A. Fletcher, Nixon's assistant secretary of labor for wage and labor standards. A lifelong civil rights activist who maintained his allegiance to the Republican Party, Fletcher is considered by many to be "the father of affirmative action." The plan continues the affirmative action goals established in the Johnson administration. Instead of imposing strict quotas for hiring, it instead allows contractors to set their own goals by examining the availability of minority workers in the local workforce.

APRIL 23, 1971   The blaxploitation film genre explodes with the release of Melvin Van Peebles's *Sweet Sweetback's Baadasssss Song*. Opening in only two cinemas, one in Atlanta, the other in Detroit, the movie's popularity grows by word

of mouth—and by Van Peebles's ingenious marketing campaign, which introduces the film as "Rated X by an all-white jury." Later that year, Gordon Parks, Sr., directs Richard Roundtree in *Shaft*, "the black private dick who's a sex machine to all the chicks." The film wins Isaac Hayes the 1971 Oscar for Best Original Song. Both movies have small budgets—$150,000 for *Sweetback* and $500,000 for *Shaft*—but are incredibly successful: Van Peebles's film becomes the most profitable independent film in history up to that point, with box office of more than $15 million. *Shaft* grosses $13 million in the United States and Canada and, writes the

Movie poster, *Sweet Sweetback's Baadasssss Song*.

Movie poster, *Shaft*.

guard already dead and forty hostages taken, Rockefeller, convinced the uprising is the work of radicals and fearful of setting a precedent of pacification, orders his state troopers to act. Of the twenty-nine inmates and ten hostages killed, all of the latter are shot by state troopers and guards. Tear gas and emotions of retribution add to the chaos. Rockefeller's tough "law and order" stance appeals to white working-class men increasingly alienated by the Democratic Party's liberal policies, but it also radicalizes prisoners and prison reformers, who pursue a class-action lawsuit against the state. In 2000, New York ends up paying $8 million to the 1,280 prisoners who suffered during the attack.[16]

OCTOBER 2, 1971 *Soul Train* premieres on television with "Want Ads," by Honey Cone. The song, recorded for the Hot Wax label founded by Eddie and Lamont Dozier and Brian Holland

Inmates protesting at Attica State Prison in New York.

film historian Donald Bogle, "single handedly save[s] MGM from financial ruin."[15]

SEPTEMBER 13, 1971 New York's four-term Republican governor, Nelson A. Rockefeller, a longtime advocate for civil rights, decides to use overwhelming force to end a five-day prison uprising at the Attica State Penitentiary in western New York instead of meeting prisoners' demands to meet with him to discuss stifling conditions at the prison, including a limit of one shower per week and one roll of toilet paper per month. Many of those jailed at Attica are African American and Puerto Rican. With one prison after leaving Motown, occupies the No. 1 spot on the *Billboard* Hot Singles chart for three weeks. Powered by its innovative impresario Don Cornelius, who conceives of the show as a sort of *American Bandstand* for a black audience, *Soul Train* will run for thirty-five years. A trendsetter in the evolution of African American music, style, and dance, *Soul Train* provides an outlet that hasn't existed before for black performers and their fans, and it also wins a large white audience.

NOVEMBER 5, 1971 With a 110–106 victory over the Baltimore Bullets, the Los Angeles Lakers, led by their thirty-five-year-old star center Wilt Chamberlain, embark on what will become the longest winning streak in NBA history. After thirty-three games, the streak ends on January 9, 1972, when the Lakers fall to the Milwaukee Bucks, 120–114, fronted by another of the game's legendary centers, Kareem Abdul-Jabbar, age twenty-four, who scores thirty-nine points in the game. Later in the season, the Lakers get their revenge on the Bucks, beating them in the Western finals and going on to win the NBA championship, their first for the city of Los Angeles. According to the *NBA Encyclopedia: Playoff Edition*, the 1971–72 Lakers squad "won more games than any team in NBA history, with a 69–13 record, which in turn gave them the best winning percentage ever at .841. They had the most regular-season victories on the road, with 31, and the most at home, with 38." On January 30 of that magical season, Chamberlain surpasses Celtics great Bill Russell to become the league's all-time rebounder, with 21,734 to his name. By the time Chamberlain retires in 1973, he grabs 23,924, a record that stands to this day. "I rate consistency very high in athletics," Chamberlain tells the press after his record-setting game. "I admire the great athletes like Aaron, Mays, Unitas and Marichal who do it 12 and 13 years, not just for a couple of years. . . . There are so many big agile men around today,"

Actors James Caan and Billy Dee Williams run past Chicago Bears players. Williams plays running back Gale Sayers in the ABC television movie *Brian's Song,* airing in late 1971.

Chamberlain adds, "that it will be difficult for one man to dominate like Russell and myself."[17]

NOVEMBER 30, 1971 *Brian's Song*, a made-for-television movie about the close interracial friendship between Chicago Bears legend Gayle Sayers and the late Brian Piccolo, premieres as the ABC Movie of the Week in prime time. The film's two lead actors, Billy Dee Williams (Sayers) and James Caan (Piccolo), both receive Emmy nominations, and the film goes on to win five Emmy Awards, including Outstanding Single Program—Drama or Comedy. Williams, one of the decade's most magnetic leading men, will soon star alongside Diana Ross in a pair of films, 1972's *Lady Sings the Blues* and 1975's *Mahogany*, and in 1980, he will take on the prominent role of Lando Calrissian in the blockbuster science fantasy film *Star Wars: The Empire Strikes Back*, later reprising the part (and copiloting his character's old ship, the *Millennium Falcon*, in battle) in *The Return of the Jedi* in 1983.

DECEMBER 25, 1971 Jesse Jackson establishes his own organization, PUSH (People United to Save Humanity), in Chicago after tensions over the future direction of the SCLC emerge with Rev. Ralph Abernathy, immediate successor to Martin Luther King, Jr. A young ally of Jackson's in New York City, Rev. Al Sharpton, also leaves SCLC, and founds the National Youth Movement.

1971 IN MUSIC Marvin Gaye releases *What's Going On* in May. Motown founder Berry Gordy doubts the album's overt politics and musical experimentation will sell, but he is proved wrong when the album reaches No. 6 on the *Billboard*

Sly and the Family Stone.

Pop chart and the top of US Hot Soul. Sly and the Family Stone, displaying a darker edge than they did on earlier hits like "Everyday People," respond to Gaye by naming their November album *There's a Riot Goin' On.* Although Charley Pride's music stands in stark contrast sonically and politically to that of Sly and the Family Stone and Gaye, his selection as Country Music Association (CMA) Entertainer of the Year suggests that even in Nashville, *something* is going on. Despite the overt influence of black country blues on hillbilly music, including DeFord Bailey and Rufus "Tee Tot" Payne this is the first time an African American artist wins the CMA award.[18]

1972

JANUARY 14, 1972 *Sanford and Son*, starring Redd Foxx and Demond Wilson, debuts on NBC. The series, following the misadventures of a junk dealer and his son, runs for more than six seasons and is one of the most popular sitcoms of the decade, earning Foxx a Golden Globe in 1973. Foxx's wisecracks and wicked one-liners are comic gold.

JANUARY 25, 1972 Representative Shirley Chisholm (D-N.Y.) becomes the first woman and the first African American congressperson to seek the Democratic Party's nomination for president. The child of West Indian immigrants,

Demond Wilson and Redd Foxx in *Sanford and Son*.

Shirley Chisholm campaign poster.

Chisholm has a reputation for feisty independence that is captured in her campaign slogan, "Unbought and unbossed." During the Democratic primaries, she earns more than 430,000 votes but is unable to get on the ballot in several states. When roll is called at the 1972 Democratic National Convention in Miami Beach, Florida, Chisholm places fourth, with 5 percent of the delegates, behind the winner, George McGovern; Henry "Scoop" Jackson; and Alabama's ex-segregationist governor George Wallace. Chisholm later visits Wallace as he recuperates from an assassination attempt and works with him to support the first minimum-wage law covering domestic workers.[19]

FEBRUARY 19, 1972 The black entertainer Sammy Davis, Jr., appears as himself on an episode of Norman Lear's provocative, critically acclaimed television sitcom *All in the Family*. After riding as a passenger in the taxicab of Carroll O'Connor's bigoted but funny and loveable white character Archie Bunker, Davis, hip to his new "friend's" prejudices, plants a kiss on Archie's cheek during a photo op at the Bunkers' front door. Davis plays the scene for laughs as he exits with a clenched fist, saying, "Peace and love."

MARCH 10–12, 1972 Several thousand attend the first National Black Political Convention, held in Gary, Indiana, a majority-black city. Prominent attendees include Coretta Scott King and Betty Shabazz, widows of Martin Luther King and Malcolm X; Barbara Jordan (D-Texas), Ron Dellums (D-Calif.), and other members of the Congressional Black Caucus; Rev. Jesse Jackson of Operation PUSH; the minister Louis Farrakhan of the Nation of Islam; and the actor

Sammy Davis, Jr., kisses Archie Bunker (played by Carroll O'Connor) on the TV sitcom *All in the Family*.

Richard Roundtree of *Shaft* fame. The issues on their mind: school desegregation, national health insurance, and black electoral power and representation. "At every critical moment of our struggle in America we have had to press relentlessly against the limits of the 'realistic' to create new realities for the life of our people," the convention's agenda states. "This is our challenge at Gary and beyond, for a new Black politics demands new vision, new hope and new definitions of the possible. Our time has come. These things are necessary. All things are possible." The Agenda is a blueprint for change, however remote its chances of success.[20]

MARCH 24, 1972 Congress enacts the Equal Opportunity Act, broadening the powers of the Equal Employment Opportunity Commission to initiate lawsuits against companies that dis-

James Reynolds, director of the Colorado Civil Commission, discusses the Equal Employment Opportunity Act with other panelists.

criminate on the basis of race and gender. It also expands the EEOC's jurisdiction to federal, state, county, and municipal workplaces.[21]

MARCH 27, 1972 Diana Ross and Cicely Tyson are nominated for Best Actress Oscars for *Lady Sings the Blues* and *Sounder*, respectively.

APRIL 27, 1972 At age seventy-seven, Alma Thomas becomes the first African American woman to have a solo exhibition at New York's Whitney Museum of American Art. Her work is influenced by abstract expressionism and by the natural colors of the rural South. "A world without color would seem dead," she observes. "Color is life."[22] A major retrospective of her work is also held that year at the Corcoran Gallery in Washington, DC.

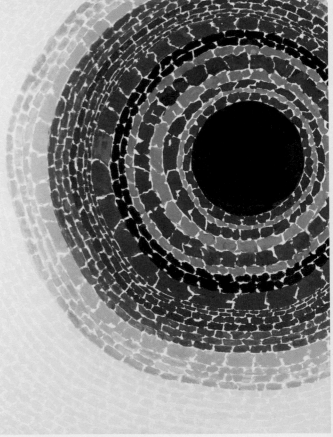

The Eclipse, painted by the abstractionist Alma Thomas.

Herman Shaw, one of the surviving subjects of the Tuskegee Syphilis Study, embraces President Bill Clinton at the White House.

JULY 25, 1972 The Associated Press publishes details of the Tuskegee Syphilis Experiment, revealing that over a period of forty years, the US Public Health Service withheld treatment from six hundred African American men in Alabama, two thirds of whom were infected with syphilis. Years later, in May 1997, the US government will issue a full and public apology, with President Bill Clinton admitting that the Tuskegee study was "racist" and "profoundly, morally wrong."[23]

AUGUST 1972 Ishmael Reed publishes his third novel, *Mumbo Jumbo*. Set in New York during the Harlem Renaissance, it introduces the concept of Neo Hoodooism, celebrating the role of traditional healing practices among Africans descended in the Americas. Critics regard it as Reed's greatest work, and it is cited as an influence by George Clinton, the leader of the music group Parliament-Funkadelic.

SEPTEMBER 9, 1972 Bill Cosby's *Fat Albert and the Cosby Kids*, based on his childhood memories of growing up in North Philadelphia, premieres as an animated series running on and off through 1985. Cosby voices many of his characters, including the eponymous star of the series, "Fat Albert" Jackson, whose indelible tagline is "Hey, hey, hey." The show overlaps for a month on television with another black animated series, *The Jackson 5ive*, coproduced by Motown and Rankin/Bass, which debuted a year earlier on ABC.

SEPTEMBER 27, 1972 Jesse Jackson and PUSH establish the first Black Business Exposition in Chicago to highlight black business success and cultural efforts in the Second City. Five hundred black businesses participate. The theme of the PUSH Expo is "Save the Children," and among the headliners performing are the Staple Singers, Gladys Knight and the Pips, and Sammy Davis, Jr.[24]

Ishmael Reed, author of *Mumbo Jumbo*.

NOVEMBER 3, 1972 US president Richard Nixon secures reelection in a landslide, defeating Democrat George McGovern in every state except for Massachusetts and the District of Columbia. Despite some prominent African American backers, including Floyd McKissisck, Sammy Davis, Jr., and the soul singer James Brown, Nixon wins only 13 percent of the black vote.

1972 IN MUSIC The Sound of Philadelphia emerges under the producers and writers Kenny Gamble and Leon Huff at Philadelphia International Records. Four No. 1 hits mark this inaugural year: "Back Stabbers" and "Love Train" by the O'Jays; "If You Don't Know Me by Now" by Harold Melvin and the Blue Notes; and the Grammy-winning "Me and Mrs. Jones" by Billy Paul. Gamble and Huff dominate the soul charts of the early 1970s. Among black music labels, only Motown enjoys greater sales than Philadelphia International by 1975. Another No. 1 hit, the instrumental "TSOP" by MFSB (Mother, Father, Sister, Brother), Sigma Sounds Studios' house band, will be used as the theme tune for *Soul Train*. The historian John Jackson has described the Philly sound as "a multilayered, bottom-heavy brand of sophistication and glossy urban rhythm and blues, characterized by crisp, melodious harmonies backed by lush, string-laden orchestrations and a hard driving rhythm section."[25] This year also witnesses the release of Aretha Franklin's live double album, *Amazing Grace*, marking a return to her gospel roots. The LP, her greatest popular suc-

Bill Withers.

cess, also features her father, Rev. C.L. Franklin, and a documentary film of the recording of the album is planned for release as a double bill with the blaxploitation movie *Superfly*, directed by Gordon Parks, Jr. Curtis Mayfield's *Superfly* soundtrack album is a watershed on the music scene in 1972, replacing Bill Withers's *Still Bill* atop the soul LP charts. Rounding out the leading album releases of the year are Al Green's *Let's Stay Together* and *I'm Still in Love with You*, which claims the No. 1 spot for a total of fifteen weeks.

1973

JANUARY 3, 1973 In his State of the State address in Albany, New York, Governor Nelson Rockefeller announces that, after spending $1 billion on programs to alleviate the growing drug-addiction epidemic in his state, the situation is only getting worse. "Whole neighborhoods have been as effectively destroyed by addicts as by an invading army. We face the risk of undermining our will as a people—and the ultimate destruction of our society as a whole." Pivoting to harsher punitive measures, Rockefeller proposes a series of "hard drug laws," including mandatory life imprisonment for drug dealers and for addicts who commit violent crimes. What become known as the Rockefeller Drug Laws profoundly shape the nexus between race and criminal justice in the country. Over time, other get-tough reforms feature mandatory prison sentences for possession of even small amounts of marijuana, cocaine, and heroin. Many commentators point to the connection between the Rockefeller Drug Laws, as they are known, and the seemingly ever-expanding "American prison industrial complex" by century's end.[26]

FEBRUARY 8, 1973 The growing black Caribbean influence on African American culture is seen in the US release of the film and

Bob Marley.

Ben Vereen as Judas in the Broadway rock opera *Jesus Christ Superstar.*

soundtrack to *The Harder They Come*, starring Jimmy Cliff, Desmond Dekker, Toots Hibbert, and other Jamaican ska and reggae artists. Later in the year, another Jamaican band, the Wailers—featuring Bob Marley, Bunny Livingston, and Peter Tosh—play their first concerts in Boston and New York City as part of their Catch a Fire tour. On October 20, in his piece titled "Wailers Wailin' Their Message to Third World People," D. J. Matthews of the *Philadelphia Tribune* writes, "As with any new sound, reggae has whispered its way onto our music world, and it is inevitable that pretty soon, we'll be singing its praises."

MARCH 25, 1973 Ben Vereen wins the Tony Award for his standout role as the lead performer in the Bob Fosse–directed Broadway musical *Pippin*. Vereen was nominated the previous year

for his performance as Judas in the Andrew Lloyd Webber rock opera *Jesus Christ Superstar*. The following year the Tony for Best Musical goes to *Raisin*, a musical adaptation of Lorraine Hansberry's 1959 Broadway drama classic, *A Raisin in the Sun*.

MAY 7, 1973 Roger Wilkins, an African American civil rights leader and journalist, shares the Pulitzer Prize for Public Service in Journalism with Carl Bernstein, Bob Woodward, and the editorial cartoonist Herb Block ("Herblock") for the *Washington Post*'s coverage of Watergate. In August 1974, President Nixon will resign over his role in the scandal.

MAY 22, 1973 Stating that children are "probably more in need of representation in an organized way than any other group in America," Marian Wright Edelman founds the Children's Defense Fund. Its primary focus is to investigate the nation's failure to enroll in school 5-plus percent of the nation's school-age population, a problem even more pronounced in black, poor,

Roger Wilkins, Pulitzer Prize–winning journalist.

Marian Wright Edelman, founder and president of the Children's Defense Fund.

and rural communities. Edelman is awarded the Presidential Medal of Freedom in 2000.[27]

JUNE 21, 1973 In *Keyes v. Denver School District*, the US Supreme Court extends to Hispanics in the Southwest rights similar to the desegregation remedies enjoyed by African Americans in the South. The liberal opinion expressed by Justice William Brennan sets a notable precedent by stating that de facto segregation in the West and urban North can be seen as equally culpable as de jure segregation in the South in violating the Fourteenth Amendment's Equal Protection Clause.

MAY 20, 1973 Tom Bradley, a sharecropper's son born in Texas and a former Los Angeles

police officer, defeats the incumbent Sam Yorty in a runoff election to become the first African American mayor of Los Angeles. He will serve for twenty years, during which time he will lead his city past Chicago to become the second largest in the country, behind New York.[28]

AUGUST 15, 1973 Eight months after the Supreme Court's *Roe v. Wade* ruling upholding a woman's constitutional right to seek an abortion during pregnancy, the National Black Feminist Organization is founded in New York City. Among its founders is Eleanor Holmes Norton, a veteran of the March on Washington and a future member of Congress from the District of Columbia.

AUGUST 11, 1973 The earliest grooves and scratches of a new musical form that will come to be known as hip-hop debut from the Jamaican-born DJ Kool Herc's sound system and turntables at his nighttime back-to-school jam in New York's South Bronx. Admission is fifty cents for

Lawyer and activist Florynce Kennedy attends the National Organization for Women's national convention in 1991. One of the first African American women to graduate from Columbia Law School, Kennedy was a founding member of the National Women's Political Caucus in 1971.

The pioneers of hip-hop attend Rap Summit at Columbia University, 1993: Grandmaster Flash, DJ Kool Herc, Afrika Bambaataa, and Chuck D.

Election Day, in Raleigh, North Carolina, Clarence E. Lightner, a fifty-two-year-old funeral director, becomes the first black man elected mayor of a major southern city with a white majority. (Four years earlier, Howard Lee, in the neighboring college town Chapel Hill, became the first African American mayor of a majority-white city since Reconstruction.)

1973 IN THE ECONOMY With the country entering a recessionary environment caused by inflation and a series of oil shocks, the annual black unemployment rate registers at 9.4 percent, almost twice the national rate. Black unemployment has been consistently twice that of the national rate since 1954, when the Government Bureau of Labor Statistics began tracking it, and it will remain over 10 percent until 1998.[30]

"fellas" and twenty-five cents for "ladies." Other Bronx DJs emerging in the mid-1970s are, notably, Grand Wizard Theodore and the Barbados-born Grandmaster Flash, both of whom claim to have invented scratching around 1975. The political and Black Power influence on these early spin masters can be seen as early as 1974, when the charismatic teenage gang member Afrika Bambaataa founds the Universal Zulu Nation as an alternative to gang culture. " 'Kool Herc, Grandmaster Flash and Bambaataa are the Holy Trinity of hip-hop,' " *Forbes* staff writer Zack O'Malley Greenburg quotes the hip-hop historian Jeff Chang as saying in 2009. " 'Bambaataa had this vision of hip-hop as a force for social change.... He was the guy who articulated that hip-hop could be a cultural movement.' "[29]

NOVEMBER 6, 1973 Maynard Jackson is elected Atlanta's first African American mayor, defeating the white incumbent, Sam Massell, the city's first Jewish mayor, by a 3–2 margin. The election is the city's first in which African Americans constitute a majority of Atlantans. Also on

Pioneering hip-hop artist Afrika Bambaataa at the turntable.

1974

JANUARY 7, 1974 During his inaugural address, Atlanta, Georgia's first black major, Maynard Jackson, declares, "Everybody knows the old South is dead forever, and thank goodness. But in spite of propaganda to the contrary, we have not yet seen the birth of a really new South." To speed that birth, Jackson establishes the Minority Business Enterprise Program, which revolutionizes African American participation in public works projects, including a major expansion of the city's airport into an international travel hub. The number of contracts with black businesses rises from 1 percent in 1973 to 39 percent five years later, greatly strengthening Atlanta's black middle class and creating several African American millionaires.[31]

JANUARY 28, 1974 In a rematch at Madison Square Garden in New York City, former heavyweight champion Muhammad Ali, by a unanimous decision after twelve rounds, defeats his archrival Joe Frazier. It has been nearly three

The Evans family gathered in the kitchen, from the TV sitcom *Good Times*.

years since Frazier beat Ali in their first match at the Garden. Afterward, both boxers say they look forward to a score-settling third contest.[32]

FEBRUARY 8, 1974 *Good Times*, the first sitcom set in a gritty working-class black neighborhood (in Chicago, spinning off from the *All in the Family* spin-off *Maude*), premieres on television and runs through 1979. Esther Rolle and John Amos play the parents of the Evans family, and the show makes a star of the comedian Jimmie Walker, a onetime member of the Black Nationalist group

the Last Poets, who, as J.J. Evans, immortalizes the line "Dy-no-mite!" Also in 1974, former *Laugh-In* comedienne Teresa Graves makes history by becoming the first black actress to star as a policewoman—actually an undercover cop for the Los Angeles Police Department—in the television drama *Get Christie Love!*

MARCH 2, 1974 Roberta Flack, a former music teacher and café performer with classical training from Howard University in Washington, DC, takes home the Grammy for Record of the Year with her transfixing rendition of "Killing Me Softly with His Song." It is the first time an artist has repeated in this category: the year before, Flack had clinched Record of the Year for her version of "The First Time Ever I Saw Your Face," which also appeared on the soundtrack for the Clint Eastwood film *Play Misty for Me*. Along with her brilliant solo career, Flack in 1972 released an album of duets through Atlantic Records with her fellow Howard alum, Donny Hathaway, that included the tracks "Where Is the Love" and "Be Real Black for Me." The latter's lyrics reflect a growing black consciousness in the country—not only within relationships, but as part of a cultural yearning for music that speaks to the black experience, the black body, and love.[33]

Movie poster for *Foxy Brown*, starring Pam Grier.

Henry "Hank" Aaron hits his 715th career home run, eclipsing Babe Ruth's long-standing record.

APRIL 5, 1974 Twenty-four-year-old Pam Grier stars with top billing in the blaxploitation film *Foxy Brown* after previous turns in *Coffy* and *Black Mama, White Mama*. In *Foxy Brown*, Grier once again proves she "can handle a lover, a gun, a car, a plane, four-letter language and her enemies with ease," writes the *New York Times* critic A.H. Weiler, concerned Grier is already being typecast. Linda Gross of the *Los Angeles Times* describes the film as James Bond meets Wonder Woman, and it is a major commercial hit for American International Pictures: with a budget of $500,000, it grosses $2.5 million. *Foxy Brown* solidifies Grier's place as a style icon whose round, natural Afro is considered one of the peak moments in the history of hair, and the film signals an important milestone in the development of 1970s black consciousness.[34] "I am where I am because I took those tough roles," Grier will tell Mary Murphy of the *Los Angeles Times* in 1976. "If I held out for those sweet, pretty demure parts I'd still be waiting."[35]

APRIL 8, 1974 In his second at-bat against Los Angeles Dodgers pitcher Al Downing, the Atlanta Braves' left fielder Henry Aaron cranks his 715th career home run, shattering the former Yankee great Babe Ruth's record, in place since 1935. In the long and wearing lead-up to this milestone, Aaron and his family receive racist letters and death threats from angry white fans who do not wish to see an African American recorded as the greatest home run hitter of all time, and they are under full-time police and FBI protection. An example: "Dear Nigger, you can hit all dem home runs over dem short fences, but you can't take dat black off your face." After breaking Ruth's record, Aaron says during a midgame ceremony on the field: "Thank God it's over." Aaron retires from baseball in 1976 with a total of 755 home runs, a figure later eclipsed (albeit controversially) by Barry Bonds in 2007.[36]

MAY 28, 1974 The television adaptation of the Ernest Gaines novel *The Autobiography of Miss Jane Pittman* earns nine Emmy Awards, includ-

Coleman Young, the mayor of Detroit, addresses racial unrest in the city.

ing Best Actress for Cicely Tyson in a career-defining role. It is the first Emmy won by an African American actress.

Beverly Johnson, the first black model to appear on the cover of *Vogue* in the US.

JUNE 17, 1974 Ten months after an August 1973 *Ebony* feature on the "The Black Middle Class Defined," *Time* magazine features a cover story on "America's Rising Black Middle Class." "With little fanfare, and without the rest of the society quite realizing it," the magazine observes, "more and more blacks are achieving the American dream of lifting themselves into the middle-class."[37]

JULY 25, 1974 Twenty years after the historic *Brown v. Board of Education* school-desegregation case, the US Supreme Court, in *Milliken v. Bradley*, nullifies an attempt to integrate black schools in Detroit with those of nearby white suburbs. Justice Thurgood Marshall, in dissent, calls the ruling "an emasculation of the constitutional guarantee of equal opportunity."[38]

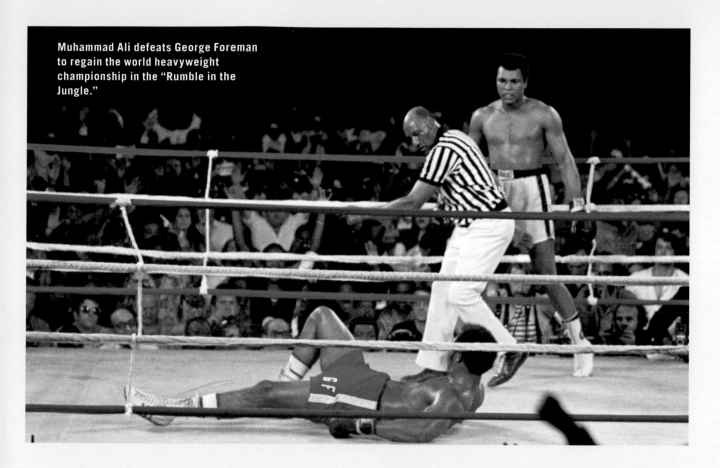

Muhammad Ali defeats George Foreman to regain the world heavyweight championship in the "Rumble in the Jungle."

AUGUST 1974 Beverly Johnson becomes the first black model to appear on the cover of *Vogue* magazine in the United States. (Donyale Luna, an African American model from Detroit, appeared on the cover of British *Vogue* eight years earlier, in 1966.)

SEPTEMBER 3, 1974 Thirty-seven-year-old Oscar Robertson, a twelve-time NBA all-star, announces his retirement to enter the broadcast booth at CBS. Robertson, who split his career between the Cincinnati Royals and Milwaukee Bucks, averaged twenty-six points a game during his career and claims the league's all-time assist record at 9,887. "No one comes close to him in the ability to break out a game," the legendary Celtics coach Red Auerbach says. "He's so great he scares me. He can beat you all

by himself and usually does." Hall of Fame point guard Jerry West, looking back in 2010, leaves no doubt: Robertson "is the best basketball player I have ever seen."[39]

OCTOBER 30, 1974 Using rope-a-dope-tactics, Muhammad Ali defeats George Foreman to regain the world heavyweight boxing title in Kinshasa, Zaire. The match is promoted by Don King and Lloyd Price with the title "From Slave Ship to Championship" to connect blacks with their African roots, but it is Ali himself who coins the more memorable phrase "Rumble in the Jungle."

DECEMBER 31, 1974 Carl Douglas's global No. 1 song, "Kung Fu Fighting," sells two million copies in its first year and is the latest dance craze to

Carl Douglas delivers a high kick while performing his hit song, "Kung Fu Fighting."

diverse world of popular music in the 1970s. It also signifies African Americans' growing interest in martial arts. Bruce Lee's kung fu movies have a huge audience among black cinemagoers, and Scatman Crothers voices the kung-fu-fighting dog and title character of *Hong Kong Phooey*, a short-lived Hanna-Barbera cartoon airing on ABC between September and December. "To dance the Kung Fu this New Year's Eve, one must be prepared to kick, jab and chop one's way across the dance floor," writes Henry Edwards of the *New York Times*.[40]

1974 IN MUSIC Gloria Gaynor's hit "Never Can Say Goodbye" is the first No. 1 record on *Billboard*'s new music chart listing top disco hits. Born in the gay, black, Latin, and Italian dance-club scene in the early 1970s and strongly influenced by the Philadelphia Sound, disco quickly emerges as a distinct genre and phenomenon. Other top disco hits that year are the Hues Corporation's "Rock the Boat" and George McCrae's "Rock Your Baby." In New York City, WPIX launches the first radio show dedicated to disco music.

usher in the new year. Written by a white Jewish American, produced by an Anglo-Indian, and sung by a black Jamaican, the song reflects the

1975–1979

George Clinton, aka Dr. Funkenstein, singing onstage with Parliament-Funkadelic, Madison Square Garden, 1977.

1975

JANUARY 5, 1975 *The Wiz*, a reworking of L. Frank Baum's children's classic *The Wizard of Oz*, debuts on Broadway with an all-black cast including Stephanie Mills, Hinton Battle, and Ted Ross. It dominates at the Tony Awards, winning seven prizes, among them Best Musical. A film version—starring Diana Ross, Michael Jackson, Nipsey Russell, Richard Pryor, and Ted Ross reprising his Broadway role of the Lion—appears three years later.

JANUARY 18, 1975 *The Jeffersons*, another spin-off of *All in the Family*, makes its television debut, with a theme song that finds George and Louise Jefferson, played by Sherman Hemsley and Isabel Sanford, "moving on up" from their working-class neighborhood in Queens to a "deluxe apartment in the sky" on Manhattan's Upper East Side. The series, which will run for a decade, earns thirteen Emmy nominations, including seven consecutive nods and one win, in 1981, for Sanford. Among the *Jeffersons* cast of characters is George and Louise's maid, Florence, played by Marla Gibbs, and the Willises, an interracial couple living as their neighbors, played by Roxie Roker and Franklin Cover. Dry-

cleaning store owner George Jefferson, famous for his three-piece suits and bouncing strut, is Archie Bunker's black analogue, prone to calling white people "honky."

Sherman Hemsley and Isabel Sanford in a promo still for *The Jeffersons*.

Nation of Islam leader Louis Farrakhan addresses his followers in Chicago.

FEBRUARY 25, 1975 The death of Elijah Muhammad in Chicago at age seventy-seven leads to a split within the Black Muslim movement. The majority of his followers join his son and successor, Warith Deen Muhammad, in moving toward a more traditional form of Sunni Islamic religious observance. One of Warith Deen Muhammad's first changes is to open up membership to whites and to disband the paramilitary Fruit of Islam. Others in the movement gravitate toward the more politi-

cally inclined Black Nationalist organization, the Nation of Islam, under the leadership of minister Louis Farrakhan.[1]

MARCH 10, 1975 The former talent agent Wally Amos establishes the Famous Amos Chocolate Chip Cookie Company, a $250 million business in the making, with his first shop on Sunset Boulevard in Los Angeles. The company's branding, with Amos in his trademark embroidered shirt and panama hat, becomes one of the more visible examples of black capitalism in action. "What I'm doing really," Amos says in a *New York Times* profile on August 16, "is combining everything I've ever learned in my life—my business college training, my show business background, my promotion experience—and applying it to selling these cookies. I manage the cookie."[2]

APRIL 18, 1975 Van McCoy's recording of "The Hustle" is released and dominates the dance floors, reaching No. 1 on both the *Billboard* Hot 100 and Hot Soul Singles charts. "The hustle," writes Dena Kleiman of the *New York Times* on July 12, "is believed to have had its origins five years ago in the black and Puerto Rican bars of

Baker "Famous Amos" holds a tray of his signature cookies.

The multiracial singing group the Village People onstage: Victor Willis, in the foreground, features prominently as the group's original lead singer.

Queens" and "is danced to 'disco,' a black-based rhythm and blues characterized by a strong, rhythmic bass guitar, that in itself is achieving wide popularity." A harsher though no less danceable musical note is struck by the Isley Brothers' "Fight the Power," which replaces McCoy at the top of the soul charts and will play a critical role in the history of hip-hop when Public Enemy samples it in their defining anthem of the same name in 1988. By the end of 1975, there are a reported ten thousand discos in the United States.[3]

AUGUST 15, 1975 A Raleigh, North Carolina, jury acquits Joan (pronounced *Jo-Ann*) Little of murder charges, finding that she was justified in using deadly force to resist her attacker, a prison officer who had raped her. That Ms. Little wins,

even though she is African American and her assailant was white, speaks to a long but often hidden history of racial and sexual oppression in which white men's abuse of black women's bodies was not only not punished but tolerated by law and custom. Angela Davis writes of the trial in *Ms.* magazine: "Those of us—women and men— who are black or people of color must understand the connection between racism and sexism that is so strikingly manifested in her case. Those of us who are white and women must grasp the issue of male supremacy in relationship to the racism and class bias, which complicate and exacerbate it."[4]

OCTOBER 1, 1975 With the title on the line, Muhammad Ali and Joe Frazier square off for a third and final contest, this time at Araneta

Parliament-Funkadelic performing as the *Mothership* lands.

Coliseum in Quezon City, Philippines. Billed as "the Thrilla in Manila," the fight does not disappoint, lasting fourteen rounds, until Frazier's trainer tells the referee his man cannot continue. "It was a war," reports the *Washington Post*, "and Ali fired the most telling and accurate shots as he pounded and pounded rights and lefts to Frazier's head in the 13th and 14th rounds that closed the challenger's eyes and had him reeling." Afterward, Ali says of his opponent, Smokin' Joe, "He is the best there is except me." Until now, Frazier is the only boxer to have defeated Ali, other than Ken Norton in 1973. "I want to retire. It's too much work; too painful," Ali is quoted saying after the fight. "I might have a heart attack. I want everyone to know that I'm the greatest fighter of all time."[5]

DECEMBER 13, 1975 Richard Pryor introduces Gil Scott-Heron during the inaugural season of the sketch-comedy show *NBC's Saturday Night* (later *Saturday Night Live*). Scott-Heron performs "Johannesburg," the opening track on his album *From South Africa to South Carolina*. In politics as well as in culture, African Americans begin to make connections between the US and apartheid South Africa. That same month, Georgia congressman Andrew Young denounces the Central Intelligence Agency's support of pro-apartheid forces in the Angolan civil war and calls for US involvement in an African development bank.[6]

DECEMBER 15, 1975 Parliament-Funkadelic releases *Mothership Connection* as a follow-up to that year's *Chocolate City*. Where the latter is an homage to majority-black cities, especially Washington, DC, *Mothership Connection* sets its sights on the equally funky farther reaches of the cosmos. With George Clinton at the helm on vocals, Bootsy Collins on bass, and Bernie Worrell on keyboards, the LP becomes a funk classic be heavily signified upon in the hip-hop era.

DECEMBER 15, 1975 *Time* magazine reports on the growing resegregation of schools in the South by way of private academies. During the year, 3,500 such academies enroll 750,000, or 10 percent, of the region's white school-age children. The trend continues throughout the rest of the century and spreads outward from the South, nullifying many of the gains achieved by busing as a way of integrating public schools following 1971's *Swann* ruling. By 2014, whites, although 78 percent of the national population, are a minority in the public K-12 system, where 50.3 percent of the students are black, Latino, or Asian.[7]

1976

JANUARY 27, 1976 Before its merger with the NBA, the American Basketball Association (ABA) launches the first Slam Dunk Contest at its All-Star Game at McNichols Sports Arena in Denver, Colorado. The masters of the universe that night are Julius "Dr. J" Erving of the New York Nets and David Thompson of the hometown Denver Nuggets. It is Erving who wins the contest with a slam dunk delivered all the way from the free-throw line. Not only does it ignite the crowds, Erving's dunk forever transforms the way the game of basketball is played and enjoyed. "We've seen better dunks since then," the player George Gervin recalls in Eric Neel's piece for ESPN's *Page 2,* "The Day the Dunk Was Born," "but David and Doc got something started that night with the 360 and the Free Throw; they showed us some amazing sights people had never seen before, and they laid a foundation for everything we see now."[8]

JANUARY–FEBRUARY 1976 During the Republican Party's primary contest in New Hampshire, the presidential contender Ronald Reagan, a former actor and governor of California, launches an attack on Linda Taylor, a so-called "welfare queen" from Chicago who, Reagan alleges, makes enough money gaming the welfare system to buy a Cadillac. Although Reagan does not explicitly state that the woman is black, observers view his remarks, which send fact checkers scurrying, as a coded appeal to white voters resentful of social welfare programs perceived as advantaging African Americans. "We lopped four hundred thousand off the welfare rolls," Reagan tells voters about his record as California governor. This is Reagan's second bid for the presidency, and in a close race, he loses the nomination to the incumbent president, Gerald Ford, who succeeded Richard Nixon after the Watergate scandal in 1974.[9]

FEBRUARY 28, 1976 *Rufus Featuring Chaka Khan* reaches the top of *Billboard*'s R&B album charts and stays there into the spring. The Chicago funk band made a breakthrough in 1974 with its version of Stevie Wonder's "Tell Me Something Good." Its twenty-two-year-old lead singer, Chaka Khan, a former member of the Black Panthers, is touted by some critics a bridge to the enduringly popular Aretha Franklin and Tina Turner. By fall, Stevie Wonder's *Songs in the Key of Life*, featuring "Sir Duke," his homage to the jazz great Duke Elling-

Tina Turner.

ton, and "Isn't She Lovely," soars to the top of the R&B charts and remains there for nineteen of the next twenty weeks.

APRIL 5, 1976 A busing crisis in Boston, Massachusetts, comes to a head when images go public of a mob of white youths attacking Ted Landsmark, a black lawyer. Their weapon of choice: a large American flag. The photo is especially poignant during the nation's bicentennial year. Racial tensions had simmered in Boston, known as "the cradle of liberty" for its historic role in the American Revolution, since 1974, when a federal ruling required the city to begin busing students to integrate its public schools. Whites opposed to the plan establish the organization Restore Our Alienated Rights (ROAR), and the period witnesses numerous racially motivated attacks, including an October 7, 1974, riot by black students in Roxbury in violent response to the beating of a black man, André Yvon Jean-Louis, by a white mob in South Boston.[10]

Chaka Khan performs with Rufus on *Soul Train*.

The Soiling of Old Glory, Stanley Forman's award-winning photo from the Boston busing crisis, shows black lawyer Ted Landsmark under attack at the point of the flag.

JUNE 25, 1976 In *Runyon v. McCrary*, the US Supreme Court rules 6–2 in support of two African American students in Fairfax, Virginia, refused admission to a private day-care facility. The case sets a precedent that private organizations, as well as public ones, can be sued for racial discrimination. The two dissents in the case flow from the pens of the Court's leading conservative, William Rehnquist, and Byron White, a former college and NFL star who believes the case will force unwanted desegregation on both black and white private organizations.

JULY 4, 1976 The bicentennial of American independence, one year after the fall of Saigon and the end of the Vietnam War, causes many to examine the ties that bind citizens to their common heritage and to each other. Black Americans reflect on the bicentennial in diverse ways, including calls for a celebration and recognition of black Revolutionary War heroes like Crispus Attucks, a victim of the Boston Massacre in March 1770. Black History Month (originating

Gerry O'Leary, William Bulger, and Louise Day Hicks, on the megaphone, at an anti-busing rally.

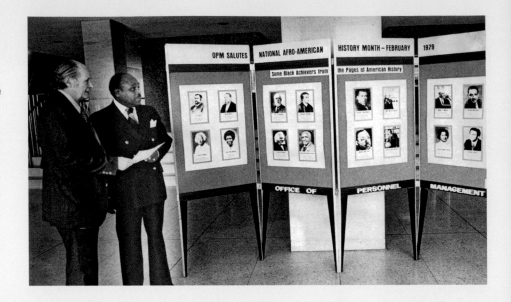

Dr. J. Rupert Picott, right, executive director of the US Office of Personnel Management, stands beside a display of Black History Month images, 1976.

in the historian Carter G. Woodson's Negro History Week in 1926) becomes a national event as part of the country's bicentennial celebration. Others take a more caustic view of this display of national pride. Gil Scott-Heron, in his poem "Bicentennial Blues," writes: "From Plymouth Rock to acid-rock / From 13 states to Watergate / The blues is grown / But not the home / The blues is grown / But the country has not / The blues remembers everything the country forgot." Or, as Richard Pryor puts it more succinctly on his Grammy-winning concert LP, *Bicentennial Nigger,* 1976 signals "two hundred years of white folks kicking ass."[11]

JULY 12, 1976 Congresswoman Barbara Jordan of Texas steps forward as the first African American to deliver the keynote address at the Democratic National Convention. Her address at Madison Square Garden in New York City reflects Democratic presidential candidate Jimmy Carter's assiduous courting of African American political leaders, especially in his native Georgia and across the South. Jordan's

US representative and keynote speaker Barbara Jordan appears on the podium with presidential candidate Jimmy Carter at the 1976 Democratic National Convention in New York.

Ntozake Shange (right) performs in her play *for colored girls who have considered suicide/when the rainbow is enuf.*

speech is an impassioned defense of the idea that Americans can make their creed of equality and justice a political reality. A panel of experts on public speeches later recognizes it as the fifth-greatest American speech of the twentieth century. "It was one hundred and forty-four years ago that members of the Democratic Party first met in convention to select a presidential candidate," Jordan tells those gathered in the hall. "Since that time, Democrats have continued to convene once every four years and draft a party platform and nominate a presidential candidate. And our meeting this week is a continuation of that tradition. But there is something different about tonight. There is

something special about tonight. What is different? What is special? I, Barbara Jordan, am a keynote speaker. . . . And I feel that notwithstanding the past that my presence here is one additional bit of evidence that the American dream need not forever be deferred."[12]

AUGUST 5, 1976 US president Gerald Ford awards the Presidential Medal of Honor, the nation's highest civilian honor, to the black Olympian Jesse Owens. Ford also appoints a senior liberal black Republican, William Coleman of Philadelphia, as his secretary of transportation, and pursues a less abrasive approach to civil rights leaders and the Congressional Black Caucus. The CBC, though less hostile to Ford than to Nixon, strongly criticizes him for his opposition to busing and for his foreign policies in Africa.

SEPTEMBER 15, 1976 After stints at a Lower East Side bar and the Public Theater, Ntozake Shange's play *for colored girls who have considered suicide/when the rainbow is enuf* makes its Broadway debut. "What does it mean to be a black woman in white America?" the *New York*

Gamers play with vintage video games, including the Atari system developed by the black entrepreneur Jerry Lawson.

Times' Mel Gussow asks in the first line of his review. "The search for self, the struggle for singularity, the anguished urging to be loved are at the root of Ntozake Shange's remarkable evening of theater." Feminist themes become more visible among other black artists such as Faith Ringgold, whose performance piece *The Wake and Resurrection of the Bicentennial Negro* is first performed at Wilson College in Chambersburg, Pennsylvania, where she is an artist in residence.[13]

OCTOBER 20, 1976 Gerald A. "Jerry" Lawson, an African American engineer who attended Queens College and the City College of New York, is asked by his company, Fairchild Camera & Instrument (later Fairchild Semiconductor International), to work on a video-game console after it learns he already has invented his own coin-operated arcade game. The result is the Fairchild Video Entertainment System (Channel F), the first video-game system to be cartridge-based and the first console to leverage a microprocessor, approved for sale by the Federal Communications Commission on this date—in time for the holiday season. In 1980, Lawson cofounds Video Soft, Inc. In 2011, the year of his death, he is celebrated by the International Game Developers Association. "The whole reason I did games was because people said, 'You can't do it,'" Lawson says, looking back on his career, which included membership in the illustrious Homebrew Computer Club of the early 1970s with Apple cofounders Steve Jobs and Steve Wozniak. "I'm one of the guys, if you tell me I can't do something, I'll turn around and do it."[14]

NOVEMBER 2, 1976 Democrat Jimmy Carter ekes out a narrow victory over the incumbent, Republican Gerald Ford. While Ford wins a majority of the white vote, Carter secures 83 percent of the black vote, which proves decisive in winning several states, notably Mississippi and Barbara Jordan's Texas.[15] Among the minor candidates for president is the Watts welfare rights activist Margaret Wright, running on the socialist People's Party ticket with the pediatrician and child psychologist Dr. Benjamin Spock; together, they garner fifty thousand votes out of eighty-one million cast.

1977

JANUARY 8, 1977 At the National Cathedral in Washington, DC, Dr. Pauli Murray, a lawyer and veteran of the civil rights sit-in movement decades earlier, becomes the first African American woman priest ordained in the Episcopal Church. Once rejected from Harvard Law School because of her gender, Murray joined Betty Friedan in founding the National Organization of Women in 1966 and served as a professor and consultant to the EEOC before turning to the priesthood. "I didn't decide to become a priest in order to do this. God decided this," Murray tells J. Wynn Rousuck of the *Sun* on April 24, 1977. "Why is it that national recognition comes to me only when I am an ordained priest? If you can answer that question you'll know why I became a priest."[16]

Rev. Pauli Murray, the first black woman to be ordained an Episcopal priest.

JANUARY 30, 1977 Representative Andrew Young (D-Ga.) is sworn in as the US ambassador to the United Nations, the first African American to hold the position. The appointment of Young, a former aide to Martin Luther King, Jr., is one of several notable black appointments in the Carter administration. Carter, who received an overwhelming percentage of the black vote in the election, now relies heavily on the advice of Washington insiders Vernon Jordan, executive director of the National Urban League, and Marian Wright Edelman, founder of the Children's Defense Fund, in vetting administration appointees. Among them are Patricia Harris, who becomes the first black woman to hold a cabinet-level position when

Rev. Jesse Jackson with Patricia Roberts Harris at her swearing-in ceremony.

Carter appoints her secretary of Housing and Urban Development (HUD); Eleanor Holmes Norton, head of the Equal Employment Opportunity Commission (EEOC); and Clifford Alexander as secretary of the Army. In his role as secretary, Alexander promotes a young African American colonel to the rank of general. His name is Colin Powell. "Black people with sterling records emerged on those lists," Alexander wrote years later. "Yes, Colin Powell was like his white fellow generals—no better, no worse. He did not get anything extra—but more important, his white colleagues did not get anything extra either."[17]

Clifford Alexander, first black secretary of the US Army.

FEBRUARY 2, 1977 One hundred million viewers watch the final episode of ABC's adaptation of Alex Haley's *Roots*, the biggest audience for a television show at the time. More than 85 percent of American households tune in to at least part of the series, which is shown over eight nights. Haley wins a special Pulitzer Prize for his original book, and the television series goes on to receive thirty-seven Emmy nominations. While Haley must confront charges of fabricating and lifting elements of his family tree, *Roots* inspires countless Americans, especially black Americans, to search for clues in their ancestry and retrace their heritage to the African continent. "I do not believe it is something I have done by myself," Haley says in his keynote address at the 1977 Opportunity Fair of the Greater Washington Business Center on February 23. "I believe that I have only been a channel, a conduit that has been used at this particular time to tell the story of a people."[18]

APRIL 1977 A gathering of leading black feminist and lesbian writers and activists pen the

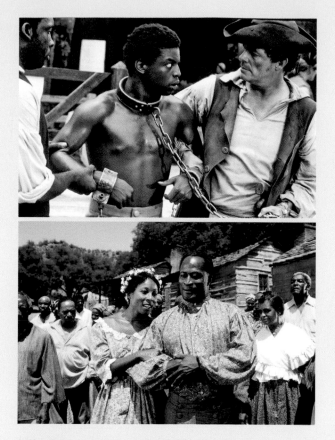

potentially most radical politics come directly out of our own identity, as opposed to working to end somebody else's oppression. In the case of Black women this is a particularly repugnant, dangerous, threatening, and therefore revolutionary concept because it is obvious from looking at all the political movements that have preceded us that anyone is more worthy of liberation than ourselves. We reject pedestals, queenhood, and walking ten paces behind. To be recognized as human, levelly human, is enough." The statement appears in Zillah Eisenstein's anthology *Capitalist Patriarchy and the Case for Socialist Feminism* (1978). The inspiration for the collective's name comes from Harriet Tubman's guerrilla campaign to free slaves during the American Civil War.[19]

LeVar Burton appears as Kunta Kinte in the groundbreaking television miniseries *Roots*. Above: Kunta Kinte in chains. Below: John Amos, as an older Kunta Kinte, marries Bell (Madge Sinclair).

JULY 1, 1977 Randall Robinson is the founding executive director of TransAfrica, a lobbying organization geared toward US policy on Africa and the Caribbean. The presence of TransAfrica reflects the Carter administration's foreign-policy focus on human rights and its pursuit of "African solutions to African problems."

Combahee River Collective Statement, a foundational document that articulates a distinct African American women's political voice. The group, organized in Boston in 1974 and continuing through 1980, includes Barbara Smith, Gloria Hull, and Audre Lorde, who together argue that "the most profound and

Randall Robinson, executive director of TransAfrica, demonstrates against apartheid outside the South African embassy. Beside him are the children of Robert Kennedy.

Justice A. Leon Higginbotham, chief judge of the Federal Court of Appeals for the Third Circuit, testifies before the House Judiciary Committee.

SEPTEMBER 19, 1977 President Carter elevates Federal District Court Judge A. Leon Higginbotham to the Third Circuit US Court of Appeals; a year later, Higginbotham publishes *In the Matter of Color*, the first scholarly examination of race and the law in American history. Should Carter have the chance to make an appointment to the US Supreme Court, many believe he will tap Higginbotham, one of the most gifted jurists of his generation. (Instead, when Carter leaves office in 1981, he will be the only president in American history to serve a full term without having the opportunity to appoint a single Supreme Court justice.[22])

UN ambassador Andrew Young plays a central role in ensuring that Carter enforces sanctions against the minority-ruled government in Rhodesia until an agreement can be reached for free elections in 1979. A year later, the independent nation of Zimbabwe is formed.[20]

SEPTEMBER 13, 1977 *The Richard Pryor Show* debuts in prime time on NBC but is canceled controversially after just four episodes. In one skit, Pryor portrays a black American president, answering reporters' questions on when he will stop dating white women. In another, he plays a white prosecutor in a southern rape trial. Although the show's ratings of twenty million viewers is deemed "poor" by NBC, the company's censorship of Pryor's material is also a factor in its demise. In the final episode of the show, only twenty-two words are broadcast from the first sixty-five minutes of Pryor's actual performance.[21]

New York Yankees slugger Reggie Jackson on the cover of the New York *Daily News*.

DJ and record producer Frankie Knuckles, known as the "Godfather of House Music."

OCTOBER 18, 1977 In the sixth game of baseball's World Series, New York Yankee Reggie Jackson, "Mr. October," hits three consecutive home runs off three different pitchers to defeat the Los Angeles Dodgers and clinch the series for his team. Babe Ruth was the only other slugger ever to smash three homers in a single World Series game, doing so twice but not in consecutive at-bats. As a sign of Jackson's popularity, Standard Brands, Inc., markets the Reggie candy bar when the next season begins.[23]

1977 IN MUSIC During a hot summer in New York City, exacerbated by a blackout on July 13–14 and a series of gruesome murders by the infamous serial killer known as Son of Sam, the twenty-year-old Bronx DJ Afrika Bambaataa provides block-party entertainment that signals the expansive cultural possibilities of the nascent musical form of hip-hop. According to a 2009 profile in *Forbes* by Zack O'Malley Greenburg, what Bambaataa concocts that summer will serve as hip-hop culture's defining ingredients—"deejaying, painting graffiti, emceeing (rapping) and b-boying (break dancing)"—to which Bambaataa "add[s] a fifth: knowledge." In Chicago, Frankie "the Godfather" Knuckles is the resident DJ at the opening night of a predominantly gay and lesbian black club called the Warehouse. Although he does not use the phrase himself, Knuckles ushers in the era of what becomes known as "house music." Other founders include Ron Hardy and Farley "Jackmaster" Funk. "Even when they're hopping up and down on the dance floor, it still has their spirit calm, because they're concentrating on having a good time, loving the music, as opposed to thinking something negative," Knuckles is quoted as saying in a profile by Greg Kot in the *Chicago Tribune* in 1991. Fast-forward to the year 2006, when the hip-hop pioneer Grandmaster Caz (aka Curtis Fisher) narrates a hip-hop history bus tour through the New York City streets for the company Hush Tours. "The rappers today," Caz says, "who can drive around in Bentleys, with their jewelry and million-dollar home. . . . They're able to live like that because cats like me and Bambaataa . . . were in the trenches back in the day, laying the groundwork and getting chased off the block by the police."[24]

1978

JANUARY 11, 1978 Toni Morrison's *Song of Solomon* wins the National Book Critics Circle Award. Its republication as the second choice of Oprah Winfrey's Book Club series in 1996 makes the novel a global bestseller.

JANUARY 31, 1978 The NASA Johnson Space Center in Houston, Texas, announces that three African Americans, Guion S. Bluford, Frederick D. Gregory, and Ronald McNair will join the space program. In October 1983, Bluford becomes the first African American in space, as part of the eighth space shuttle launch. (He was preceded three years earlier by the Cuban cosmonaut Arnaldo Tamayo Méndez, who was the first person of African descent in space, as part of the Soviet Union's Soyuz missions.)

FEBRUARY 1, 1978 Harriet Tubman is the first black woman to be honored on a US postage stamp as part of the US Post Office's Black Heritage Series. The idea for a series of postal stamps commemorating African Americans originates with Clarence L. Irving, Sr., the chairman and founder of the Black American Heritage Foundation.

Max Robinson, seen here in the ABC television studio with Frank Reynolds and Peter Jennings.

FEBRUARY 2, 1978 Faye Wattleton is appointed president of Planned Parenthood, the first African American to hold the position. At age thirty-four, she is also the organization's youngest president and the first woman to hold the post since founder Margaret Sanger in 1942. Accepting her appointment, Wattleton declares at New York press conference that she is "putting the world on notice" that under her leadership, the group will take a bolder approach in defending women's reproductive rights against the vocal, well-funded, and well-organized Right to Life anti-abortion movement that emerged in the wake of the Supreme Court's 1973 *Roe v. Wade* decision. "What's really important," Wattleton tells the press, "is that black women have equal access to determining when and how they will have children."[25]

FEBRUARY 15, 1978 At the Hilton Hotel in Las Vegas, Nevada, Muhammad Ali loses his heavyweight title to Leon Spinks in a split decision after fifteen rounds. Ali is thirty-six, Spinks twenty-four. SPINKS DETHRONES ALI, the *Los Angeles Times* headline reads the next day; SCORES SHOCKING UPSET IN ONLY EIGHTH PRO FIGHT. Analyzing his defeat, Ali tells the press, "My rope-a-dope didn't work. He was too strong. It was more a mistake in strategy. I could say a lot of things were wrong, but they would sound like excuses. But there are no excuses. It was close, but he beat me." Gracious in victory, Spinks says of Ali, "He's still the greatest. . . . I'm just the latest." Proving it, Ali defeats Spinks by a unanimous decision in a rematch at the Superdome in New Orleans on September 15, marking the third time Ali has held boxing's crown. On that night, Ali reflects, "My greatest fight was against Joe Frazier in Manila. But this was my most satisfying fight."[26]

FEBRUARY 28, 1978 Sociologist William Julius Wilson, of the University of Chicago, pens an editorial in the *New York Times* titled "Poor Blacks' Future," in which he notes a growing divergence within the African American community. "As the black middle class rides on the wave of political and economic changes, benefiting from the growth of employment opportunities and the application of affirmative-action programs in the growing corporate and government sectors of the economy," Wilson warns, "the black underclass falls behind the larger society in every conceivable respect." The following year, Wilson publishes *The Declining Significance of Race: Blacks and Changing American Institutions* a pioneering work that argues class is becoming a more important factor than race in determining the life chances of African Americans. The book inspires more than eight hundred empirical studies by 2012, and many more nonscholarly responses.[27]

JUNE 8, 1978 The long-standing policy of the Mormon Church to exclude African American men from the priesthood is reversed when church president Spencer W. Kimball receives the revelation from God that was necessary to end the ban. The change has a limited impact on black membership in the church: a 2009 Pew Forum survey of religious affiliation finds that Mormons comprise 1.7 percent of the US population, and only 3 percent of LDS members are black. The end of the ban on black Mormon priests has, however, boosted the growth of the church among blacks in the Caribbean, Latin America, and Africa.[28]

JUNE 28, 1978 In a landmark affirmative action decision, *Regents of the University of California v.*

Demonstrators protest the *Bakke* case.

Bakke, the US Supreme Court upholds the right of academic institutions to consider a variety of factors, including race, ethnicity, gender, and class, in evaluating applicants. In the same case, however, the Court strikes down UC Davis medical school's rigid quota system that sets aside places for racial minorities. In their dissent, Justices Harry Blackmun, William Brennan, Thurgood Marshall, and Byron White say they agree with the broad goal of color blindness but warn, "we cannot . . . let color blindness become myopia which masks the reality that many 'created equal' have been treated within our lifetimes

as inferior both by the law and by their fellow citizens."[29] *Bakke* signals a major turning point in the history of affirmative action with its evolution away from quotas to vaguer concepts of diversity and inclusion. The backlash against what began under the Great Society of the 1960s is now in full swing.[30]

JULY 10, 1978 Max Robinson becomes the first African American to coanchor a nightly newscast when he joins Frank Reynolds and Peter Jennings on ABC's *World News Tonight*. (In 1962, Malvin R. Goode, also of ABC News, became the first African American news correspondent on network television.) For Robinson, the appointment is "destined to illustrate a new concept in the American mindscape: blacks can read the news, too." He will later recall the racist response to his selection, but also the intense burden of being a "first": "I felt a tremendous amount of pressure when I took this job, that I could not fail, I must not fail, and that kind of burden is much too great for anybody to have to carry. To constantly be guarding against failure, almost guarantees failure." The slow but growing visibility of African Americans on local and national news programs is further boosted in 1978 when Charlayne Hunter-Gault joins the PBS *MacNeil/Lehrer NewsHour* as a national correspondent.[31]

OCTOBER 27, 1978 President Carter signs into law the Full Employment and Balanced Growth Act, known as the Humphrey-Hawkins Act after its sponsors, Senator Hubert Humphrey (D-Minn.) and Congressional Black Caucus member Gus Hawkins (D-Calif.). The Humphrey-Hawkins Act establishes the federal government's responsibility to ensure full

Civil rights pioneer and award-winning journalist Charlayne Hunter-Gault first came to national attention in 1961, when, amid turmoil and violence, she and Hamilton Holmes were the first black students to enroll at the University of Georgia.

employment, long a demand of the Congressional Black Caucus. In practice, however, the act's effectiveness is undercut by the drift of national and state politics toward cutting taxes and slashing budgets, most notably in California's Proposition 13, enacted that June.[32]

NOVEMBER 3, 1978 *Diff'rent Strokes*, a television sitcom following orphaned inner-city black brothers Willis and Arnold Jackson in their adoption by a wealthy white father living in a penthouse in New York City, premieres on NBC. The show, airing through 1986, catapults the child actor Gary Coleman to stardom. Another series with a similar class- and race-crossing adoption storyline, *Webster*, starring Emmanuel Lewis, runs on ABC from 1983 to 1987.

President Jimmy Carter signs the Humphrey-Hawkins Act.

1979

JANUARY 1979 Michele Wallace appears on the cover of *Ms.* magazine, which declares her new book, *Black Macho and the Myth of the Superwoman*, "the book that will shape the 1980s." Fiercely critical of sexism within the civil rights

Former football running back Jamal Anderson poses with female models. In her book *Black Macho and the Myth of the Superwoman*, Michele Faith Wallace critiques the role of such sexist stereotypes in contemporary black culture.

and Black Power movements, the book and article provoke a bitter response from many black academics and writers, who accuse the twenty-seven-year-old Wallace of giving succor to white racism and betraying African American men.[33]

MARCH 26, 1979 The NCAA men's college basketball final features the first matchup between Earvin "Magic" Johnson and Larry Bird, whose rivalry will go on to dominate the NBA for the next six years. While some pitch the white Bird as Rocky to Johnson's Apollo Creed, most observers come to view the rivalry as the players did themselves: fiercely competitive, but with mutual respect. The victory of Johnson's Michigan State over Bird's Indiana State also popularizes March Madness as a highly anticipated annual television event.[34]

JUNE 1979 The science-fiction writer Octavia Butler publishes her fourth novel, *Kindred*, the first work in the genre by a black female author to enter the literary mainstream. The novel follows Butler's protagonist as she travels from present-day California to slave-era Maryland

Apollo Creed, played by Carl Weathers, raises his glove next to Sylvester Stallone's Rocky Balboa following their climactic match in the Academy Award–winning film *Rocky.*

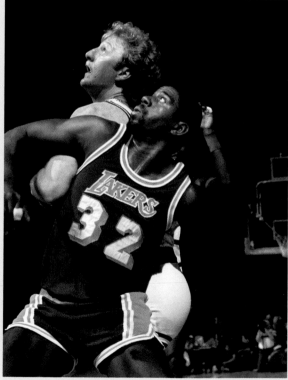

Basketball legend Magic Johnson of the LA Lakers in a storied matchup with the Boston Celtics' Larry Bird.

and draws on Butler's reading of slave narratives and 1970s black-consciousness debates. In 1995, Butler becomes the first science-fiction writer to receive a John D. and Catherine T. MacArthur Foundation "Genius Grant."

JUNE 1979 *Black Enterprise* magazine reports that in 1978, African American businesses featured on the magazine's BE 100s listing of companies surpassed the billion-dollar mark for the first time, with revenues of $1.053 billion for the year. Seventy-seven percent of the BE 100 companies have been in operation for a decade or less; 24 percent have only formed since 1975. Although concerned that many black businesses are heavily dependent on federal contracts—"the only game in town"—the magazine reports that "black business . . . is making strong and youthful strides toward profitability."[35]

JUNE 4, 1979 MIT student Jennie Patrick becomes the first African American woman to earn a PhD in chemical engineering. In 1979, black women make up only 2.4 percent of the total of all employed women with doctorates in any science and engineering fields. (In the entire segment of the workforce that holds PhDs, the overall number of women with PhDs in the sciences is 11 percent.) For the first time, the number of African American women earning doctorates in mathematics, science, and engineering exceeds that of black men, a trend that continues to the present. Four years after Patrick's achievement, Christine Darden will become the first black woman in the United States to earn a PhD in mechanical engineering, at George Washington University.[36]

JUNE 26, 1979 Muhammad Ali, now thirty-seven, says the reports are true: he is retiring from professional boxing.

JULY 12, 1979 A federal judge rules that a school district in Ann Arbor, Michigan, has denied a group of black schoolchildren equal access to education by failing to overcome communication barriers resulting from their use of so-called "Black English." The ruling requires the school district to treat speakers of Black English as it would speakers of a foreign language and introduces a new word into the lexicon: *Ebonics*. Black learning, language, and Ebonics becomes a lightning-rod issue in debates on multiculturalism in education.[37]

JULY 12, 1979 Gloria Gaynor's feminist anthem "I Will Survive" is a global No. 1 hit but in retrospect can be seen as the disco era's swan song—along with "Last Dance," a 1978 hit for Gaynor's

main rival for Queen of Disco, Donna Summer. A growing backlash against disco, some of it racist, some of it homophobic, comes to a head on Disco Demolition Night, when the Detroit Tigers square off against the Chicago White Sox at Comiskey Park on Chicago's South Side. On the field between games of a doubleheader, a local disc jockey defending rock music blows up thousands of disco records, which fans were invited to bring for a 98-cent ticket promotion. "And then all hell broke loose," Tigers pitcher Jack Morris will tell *New York Times* reporter Joe Lapointe thirty years later, on July 4, 2009. Fans, many of them high on marijuana, "charged the field and started tearing up the pitching rubber and the

General Hazel W. Johnson.

dirt. They took the bases. They started digging out home plate."[38]

AUGUST 10, 1979 Pop icon Michael Jackson's first solo collaboration with producer Quincy Jones yields the LP *Off the Wall*, a global smash hit with sales totaling more than $8 million in the United States alone. The album's first track, "Don't Stop 'Til You Get Enough," also gives Jackson his first US *Billboard* No. 1 single since 1972's "Ben" and his first solo Grammy. Jackson and Jones will collaborate again on the albums *Thriller* (1982) and *Bad* (1987). Jones, who first worked with Jackson in 1978 on the soundtrack for *The Wiz*, will say in the *Wall Street Journal* on July 1, 2009, "I saw his sensitivity and his focus. . . . There was such an innocence, but he didn't miss a thing."[39]

SEPTEMBER 1, 1979 Hazel W. Johnson is appointed brigadier general in charge of the US Army Nursing Corps, becoming the first black woman general in the history of the US military and the first to hold a doctorate. "The only way I could be happier . . . is if my parents were still alive to see it," Johnson tells the *Philadelphia Tribune*.[40]

SEPTEMBER 16, 1979 "Good Times" is the second No. 1 hit for Nile Rodgers and Chic, following 1977's "Le Freak." In September, the hypnotic bass riff from "Good Times" powers the first-ever hit hip-hop single, "Rapper's Delight," by the Sugar Hill Gang on Sylvia and Joe Robinson's Sugar Hill Records. It is a watershed moment in the history of American music. Recalling the first time he heard it, Questlove, the drummer of the hip-hop band the Roots, writes in *Rolling Stone* on December 17, 2012: "I was eight years old when 'Rapper's Delight' made its world premiere on Philadelphia radio. It happened at 8:24 p.m. on a Thursday night, after a dinner of porgies, string beans and creamed corn. Me and my sister Donn were sneaking a listen of the local soul station while we washed dishes when an army of percussion and a syncopated Latin

The Sugar Hill Gang.

Capping a prestigious career in teaching, research, and administration, Sir Arthur Lewis (second from right) receives the Nobel Prize in Economics in 1979.

piano line came out of my grandma's JVC clock radio—what appeared to be Chic's 'Good Times,' or a good duplicate of it. How was I to know that my world would come crashing down in a matter of 5, 4, 3, 2, 1? . . . Philadelphia row house walls were thin, so I could hear the neighbors on both sides blasting this jam on their stereo. My friends starting calling, way past grandma's weeknight deadline: 'Did you just hear that!?' It was like our version of Orson Welles's *War of the Worlds*. The next night, I was prepared, with a prehistoric tape recorder in hand and a black-and-white composition notebook. This song single-handedly made me the man in my fourth grade lunchroom." Two years later, Sugar Hill Records releases "The Adventures of Grandmaster Flash on the Wheels of Steel" as the first-ever live DJ mix recording; it, too, will feature the hook from "Good Times."[41]

OCTOBER 16, 1979 Sir Arthur Lewis, a St. Lucian economics professor at Princeton, wins the Nobel Prize for his work examining the causes of poverty and uneven economic progress in the developing world. He is the first black winner of a Nobel Prize in Economics.

NOVEMEBER 11, 1979 The Mary McLeod Bethune Memorial Museum and National Archives for Black Women's History (BMA) opens in Washington, DC. It is the nation's first institution devoted solely to the collection and preservation of African American women's history. The opening is a result of the long-standing efforts of Bethune during her lifetime, as well as a growing cohort of African American historians, notably Bettye Collier-Thomas. The year 1979 also sees the founding of the Association of Black Women Historians.[42]

1980–1984

Jean-Michel Basquiat.

1980

JANUARY 25, 1980 Robert Johnson, the Urban League's former director of communications and a lobbyist for the National Cable Television Association, launches Black Entertainment Television (BET), the first and only black-owned cable television network. Its pitch: "programming that features blacks in lead or dominating roles or addresses itself in fact or fiction to black cultural themes or lifestyles." Its reach: 3.7 million outlets and climbing when Johnson adds into the mix a sports package featuring black colleges. The sponsors he gathers include Pepsi, Sears, and Phillips Petroleum. African American consumption is a $75 billion-a-year proposition, Johnson knows, but that's not his only motivation. "You make it sound like a business venture instead of a culturally uplifting thing for blacks," he tells students at Howard University later in the year. Twenty years later, Johnson sells BET to corporate giant Viacom for a reported $3 billion. [1]

MAY 17, 1980 Eighteen people—ten black, eight white—are killed and more than two hundred are injured in riots in the Liberty City neighborhood of Miami, Florida. Like the civil rights–era clashes in Watts, Newark, and Detroit, the Miami uprising is rooted in long-standing tensions between white police officers and African American. Another factor is changing demographics in Dade County, Florida, with an influx of Cuban and Haitian immigrants intensifying the competition for jobs and benefits. The immediate catalyst for blacks' outrage is the acquittal by an all-white jury of white policemen accused of fatally beating a black motorist, ex-marine Arthur McDuffie, despite his attempted surrender. In the ensuing clash, with "McDuffie" as the battle cry, 850 arrests are made and $100 billion worth of property is damaged. "We just went back 100 years last night," Robert Hall of the R&B and gospel station WMBM is quoted as saying in the *Washington Post* on May 19. Hall adds: "An injustice has been done in the Arthur McDuffie case, but do we rectify it with the bullet or the ballot? I say the ballot." [2]

AUGUST 3, 1980 Republican presidential nominee Ronald Reagan opens his general election campaign at the Neshoba County Fair near Philadelphia, Mississippi. The optics of Reagan's choice of location, near the site of the 1964 murders of civil rights workers James Chaney,

An armed soldier stands in front of the northwest section of Miami during the spring uprising caused by the death of Arthur McDuffie at the hands of white policemen.

Andrew Goodman, and Michael Schwerner, suggests the GOP's courting of southern white voters who once supported states' rights candidates like Alabama's former segregationist governor George Wallace, a Democrat. At the heart of Reagan's speech is his pledge to "restore to states and local governments the power that properly belongs to them." In taking aim at the federal government that unleashed the Great Society once of the 1960s, Reagan diminishes his appeal to African American voters, despite his announced plan to meet in New York the next day with the National Urban League president Vernon Jordan, convalescing from a gunshot wound he received in Indiana. On Election Day 1980, Reagan defeats incumbent president Jimmy Carter but wins only 14 percent of the black vote. The conservative Reagan Revolution is about to begin.[3]

SEPTEMBER 12, 1980 Stevie Wonder's "Master Blaster (Jammin')," a reggae-inflected homage to Bob Marley and a celebration of Zimbabwe's independence, is a No. 1 hit across the United States and Europe.

OCTOBER 2, 1980 Coming out of retirement to pursue a fourth heavyweight title, Muhammad Ali suffers a devastating defeat at the hands of the current champ, Larry Holmes, at Caesars Palace in Las Vegas. "I'm stopping the fight," Ali's faithful trainer and corner man, Angelo Dundee,

Eddie Murphy as Mr. Robinson, one of his breakout creations as a cast member on *Saturday Night Live*.

tells the referee after the tenth round. "It was sad to watch the end to what had been a legendary career," the Associated Press report reads. "After the fight was stopped, Ali sat for several minutes on his stool, his face badly marked below both eyes and those eyes glazed—as if in a dream, a bad dream." Ali attempts one more comeback the following year, against Trevor Berbick, but again suffers defeat by a unanimous decision after ten rounds in the Bahamas. "I could feel the youth," Ali, by then thirty-nine, says afterward. "Age is slipping up on me." The following day, December 12, 1981, Ali announces he is retiring for good. Making light of what is a momentous decision, Ali tells reporters, "I'm happy because I'm still nice looking."[4]

NOVEMBER 22, 1980 Nineteen-year-old Eddie Murphy makes his first appearance on the second episode of the sixth season of *Saturday Night Live*

in a non-speaking role in the sketch "In Search of the Negro Republican." He quickly assumes a full-time slot, writing much of his own material and, in doing so, helps sustain the series through a difficult transition following the departure of original cast members and the hiatus of the

Economist Thomas Sowell, organizer of the Fairmont Conference of black conservatives, held in San Francisco, California.

show's creator, Lorne Michaels. Asked about his meteoric success, Murphy, a Brooklyn native who has been doing stand-up comedy since age fifteen, tells Andy Edelstein of the *New York Times,* "Black comedians are not a commodity. You don't have too many of them in the city, so things started to progress quickly." By the time he exits the show for a film career in 1984, Murphy has created an unforgettable cast of characters including Mr. Robinson, Buckwheat, and Gumby, as well as his uproarious impression of James Brown and a head-turning spot in which he goes undercover, in full makeup and three-piece suit, as a white man, conveniently named Mr. White, in "White Like Me." Along the way, Murphy also fits in hit cinematic roles in *48 Hrs.* and *Trading Places.*[5]

DECEMBER 13–14, 1980 A two-day conference organized by the conservative Institute for Contemporary Studies at the Fairmont Hotel in San Francisco draws 125 members of America's growing black professional ranks. A combination of lifelong Republicans and disaffected Democrats, the attendees find common cause "in the belief," as Herbert Denton of the *Washington Post* writes, "that liberal philosophies of government intervention in behalf of blacks and creation of social programs for the poor had not worked." In other words, "They are the voices that were drowned out in the rhetoric of revolution and protest in the 1960s and early 1970s"—voices that now see the potential for reform working with the new Reagan administration. The leading academics at the conference are economist Thomas Sowell and Temple University professor Walter Williams, who level their opposition to issues traditionally favored by African Americans: school busing, affirmative action, and the minimum wage. Joining them is a senatorial aide to John Danforth of Missouri named Clarence Thomas, quoted by Denton as saying, "It's really kind of good to be here because someone might agree with me for a change."[6]

1981

JANUARY 15, 1981 Hall of Fame slugger Frank Robinson, the first black manager of an American League baseball team with the Cleveland Indians (1975–77), is appointed manager of the San Francisco Giants, becoming the first African American to hold that position with a National League team. By the time Robinson retires as manager of the Washington Nationals in 2006, he will have notched a total 1,065 wins.

JANUARY 20, 1981 President Ronald Reagan takes office and in his first year appoints twenty-four black Republicans to administration roles, including ten that require Senate confirmation—fewer than the thirty-seven in place when former president Jimmy Carter left the White House. Many of those Reagan brings in are committed to rolling back affirmative action and other policies they criticize as a wrongheaded, ineffective form of "reverse discrimination." Among them are Thomas Sowell, a member of Reagan's economic policy board, and Clarence Thomas, first as assistant secretary of civil rights within the Department of Education and later as head of the Equal Employment Opportunity Commission. Mark-

ing the ascent of this group is Clarence Pendleton at the US Commission on Civil Rights. Other black conservatives prominent in the orbit of the Reagan White House include Glenn Loury, Shelby Steele, Stephen Carter, Armstrong Williams, and Alan Keyes.[7]

APRIL 9, 1981 Links between the Manhattan art and Bronx hip-hop scenes are forged in the Downtown 500 collaborations of black and white artists. A central player in the scene is Fab Five Freddy, who curates the graffiti-related art show *Beyond Words* at the Mudd Club in TriBeCa. The show features his own work as well as works by Jean-Michel Basquiat and Rammellzee. Basquiat, who first gained notoriety as the graffiti artist SAMO© in New York, sees his big breaks come at the 1980 Times Square Show and at the P.S. 1 New Wave Show in Queens in 1981. Basquiat's prolific phase as a painter begins in 1982, when the savvy art dealer Annina Nosei sets him up in her SoHo gallery basement in exchange for the right to sell his art. At the cutting edge of art and what will become hip-hop music, Fab Five Freddy and Basquiat feature in the first hip-hop-influenced video to air on TV: Blondie's 1980 hit

Hip-hop artist and filmmaker Fab Five Freddy in front of a mural extolling the relevance of graffiti art. The work is later painted over by city authorities.

MAY 18, 1981 Henry Louis Gates, Jr., a thirty-year-old literary critic and assistant professor of English and Afro-American Studies at Yale, is one of twenty-one individuals chosen in the first class of "prize fellows" to receive what will become known as the MacArthur "Genius Grant," created by the John D. and Catherine T. MacArthur Foundation to support "exceptionally talented individuals." What distinguishes the prize is the anonymous hundred-member selection committee, the fact that fellows are selected without any action on their part (there is no application), and that the prize itself is designed to stimulate creativity without requiring fellows to stay within their field. Gates, with a history degree from Yale and a PhD in English language and literature from Cambridge University, is the first African American scholar to receive the award and joins three other African Americans in his inaugural class: the educator Elma Lewis, the writer James Alan McPherson, and the Carribean poet and playwright Derek Walcott. "I am surprised they knew of me. I still have no idea how I was nominated, or who nominated me," Gates tells Dick Davies in the June 7 *New York Times*. "I am especially pleased because the award shows that some of the choices I've made for myself in the past have been good ones."[9]

"Rapture." Asked to recount the most important milestones in hip-hop, the music critic Greg Tate surprisingly responds, "I think you can't discount the '70s—especially because all-city-wide subway writing was the world's first wake-up call that a corner had been turned in terms of how a generation expressed itself. But far as the '80s, I'm going to go radical and say the phenomenal career of Jean-Michel Basquiat." To Tate, Basquiat is "hip-hop's greatest contribution to modernism."[8]

DECEMBER 21, 1981 Michael Bennett's *Dream-girls*, a musical loosely based on the origin story of Motown's group the Supremes, debuts on Broadway. In his review, *New York Times* critic Frank Rich describes the "seismic emotional jolt" through the audience that comes with Jennifer Holliday's show-stopping "And I'm Telling You I'm Not Going." Holliday goes on to win the 1982 Tony for Best Performance by a Leading Actress in a Musical, with *Dreamgirls* taking home a total of six awards. Also premiering in 1981, Charles Fuller's drama *A Soldier's Play* wins the Drama Critics' Circle Award for Best American Play and a Pulitzer Prize for Drama in 1982.[10]

1981 IN MUSIC Rick James's album *Street Songs* is certified platinum; it will top the Black Album charts for twenty weeks and include his signature dirty, funky classic "Super Freak." The Jacksons' forty-two-date Triumph tour of North America is one of the most successful concert tours of the decade, and "Endless Love," a duet by Diana Ross and Lionel Richie, tops the *Billboard* Hot 100 and Hot Soul Singles charts for two months.

1981 IN THE ECONOMY The economic recession, particularly severe in the automotive sector, results in more than a third of black Ford dealer-

Michael Jackson in performance during the *Triumph* tour, Madison Square Garden, New York City.

ships going out of business. The overall growth trend among black-owned businesses remains positive, however, as African American companies on *Black Enterprise*'s BE 100s list report revenues of $1.53 billion for the year.[11]

1982

JANUARY 7, 1982 *Fame*, a television series following teachers and students at the illustrious New York City High School for the Performing Arts, premieres on NBC. The musical drama, adapted from the big screen and featuring a diverse cast, is choreographed by Debbie Allen, a Houston native who graduated from Howard University before pursuing her passion for dance and theater on Broadway, including turns in *Purlie*, *Raisin*, and *West Side Story*. Allen, who also stars in *Fame* as dance instructor Lydia Grant, tells Jamie Gold of the *Washington Post*, "Your body is your instrument." *Fame* receives critical acclaim and five Emmy Awards in its first season, including one for Allen for Outstanding Achievement in Choreography. It remains on television until 1987.[12]

FEBRUARY 1982 In a report titled *The Decline of Black Farming in America*, the US Commission on Civil Rights projects that at the current rate of loss of black farmland, there will be "virtually no blacks operating farms in this country" by the year 2000. The following year, the Reagan administration closes the Office of Civil Rights at the US Department of Agriculture, undercutting the department's ability to respond to discrimination complaints filed throughout the decade.[13]

MARCH 12, 1982 Richard Pryor's *Live on the Sunset Strip* captures his first concert performance since being badly burned while freebasing cocaine. It wins a Grammy for Best Comedy

Richard Pryor, *Live on the Sunset Strip.*

Record. On the album, Pryor recalls his recent trip to Kenya, where, observing the interactions among Africans, he decided to cease using the "N-word" in his comedy. Pryor raises the same point in his autobiography, *Pryor Convictions*, calling it "a wretched word. Its connotations weren't funny, even when people laughed. To this day I wish I'd never said the word. I felt its lameness. It was misunderstood by people. They didn't get what I was talking about. Neither did I. . . . So I vowed never to say it again." Pryor's standup film "is a rare experience of its kind," writes Vincent Canby of the *New York Times*, "often hilarious but also frightening and, without asking for it, very moving."[14]

JUNE 28, 1982 The author Alice Walker releases her epistolary novel *The Color Purple*, set in rural Georgia at the height of Jim Crow and told through the letters its main character, Celie, writes to God and to the sister taken from her. Walker's novel ignites controversy over its portrayal of black families. Some say it is damaging to the image of black husbands and fathers, while others see it as confronting the gender gap in how institutional racism is felt and inflicted. Still others are threatened by its revela-

tions about black female homosexuality in the relationship between Celie and her abusive husband's lover, Shug Avery. The book's literary merits are undeniable, though, and the novel goes on to win both the Pulitzer Prize for fiction and the National Book Award for fiction both firsts for an African American woman. "Why shouldn't I be tough on men?" Walker asks in an interview with Megan Rosenfeld in the *Washington Post* on October 15. "This is a country in which a woman is raped every three minutes, where one out of three women will be raped during their lifetimes, and a quarter of those are children under twelve. If I write books that men feel comfortable with,

top: Nettie (Akosua Busia) plays with her sister Celie (Desreta Jackson) in a scene from the film *The Color Purple*.
bottom: Alice Walker, producer Scott Sanders, and Oprah Winfrey attend the premiere of the theatrical adaptation of *The Color Purple*.

then I have sold out. If I write books that whites feel comfortable with, I have sold out."[15] Another addition to the growing array of black women's voices in literature in 1982 is Gloria Naylor's *The Women of Brewster Place,* which examines the interconnected lives of seven working-class African American women. In 1983 Naylor wins the National Book Award for First Novel.

JULY 1, 1982 Grandmaster Flash and the Furious Five release "The Message," this day regarded as the most important and influential hip-hop recording of all time. The song, advocated for by Sylvia Robinson of Sugar Hill Records, marks a departure from the band's earlier releases by featuring Melle Mel's socially conscious spoken rap. Limited at first to black dance parties and radio stations, the song is eventually embraced by rock fans, and the record turns gold. "Grandmaster Flash and his group, the Furious Five, have a revolutionary edge to their music," writes Robert Hilburn of the *Los Angeles Times* on March 27, 1983. Twenty-five-year-old Grandmaster Flash (born Joseph Saddler) tells Hilburn, "Until then, rap had a limited audience—something that was either a novelty for kids or dance music just for the black audience. We had always felt we could reach all people, regardless of age or color. That's what 'The Message' did for us." Melle Mel (born Melvin Glover) puts it this way: "I think people outside the ghetto were curious about what life in the ghetto is like and that people who were raised in the ghetto identified with the song."[16]

AUGUST 10, 1982 More than five hundred demonstrators are jailed protesting the creation of a polychlorinated biphenyl (PCB) waste fill in the rural black belt of Warren County, North Carolina. Of all counties in the Tar Heel State, Warren County has the highest percentage of minority residents. Tracking the situation, the North Carolina NAACP files for a preliminary injunction in federal court under the Civil Rights Act of 1964 in a landmark case connecting racism and environmental justice. Though the suit to stop the landfill, *NAACP v. Gorsuch,* proves unsuccessful in a district court ruling, the effort brings together civil rights and environmental protesters and sparks a national environmental justice movement, resulting in landmark studies by the General Accounting Office and United Church of Christ Commission on Racial Justice that reveal a pattern of locating environmentally hazardous landfills in minority communities. "Whenever land is needed for some public function, the Black community, whether urban or rural, has always been

Hip-hop pioneer Grandmaster Flash speaks during a press conference to announce the launch of the Smithsonian's *Hip-Hop Won't Stop: The Beat, the Rhymes, the Life* at the Hilton Hotel in New York City.

the first to be victimized," Dr. Charles E. Cobb writes in the *Philadelphia Tribune* on September 28, 1982. "The depositing of toxic waste within the Black community is no less than attempted genocide."[17]

SEPTEMBER 30, 1982 Music legend Marvin Gaye releases his now-classic single "Sexual Healing" on Columbia Records, his first venture after leaving the Motown label. The song holds the No. 1 spot on the R&B charts for ten weeks. Less than two years later, Gaye will be shot and killed just one day shy of his forty-fifth birthday by his father, Marvin Gay, Sr., following an argument at their Los Angeles home.

OCTOBER 27, 1982 Twenty-four-year-old Prince Rogers Nelson, better known by the singular name Prince, releases his fourth album, *1999*. With the crossover appeal of hits like "Little Red Corvette" and "1999," his unique fusion of rock, funk, and R&B proves popular with a wide audience. Prince's 1984 follow-up, *Purple Rain*, will be an even bigger commercial success and catapult him into a level of stardom rare for a black artist. Accompanying the album is a feature film in which he stars and for which his music is the soundtrack. "The most important thing is to be true to yourself," Prince tells Robert Hilburn of the *Los Angeles Times*. "But," he adds, "I like danger.... That's what is missing from pop music today. There's no excitement and mystery.... I'm not saying I'm better than anybody else, but I don't feel like there are a lot of people out there telling the truth in their music." Hilburn writes of him in his profile "The Renegade Prince": "He's a serious artist and a skilled craftsman who may become the biggest black star in rock since Sly Stone."[18]

Marvin Gaye.

NOVEMBER 2, 1982 Opinion polls project Los Angeles mayor Tom Bradley, a black Democrat, as the winner of California's gubernatorial race, but when the votes are counted, he loses to his Republican opponent. The false projections give rise to the term the "Bradley effect" to describe the perceived phenomenon of whites who misinform pollsters about their willingness to support black candidates. In this case, it is also suspected that Bradley is the victim of gun-control politics and a surge in Republican absentee voting. In contrast, in Alabama, the former segregationist governor George Wallace, having asked for forgiveness for his past opposition to civil rights, ends up winning 90 percent of the black vote in

Prince.

his successful return to the state's highest office.[19]

NOVEMBER 8, 1982 After purchasing an obscure 1859 novel in a New York City bookstore, Yale University professor Henry Louis Gates, Jr., authenticates it as the first known novel published by a black woman in the United States: *Our Nig.* Its author, Gates discovers, is Harriet E. Wilson, a black widow born in 1808 in Fredericksburg, Virginia, before landing in Philadelphia, then Boston. More than a century after Wilson's death, Gates's detective work pushes the timeline of African American literary history back to before the Civil War from what had been previously believed to be the first novel published by a black woman: 1892's *Iola Leroy,* by Frances E. W. Harper. "To add 33 years to a tradition that is young is a hell of a big leap backward," Gates tells Leslie Bennetts of the *New York Times,* "and it probably means there are other books we don't know about as well."[20]

1982 IN DANCE Bill T. Jones/Arnie Zane and Company, an avant-garde, multiracial dance troupe, is founded in New York. Provocative and irreverent, the company works with the graffiti artist Keith Haring and incorporates elements of martial arts, vaudeville, and social dance in its energetic performances. The company wins the New York Dance and Performance Award in 1986.

An unidentified youth dances in front of the *Crack is Wack* mural in New York City. The work is painted by the graffiti artist Keith Haring.

1983

APRIL 11, 1983 Louis Gossett, Jr., wins the Best Supporting Actor Oscar for his performance as a drill sergeant in the film *An Officer and a Gentleman*. Known to many for his roles in the television miniseries *Roots* and *Backstairs at the White House*, Gossett is the first African American to win an Academy Award for acting in the post–civil rights era, and only the third African American to win an acting award overall, after Hattie McDaniel for Best Supporting Actress in 1940 and Sidney Poitier for Best Actor in 1964.

APRIL 12, 1983 US Congressman (D-Ill.) Harold Washington, Jr., is elected Chicago's first black mayor. His margin of victory is due to overwhelming support in black and Latino neighborhoods, many of these residents added by a major voter-registration campaign he initiated

Harold Washington being sworn in as the first black mayor of Chicago.

Jamaica Kincaid.

the year before. The year 1983 also sees the election of Wilson Goode as the first black mayor of Philadelphia, following a racially divisive primary fight against the city's former police chief and mayor, Frank Rizzo. In Charlotte, North Carolina, a coalition of African Americans and white corporate leaders also secures the election of the architect Harvey Gantt as the city's mayor. In declaring victory early in the morning on April 13, 1983, Harold Washington as mayor-elect, tells a crowd of fifteen thousand well-wishers: "Today Chicago has seen the bright day break for this city and perhaps for the entire country. . . . Out of the crucible of this city's most trying election . . . blacks, whites, Hispanics, Jews, gentiles, Protestants and Catholics of all stripes have joined hands to form a new Democratic coalition."[21]

MAY 3, 1983 Author Jamaica Kincaid's first book, a short-story collection titled *At the Bottom of the River*, marks the emergence of a distinct black Caribbean voice in American letters. The title story, like others in the collection, first appears in the *New Yorker* on May 3. Kincaid's exquisitely crafted, often surreal short stories earn her the 1984 Morton Dauwen Zabel Award of the American Academy of Arts and Letters, a prize given to "a poet, writer of fiction, or critic, of progressive, original, and experimental tendencies."[22]

MAY 16, 1983 Michael Jackson wows audiences around the country when he debuts his signature dance move, the moonwalk, during a live performance of his hit single "Billie Jean" on *Motown 25: Yesterday, Today, Forever*, an NBC-televised retrospective about the record label's first quarter century. "Billie Jean" is one of six Top 10 hit singles from Jackson's second collaboration with Quincy Jones, the LP *Thriller*, first released in 1982. With sales of more than forty million by 2010, *Thriller* is the best-selling LP of all time and certifies Jackson as the new "King of Pop" at age twenty-four. Reviewing the album for *Vogue* on March 1, 1983, David Sargent writes: "In a time in which the pall of de facto segregation has once again settled over American radio play lists and record marketing, Jackson is one black artist who appeals strongly across every racial barrier. He does this through his sheer excellence but also through the remarkable synthesis of contemporary pop styles that he and Jones have achieved." Further proof of Jackson's impact on the culture comes with the release of his music videos for

Michael Jackson does his signature moonwalk.

JUNE 6, 1983 *Reading Rainbow* with LeVar Burton debuts on PBS. Burton starred as the young Kunta Kinte in the TV adaptation of *Roots* and will go on to portray chief engineering officer Gordi La Forge on *Star Trek: The Next Generation.* Running for twenty-three seasons, *Reading Rainbow* wins twenty-six Emmys and inspires a generation of American children to read, enjoy, and understand books.

SEPTEMBER 17, 1983 Miss New Jersey Vanessa Williams becomes the first African American to be crowned Miss America, fifty-seven years after the contest debuted and thirteen years after Miss Iowa Cheryl Brown became its first black contestant. Following the publication of nude photos of her in *Penthouse,* Williams is forced to resign her

Vanessa Williams, the first black winner of the Miss America pageant, held in Atlantic City, New Jersey. Williams later will be forced to renounce her title.

"Billie Jean," "Beat It," and "Thriller," the first of which, Robert Palmer writes in his "Year in Review" for the *New York Times,* "finally brought black music to MTV, softening up the influential cable television channel, and rock radio, for other black music." Palmer calls 1983 "the most change-filled year in recent pop-music history." Jackson's red leather jacket and sequined glove are stylistic obsessions across nearly every demographic and hearken to a pop-icon status unseen in the culture since Sinatra, Elvis Presley, and the Beatles.[23]

Mary Frances Berry, a member of the US Commission on Civil Rights.

crown in July 1984. Runner-up Suzette Charles, also African American, serves out the remainder of Williams's term, with Williams pursuing a successful acting and singing career, which includes her 1992 hit single "Save the Best for Last."

OCTOBER 25, 1983 When a majority of members of the US Commission on Civil Rights charge that the Reagan Justice Department is seeking to end affirmative action as the country knows it, Reagan "terminates the appointments" of the commission's three Democratic members. Two, Mary Frances Berry and Blandina Cardenas Ramirez, successfully bring suit against the president and are restored to the commission.[24]

OCTOBER 30, 1983 During a taped interview for CBS's *60 Minutes*, the forty-two-year-old minister and activist Jesse Jackson announces he will seek the Democratic Party's nomination in the 1984 presidential race. He makes it official in Washington, DC, later that week. His reason: "I want to help again measure greatness by how we treat children in the dawn of life, how we treat poor people in the pit of life, and how we treat old folk in the sunset of life." It's not clear if Jackson will garner endorsements from influential black leaders already committed to former vice president Walter Mondale. To win, Jackson sets as his goal the closing of the gap between eligible black voters nationwide, who number around some eighteen million, and those already registered, approximately ten million. While Jackson is not initially considered a serious candidate with any real chance of winning, the rationale for his run is found in a memo drafted by his press secretary, Frank Watkins, a year before: "Blacks must deal from a position of political power or they will simply be negotiating for the crumbs as in the past. . . . And the only way to negotiate from a position of power—to be taken seriously into account—is to create a political vehicle, a person around which people can give political allegiance and expression."[25]

NOVEMBER 2, 1983 President Reagan, who earlier stalled plans to turn the birthday of Martin Luther King, Jr., into a federal holiday, signs a bill doing just that. Reagan's move comes after attempts by Senator Jesse Helms (R-N.C.) to filibuster the proposed law and a House vote of 338–90 in support of it.[26]

DECEMBER 15, 1983 In May 1983, Richard Pryor signs a $40 million deal with Columbia Pictures, backed by Coca-Cola, to produce, direct, and write eight feature films. It is a boon for the production company Pryor has launched, Indigo Productions. To head it, Pryor chooses the actor and football Hall of Famer Jim Brown as president, but his plans to establish a "Black Hollywood" presence soon founder. Pryor's firing of Brown on December 15 over "creative differences" causes a furor in the black community, with some charging that Pryor's hand was forced by his corporate funders, a charge Pryor denies. Indigo eventually folds after making only two films, including Pryor's semi-autobiographical directorial debut, *Jo Jo Dancer, Your Life Is Call-*

ing (1986). Among the films passed up by the company is Prince's *Purple Rain*.[27]

1983 IN THE ECONOMY The economic recession of the early 1980s reaches its peak with nearly one in five black workers (19.5 percent) unemployed; the white rate is 8.4 percent. At the same time, *Black Enterprise*'s BE 100s index of black-owned businesses exceeds $2 billion for the first time, and the magazine reports that the health and beauty-aids industry is the fastest-growing black business sector, "driven largely by the curly, wet-look hairstyle craze called the Jheri Curl." Among hair-care-product manufacturers, the Chicago-based SoftSheen company registers sales of $55 million to enter the BE 100s for the first time. Meanwhile, the decline of labor union membership among industrial workers in the late 1970s and early '80s is offset by a rise in public service unions, many members of which are African American. By 1983, nearly 31.7 percent of black workers belong to unions, compared to just 22.2 percent of white workers. Union membership as a whole declines in the Reagan era and the 1990s, with only 16 percent of black workers paying union dues in 2006—again, higher than the nation as a whole, with only 12 percent.[28]

1984

JANUARY 3, 1984 Jesse Jackson's upstart presidential bid receives a significant boost when he negotiates the release of a US Navy bombardier-navigator from the government of Syria during a humanitarian mission to Damascus. Though Jackson fails to receive endorsements from high-profile black big-city mayors around the country (including Harold Washington, Tom Bradley, and his former colleague in Martin Luther King's circle, Andrew Young, now the mayor of Atlanta), in the long primary race that follows, he wins the popular vote in Washington, DC, Virginia, South Carolina, Louisiana, and Mississippi. Jackson's campaign is not without controversy. Relations with Jewish Americans, a key Democratic constituency, become tense after he is caught on tape using derogatory language, and, in the minds of many voters, his affiliation with Louis Farrakhan's Nation of Islam is uncomfortably close. Heading into the Democratic Party convention in San Francisco, Jackson has amassed 21 percent of the popular vote, yet only 9 percent of the delegates. Still, he refuses to concede the race until a final vote is taken from the floor. "He has rolled up impressive margins in the black community, usually getting 70 to 80 percent of the black vote," George Curry writes in the *Chicago Tribune* on June 3, and "some estimates are that 20 percent of the blacks voting for Jackson have never voted before."[29]

Rev. Jesse Jackson speaks during his 1984 presidential bid.

APRIL 2, 1984 John Thompson becomes the first black coach to win an NCAA basketball championship, with the Hoyas' star center Patrick Ewing claiming victory over his rival, Hakeem Olajuwon, of the University of Houston. Olajuwon will be that year's first overall NBA draft pick, by the Houston Rockets, ahead of North Carolina's Michael Jordan, drafted third by the Chicago Bulls, and Auburn's Charles Barkley, drafted fifth by the Philadelphia 76ers. Ewing will follow Olajuwon as the number-one draft pick a year later, when he joins the New York Knicks.

JULY 19, 1984 Jesse Jackson addresses the Democratic National Convention in San Francisco in a speech few on the floor will forget. Though it is clear that Walter Mondale will be the party's nominee, Jackson asks delegates to cast their votes for him during the first roll call as an expression of their support for the issues he has advanced. "My constituency is the desperate, the damned, the disinherited, the disrespected, and the despised," Jackson declares. "They are restless and seek relief. They have voted in record numbers. They have invested the faith, hope, and trust that they have in us. The Democratic Party must send them a signal that we care. I pledge my best not to let them down." Acknowledging his own shortcomings as a candidate, Jackson tries to find renewed common ground between blacks and Jews inside the party and signals he is not done with politics yet. "We must leave the racial battleground and come to economic common ground and moral higher ground," Jackson closes. "America, our time has come." Jackson's campaign has been successful in forcing party leaders to take seriously the priorities of black voters; more importantly, it has begun to redefine the electoral landscape by register-

Carl Lewis sprints at the 1984 Summer Olympics in Los Angeles.

ing unprecedented numbers of African American voters, a drive Jackson will carry into the fall campaign as he attempts to rally voters behind Mondale. It's a steep climb, with President Reagan winning reelection in a landslide in November, despite netting just nine percent of African American votes cast nationwide. Still, the progress is marked: in 1980, 9.8 million blacks stand registered to vote in the country; four years later, that number jumps to 12.2 million, representing 66 percent of eligible black voters, a level unseen since the 1968 and 1972 cycles.[30]

JULY 28–AUGUST 12, 1984 African American athletes dominate the Summer Olympics in

Los Angeles. Attention focuses on track-and-field star Carl Lewis, who nets four gold medals, matching the number won by Jesse Owens at the 1936 Berlin games. Edwin Moses, the dominant 400-meter hurdler of his era, earns his second Olympic gold. Black women dominate the sprints, with Evelyn Ashford and Valerie Brisco-Hooks winning five golds between them.

SEPTEMBER 11, 1984 Basketball player Cheryl Miller, a championship-winning forward at the University of Southern California, and volleyball player Flo Hyman, both Olympic medalists, testify before Congress in support of strengthening Title IX, the 1972 provision prohibiting dis-

crimination by gender in federally funded college athletic programs. The following year, *Sports Illustrated* names Miller the nation's top college basketball player, male or female.[31]

SEPTEMBER 20, 1984 *The Cosby Show* makes its debut on NBC and soon becomes the anchor for the network's Thursday-night lineup. Two hundred and two episodes later, it is one of the most successful—and consequential—series in the history of television. The series follows Bill Cosby as Cliff Huxtable, an obstetrician, and his wife, Clair, an attorney played by Phylicia Rashad, as they raise their children in a New York City brownstone. *The Cosby Show* is the first sitcom to feature a black family of the professional class, and one that, for a rising generation of viewers, is the quintessential American family. For white and black viewers, the show is universal and accessibly mainstream even as it provides subtle exposure to African American culture and history, most memorably when the Huxtables dance down their staircase to Ray Charles's rendition of "Night Time Is the Right Time" and pause in front of their living-room television to watch a clip of Martin Luther King's "I Have a Dream" speech during an episode airing in January 1986, just before the first federal King holiday. In its first season, *The Cosby Show* earns three Emmy Awards, including one for Outstanding Comedy Series, and according to the Nielsen ratings is the third-most-watched show. It will be the top-ranked show for its next five seasons and will go on to win a Peabody Award in 1986. In responding to the series in a piece for the *New York Amsterdam News* on October 13, 1984, titled "Cosby Show Opens White America's Eyes," Charles E. Rogers writes, "No longer will the networks be able to use the feeble excuse that America won't

Riverdale Baptist players drive the ball down the court during the National Title IX Holiday Classic.

A scene from the *Cosby Show*: Cliff and Clair Huxtable (Bill Cosby and Phylicia Rashad) with their youngest daughter, Rudy (Keshia Knight Pulliam).

buy realistic non-stereotypical portrayals of Black families."[32]

OCTOBER 11, 1984 *Ma Rainey's Black Bottom* makes its Broadway debut at the Cort Theatre—a first for its thirty-nine-year-old playwright, August Wilson, a Pittsburgh native who relocated to St. Paul, Minnesota, in 1978. *New York Times* drama critic Frank Rich lavishes praise on the production, notably its young star, Charles Dutton, "who careens about with unchecked, ever escalating turbulence." Directing the play is Lloyd Richards, who oversaw the original production of *A Raisin in the Sun* on Broadway in 1959 and nurtured Wilson's talent through his role as artistic director of both the National Playwrights Conference at the Eugene O'Neill Theater Center and the Yale Repertory Theatre in Connecticut. In a profile in the *Times* by Herbert Mitgang on October 22, Wilson reflects, "My generation of blacks knew very little about the past of our parents. . . . They shielded us from the indignities they suffered. They lived in a society that refused to recognize your worth. You don't tell your kids that when you went into the five-and-ten-cent store they let you buy but wouldn't give you a paper bag if you were black. But what you pick up in your childhood you remember. Sometimes what you discover comes back to you long afterward when you're looking for a direction or a story or a play." Wilson is in the middle of writing a cycle of plays that will cover every decade of history in the twentieth century, with *Fences* following the next year and *Joe Turner's Come and Gone* and *The Piano Lesson* by 1984 and 1986. Follow-

A scene from August Wilson's play *Ma Rainey's Black Bottom*.

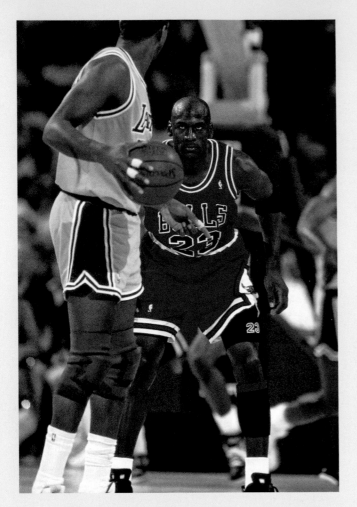

Michael Jordan of the Chicago Bulls guards the basket in the NBA Finals.

ing Wilson's death in 2005, the Virginia Theatre on Broadway is renamed in his honor.[33]

OCTOBER 26, 1984 Michael Jordan plays his first NBA game, netting sixteen points, seven assists, and six rebounds as his Chicago Bulls defeat the Washington Bullets, 109–93. It is an uneven performance, but Jordan "brought back fun to the Stadium," writes Bob Sakamoto in the *Chicago Tribune*. Famously cut from his high school basketball team his sophomore year, Jordan became a star college player under head coach Dean Smith at the University of North Carolina, winning the

men's national championship in 1982 and leading the 1984 US Olympic men's basketball team. Though the Bulls struggle during his rookie season, Jordan establishes himself as a rising star in the league and gains attention for his incredible slam dunks. In 1985 he signs an endorsement deal with Nike, which begins to manufacture his Air Jordan sneakers. The sneaker, emblazoned with Jordan's "jumpman" logo, becomes a phenomenon, popular across races, thanks to Jordan's skill and charisma and a popular series of ads directed by Spike Lee and starring Lee's Mars Blackmon character. On the hardwood, in a playoff game against the Boston Celtics on April 20, 1986, Jordan scores an astonishing sixty-three points, prompting Larry Bird to quip, "I think he's God disguised as Michael Jordan." Though the Celtics win the NBA championship that season, Jordan's Bulls are ascendant, and in 1991, he and another future Hall of Famer, Scottie Pippen, along with head coach Phil Jackson, lead the Chicago team to their first NBA title. Jordan goes on to win five more, broken up only by a brief detour into baseball in 1993–94 and a playoff loss to the Orlando Magic in 1995. He also captures a total of five MVP awards. Jordan retires again in 1998, though he suits up for the Washington Wizards, a team he partially owns, from 2001 through 2003 before buying an ownership stake in the Charlotte Bobcats (later the Hornets) in 2006 and becoming the franchise's controlling owner in 2010. On September 11, 2009, Michael Jordan is inducted into the Naismith Memorial Basketball Hall of Fame. Many consider him to be the greatest player—and competitor—of his or any generation.[34]

NOVEMBER 17, 1984 *Billboard* magazine announces the launch of Def Jam, a new record label based in New York City. Cofounded by Russell

LL Cool J.

Simmons, a black twenty-seven-year-old native of Queens managing the rap group RunD.M.C., and his twenty-one-year-old partner, Rick Rubin, a white Jewish Long Islander whose New York University dorm room doubled as a music laboratory, Def Jam Records is the music industry's first major rap label, with a slate of talent that already includes Jazzy Jay, TLA Rock, Jimmy Spicer, and the Beastie Boys. The long-range influence the label will have on rap is foretold in its first, auspiciously launched hit single, LL Cool J's "I Need a Beat." LL's *Radio* LP, released the following year, becomes Def Jam's first album to reach gold (it eventually goes platinum). "The purpose of this company," Simmons says in the *Billboard* article, "is to educate people to real street music by putting out records nobody in

the business world would distribute but us." The founding of Def Jam is as significant as any new label's since Berry Gordy started the Motown Record Corporation twenty-four years before.[35]

NOVEMBER 21, 1984 Pleading for the release of nine South African labor leaders an ocean away, the District of Columbia's recently elected congressional delegate, Walter E. Fauntroy, along with Randall Robinson of TransAfrica and Civil Rights Commissioner Mary Frances Berry, are arrested at a sit-in inside the office of South African ambassador Bernardus G. Fourie in Washington, DC. Speaking for the group, Eleanor Holmes Norton, then a professor at Georgetown, tells the press, "If there was a government in Washington that looked like it was going to use its pressure, even diplomatically, on the government of Pretoria, we wouldn't have been here tonight."[36] By the end of 1985, more than 4,500 people will be arrested in similar protests against the apartheid regime in South Africa.[37]

DECEMBER 22, 1984 Bernard Goetz, a white New York City resident, shoots four black teen-

Eleanor Holmes Norton.

New York City subway car where four black youths are shot by white passenger Bernie Goetz.

agers, paralyzing one of them, on a crowded downtown Manhattan subway car. At first, the case unites a broad swath of New Yorkers grown weary of the city's high crime rate. Yet by the time the trial ends with Goetz's exoneration on all but a minor weapons charge in 1987, a clear racial divide has emerged. Whites continue to find Goetz justified in his actions, while African Americans are inclined to view his motives, and the verdict, as racially biased. The view of Congressman Floyd Flake (D-N.Y.) is typical: "I think that if a black had shot four whites, the cry for the death penalty would have been almost automatic."[38]

1984 IN BUSINESS Sales on the *Black Enterprise* BE 100s index of companies reach $2.3 billion. For the first time since the BE index began in 1973,

Motown Records is dethroned from its position as the leading black-owned company. Johnson Publishing now assumes the top spot, with sales of $118 million, $10 million more than Motown.[39]

1984 IN TELEVISION In a year that witnesses the debut of *The Cosby Show*, actress Diahann Carroll, who broke ground as nurse Julia Baker on TV in 1968, establishes another new mark on the small screen when, in the role of Dominique Deveraux on *Dynasty*, she becomes the first African American actress to star as a high-powered diva (opposite Joan Collins) in a prime-time soap. Also in 1984, Philip Michael Thomas plays detective Rico Tubbs alongside Don Johnson's James Crockett in the NBC crime drama *Miami Vice*, shining a light on the drug trade in south Florida.[40]

1985-1989

Whitney Houston in concert
in London for Mandela.

1985

FEBRUARY 14, 1985 Twenty-one-year-old Whitney Houston, the daughter of gospel singer Cissy Houston, releases her eponymous debut album on producer Clive Davis's Arista label. With three No. 1 singles including "The Greatest Love of All," *Whitney Houston* reaches No. 1 on the *Billboard* charts. *Rolling Stone* magazine says Houston is "blessed with one of the most exciting new voices in years." Soon, she will be known to the world as "the Voice." A product of Newark, New Jersey, Houston developed her craft as a member of the New Hope Baptist Church choir, with early exposure to the top singers of the day, including her godmother Darlene Love and her honorary aunt Aretha Franklin, and not least her own mother and her cousin, Dionne Warwick. As a model, Houston has already graced the cover of *Seventeen* magazine, but it is her voice that will eventually rank her among the greatest talents of all time. Houston's success only grows two years later with the release of *Whitney*, the first album from a female artist to enter the charts at No. 1, where it stays for eleven weeks. Its four chart-topping singles give Houston an unprecedented seven straight No. 1 hits. "We all came up through the church," Houston tells Mike Joyce of the *Washington Post* for a June 28, 1985, profile. "My mother taught me not only how to sing . . . but to discover what each song is about, and what music, any music, really requires to sing it properly." Yet as long a runway as Houston appears to have before her, she also makes clear, "I can't imagine myself performing for the rest of my life . . . even though I love it right now. I want to sit down at one point and enjoy what I've done."[1]

MARCH 7, 1985 "We Are the World," is released, and within ten days, an initial run of 800,000 copies sells out with another 500,000 on the way, making it one of the top—and fastest—selling singles of all time. Conceived by Harry Belafonte, produced by Quincy Jones, managed by Ken Kragen, and written by Lionel Richie and Michael Jackson, the song is recorded by USA for Africa, forty-six star performers, among them Stevie Wonder, Diana Ross, Bob Dylan, and Bruce Springsteen, who donate their diverse talents at a recording session in Los Angeles on January 28 to raise money for African hunger relief. The song, which is accompanied by an hour-long "making of" documentary on HBO, nets three Grammys, and the project raises more than $50 million. Also in 1985, Arthur Baker and Steven Van Zandt organize Artists against Apartheid, protesting the political situation in South Africa with the song "Sun City." Bob Geldolf's Live Aid concerts, held simultaneously in London and Philadelphia on July 13, also raise millions to fight famine in Africa. "Black artists should be doing more," Belafonte is quoted as saying in the *Los Angeles Times* on February 13. "If Jews were starving to death in Israel, you can bet American Jews would organize and raise millions to feed their foreign brethren. I wish blacks in this country had that same spirit."[2]

Gwendolyn Brooks.

APRIL 24, 1985 *Newsday* reporters Dennis Bell and Josh Friedman and photographer Ozier Muhammad win the Pulitzer Prize for International Reporting for their series of stories on famine in Ethiopia.[3]

MAY 6, 1985 Gwendolyn Brooks, the writer of the Pulitzer Prize–winning book of poetry *Annie Allen*, the novella *Maud Martha*, and the iconic poem "We Real Cool," becomes the first black woman selected as Poetry Consultant to the Library of Congress. The position is renamed Poet Laureate the following year.[4]

MAY 13, 1985 Philadelphia police bomb the headquarters of MOVE, a black radical organization. MOVE and local police had a violent confrontation in 1978, and, after tensions rise again in 1985, Wilson Goode, the city's black mayor, authorizes a raid on the group's base. When police cannot break down the door, they drop a bomb from a helicopter. The resulting fire kills eleven MOVE members and destroys sixty-one homes. Although the police face no criminal charges, MOVE members and their relatives later secure $5 million in civil damages. "We should have and could have done better," Mayor Goode tells a hearing of the Philadelphia Special Investigation Commission on November 6. "I shall carry this burden, grief, and sorrow for the rest of my life."[5]

JULY 30, 1985 After years of living in self-sought exile abroad in response to the racism she felt in America, the folk singer Nina Simone, her bluesy, jazzy voice indelibly linked to the civil rights movement of the 1960s, returns home to the United States—not to her native North Carolina but to her adopted home city of Los

West Philadelphia row houses after the police action against MOVE.

Angeles, where she begins a six-night engagement at the Vine St. Bar & Grill. Regarded as the "High Priestess of Soul" by those who followed her decades earlier through such hits as "Four Women" and "To Be Young, Gifted and Black," Simone tells Don Heckman of the *Los Angeles Times*, "The country has treated me entirely differently this time, and my attitude *about* the country is completely different." Simone adds: "Music hasn't made me happy. It makes *life* happy." Simone's influence on the evolution of black female singers is unmistakable.[6]

OCTOBER 5, 1985 With his 324th career victory clinched in a 27–7 win over Prairie View at the

Cotton Bowl in Dallas, Texas, Grambling State's head coach Eddie Robinson, at age sixty-six, breaks the all-time college football wins record previously held by Alabama's Bear Bryant. Back home, the state of Louisiana declares the day Eddie Robinson Day. In the NFL, future Hall of Famer Walter "Sweetness" Payton leads the Chicago Bears to a Super Bowl championship in the 1985–1986 season, cemented in memory by the team's promotional video featuring the rap song "The Super Bowl Shuffle." That year, blacks comprise 52 percent of NFL players.

NOVEMBER 29, 1985 A *New York Times* cover story written by the journalist Jane Gross about crack, a "new form of cocaine" that has "a tendency to accelerate the abuse of the drug," introduces the drug to a national audience. Until now, crack has been unfamiliar to most Americans, though it has already infiltrated New York and other cities. Explains Gross: "Experts estimate that there are at least five million regular cocaine users in the United States, with perhaps a million of them in the [New York] metropolitan region." Most used to "snort" cocaine, but now, with the introduction of this new smoked "rock" form, the trend is certain to change, with adolescents most at risk. Kevin McEneaney, a director at Phoenix House, whom Gross consults, says, "The behavioral stuff we're hearing about . . . drives home that what we're dealing with, and not in the physical sense, is the most powerful drug we've ever seen." The following year, Congress makes the penalties for possession of crack much more severe than those for powdered cocaine.[7]

DECEMBER 16, 1985 The film version of Alice Walker's *The Color Purple* opens in New York City. Directed by Steven Spielberg and starring Whoopi Goldberg, Danny Glover, and Oprah Winfrey, the film earns eleven Academy Award nominations, even as it portrays difficult, often harrowing subject matter. Roger Ebert writes that it "moved me and lifted me up as few films have" and declares it the best film of 1985. Twenty years later, it becomes a Broadway musical that earns eleven Tony nominations.[8]

1986

JANUARY 8, 1986 Desmond Tutu, the archbishop of Johannesburg and the 1984 Nobel Peace Prize winner, arrives in Washington, DC, for a two-

Archbishop Desmond Tutu speaks at an anti-apartheid rally in New York City. David Dinkins, the first black mayor of Gotham, stands behind him.

week, twelve-city tour of the United States. His first visit is to the South African embassy, the site of a yearlong protest campaign against apartheid. Standing on a "cardboard box" in the bitter cold, striking in his religious garb, Tutu describes the South African regime as "a vicious, immoral, un-Christian and totally evil system." Twelve protesters expressing solidarity with Tutu and the South African people are arrested at the embassy that very day, while Mayor Marion Barry announces legislation to rename that portion of Washington Avenue for Nelson and Winnie Mandela.[9] In October, Congress passes economic sanctions against South Africa over President Reagan's veto. By this point, some twenty-eight American companies have divested from South Africa, and American banks refuse to roll over $14 billion in loans to the country.[10]

JANUARY 20, 1986 The first national Martin Luther King holiday is observed. At a three-hour ecumenical service at Ebenezer Baptist Church in Atlanta on January 19, the same church where King and his father once ministered, Coretta Scott King awards Desmond Tutu the King Center's Nonviolent Peace Prize, making clear her intentions for the holiday: "We want this to be the launching pad of a new and intensified phase in the struggle to end apartheid. We will not rest until apartheid is finally abandoned."[11]

JANUARY 23, 1986 The Rock and Roll Hall of Fame in Cleveland, Ohio, inducts a number of black performers in its inaugural class. Illustrating rock's roots in African American musical forms, the hall welcomes Chuck Berry, Fats Domino, James Brown, Ray Charles, Sam Cooke, and Little Richard and offers tributes to Robert Johnson and Jimmy Yancey. The following year, Aretha Franklin becomes the first woman inducted.[12] The resiliency, and timelessness, of black musical expression is witnessed again in 1986, when, twenty-five years after its original release, Ben E. King's soul classic, "Stand by Me," breaks into the top ten when it is re-released on the soundtrack of the coming-of-age film, directed by Rob Reiner, that bears its name, *Stand by Me*. "What's interesting to me," King, forty-eight, tells Daniel Brogan of the *Chicago Tribune*, "is that a song I wrote as a love song is being adopted by kids everywhere as a song about friendship. I think that's interesting: two generations listening to the same song are getting different, but equally positive, meanings from it."

JANUARY 28, 1986 The space shuttle *Challenger* explodes, kill-ing all seven crew members onboard, among them thirty-five-year-old African American astronaut Ronald E. McNair in what would have been his second trip into space. McNair, who once toiled as a child in the cotton and tobacco fields of Lake City, South Carolina, earned his doctorate at MIT and was a specialist in laser physics. In a commencement address at the University of South Carolina in 1984, McNair, a husband and father of two, advised graduates: "You may not come from a well-to-do financial background, you may not come from an affluent social background, you may not have glided through the University of South Carolina with the greatest of ease. But if you're willing to work hard, sacrifice and struggle, then I proclaim today that you're better than good enough."[13]

FEBRUARY 15, 1986 Carl Weathers, a former football standout at San Diego State known to movie fans as boxer Apollo Creed from the *Rocky* series, premieres on ABC in the title role of the detective action drama *Fortune Dane*. This marks the first time that an African American man stars in an independent leading role in a television drama series. Weathers also serves as

NASA astronaut Ron McNair plays his saxophone aboard the *Challenger* space shuttle during his first mission in 1984.

a producer on the show. "Here's a kid from New Orleans whose parents may never have reached the tens of thousands of dollars in yearly earnings," Weathers is quoted in a *Washington Post* cover story on March 16. "It's a long way for me to be the producer of a TV show." *Fortune Dane* faces stiff competition in its time slot against *The Golden Girls* on Saturday nights and is canceled by season's end. Weathers returns to the big screen the following year in *Predator* and in 1988's *Action Jackson*.[14]

MAY 15, 1986 Run-D.M.C. release their album *Raising Hell*, featuring a collaboration with Aerosmith on a fresh interpretation of the rock band's hit "Walk This Way." The new version dominates MTV with its fusion of rap and rock music. The year in music also witnesses the ascendancy of Michael Jackson's sister, Janet Jackson, whose album *Control* gains critical acclaim and commercial success. *Rolling Stone* declares that with *Control*, Janet "states that she's not the Jacksons' baby sister anymore." With five No. 1 singles, *Control* suggests that Janet Jackson will continue the family's pop dynasty. Also in 1986, the rap group N.W.A's album *Straight Outta Compton* introduces gangsta rap to a wider audience for the first time. With songs like "Fuck tha Police," N.W.A, fronted by the talents of Ice Cube and Dr. Dre, gives voice to the anger of poor blacks and ignites an East Coast–West Coast rivalry for influence over the direction of the art form.[15]

JUNE 19, 1986 Twenty-two-year-old Len Bias, an All-American basketball player at the University of Maryland and a prize Boston Celtics draftee, dies of a cocaine overdose. The high-profile case makes the dangers of cocaine

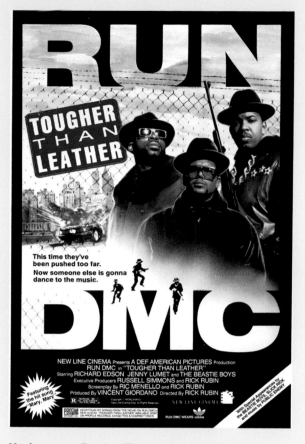

Movie poster, *Tougher Than Leather*, starring Run-D.M.C.

a topic of national political discussion. "God has called him to a higher purpose—to get the attention of this generation and save it," Jesse Jackson is quoted as saying in the *Washington Post* on August 2. Later in the article, the Drug Enforcement Administration's chief of congressional and public affairs, William Alden, notes that Bias, a young man with such a promising career in his future, defied the commonly held beliefs about cocaine users. "The myths have been quickly removed," he says. "All of a sudden people are saying cocaine can kill."[16]

SEPTEMBER 8, 1986 *The Oprah Winfrey Show* begins its run in national syndication. Winfrey,

President Barack Obama and First Lady Michelle Obama appear on *The Oprah Winfrey Show.*

thirty-two, started in television in Nashville and Baltimore, where she was an anchorwoman and talk-show host from the mid-1970s into the early '80s. In 1984, she began hosting *AM Chicago*, which became *The Oprah Winfrey Show* the following year. Now the Oscar-nominated actress will reach a national audience that embraces her as strongly as Chicago has. Two years later, Winfrey establishes Harpo Studios, making her the third woman in the American entertainment industry (after Mary Pickford and Lucille Ball) to own her own studio. And out of a crowded field that includes fellow talk-show hosts Phil Donahue, Geraldo Rivera, and Sally Jesse Raphael, Winfrey, through her evolving, purpose-driven content and philanthropic work, will become a figure of unparalleled influence and the host of the highest-rated daytime talk show in history. In a September 20, 1986, article in the Baltimore *Afro-American* titled "Oprah Winfrey's Hotter Than Hot," Winfrey is quoted as "say[ing] her life is 'good, getting better and will continue to get better. The main reason is because I believe it will.'"[17]

OCTOBER 24, 1986 *Soul Man*, a comedy about a white student who disguises himself as black in order to receive a scholarship to Harvard Law School, opens in movie theaters. It grosses more than $27 million but faces criticism over its glib treatment of discrimination and the fact that its lead actor, C. Thomas Howell, wears makeup resembling blackface. African American students at UCLA protest the film's launch, while the Beverly Hills chapter of the NAACP issues a formal statement. Van Scott, head of the Black Student Alliance at UCLA, tells John Voland of the *Los Angeles Times* on October 29, that *Soul Man* "makes fun of the things we have to struggle with every day: the jokes, the hassles, the preconceptions and the demands." The film stands in sharp contrast to the black auteur Spike Lee's debut feature, *She's Gotta Have It*, also released in 1986, which, on a $175,000 bud-

Movie poster, *She's Gotta Have It.*

audiences. "I think a lot of black artists get trapped in this whole crossover mentality," Lee tells the *Post*. "If I say that I do my films specifically for black audiences, there's this uproar like, you know, you shouldn't limit yourself and all this other stuff. But I don't really see why I have to defend it."[18]

NOVEMBER 4, 1986 John Lewis, the former chair of the Student Nonviolent Coordinating Committee (SNCC), wins election to the United States House of Representatives from Georgia's Fifth District, having defeated Julian Bond, another former SNCC leader, in a tight primary race in September. Lewis's unflagging commitment to civil rights earns him the nickname "the conscience of the Congress." Lewis maintains a commitment to ensuring that the Voting Rights Act of 1965, legislation he fought for as an activist, continues to protect black voters in the twenty-first century.[19]

NOVEMBER 22, 1986 Twenty-year-old "Iron" Mike Tyson, from Catskill, New York, defeats

get, interrogates black culture on its own terms and is the delight of the Cannes Film Festival in France. Lee, a Brooklyn native with degrees from Morehouse College and NYU Film School, represents a new crop of black storytellers forcing audiences to confront structural inequalities at the core of American society in works of art without easy resolutions. The name of his production company, Forty Acres and a Mule, signals the seriousness of his mission. "I'm just not here to take everything in sight," Lee is quoted as saying in a *Washington Post* profile on October 22. "I don't want to be guest host of *Hollywood Squares* or *Love Boat* another three years from now." Lee is particularly resistant to box-office pressures to tailor his work to white

Rep. John Lewis and Rep. John Conyers, cochairs of the Civil Rights Taskforce of the Congressional Black Caucus.

Trevor Berbick to become the youngest heavyweight champion in boxing history. By August 1987, the undefeated Tyson unifies all three heavyweight championships. His dramatic knockouts make him a pop-culture phenomenon; he even has his own video game, Mike Tyson's Punch Out!, which captivates users of the Nintendo Entertainment System in their quest to face off against Tyson through their television screens. But Tyson's fortunes turn sharply. His ex-wife, the actress Robin Givens, charges him with abuse in 1988; he loses the title to Buster Douglas in 1990; and he spends 1992 through 1995 in prison on rape charges. When Tyson returns to boxing in 1996, he invites further infamy by biting his opponent Evander Holyfield's ear during a match. Following another term in jail, Tyson vies for the title again in 2002 but is clobbered by Lennox Lewis. He retires from the sport in 2005 with a record of 50-6 and remains in the public eye with cameo appearances in blockbuster Hollywood films like *The Hangover* and one-man show on Broadway directed by Spike Lee. On the night he becomes champ for the first time, with his future notoriety unbeknownst to him, Tyson announces, "I'm the youngest heavyweight champion of the world and I'm going to be the oldest."[20]

DECEMBER 20, 1986 A dozen white men attack three black men in the Howard Beach neighborhood of Queens, New York. One victim, Timothy

Mike Tyson fights Trevor Berbick in the second round.

Rev. Al Sharpton leads demonstrators through Howard Beach, Queens, New York.

Grimes, escapes. Another, Cedric Sandiford, is severely beaten. The third, Michael Griffith, is hit by a car and killed when he tries to flee across a busy highway. The Howard Beach incident leads to national outrage, with Rev. Al Sharpton organizing a series of protests that reflect and, some believe, exacerbate the racial divide in New York's outer boroughs. At a march through Howard Beach on December 27, Sharpton and the throng of 1,200 he leads are met by a torrent of opposition, and the shouting goes both ways. On one side, marchers chant, "Segregation Here. Apartheid There. Smash Racism Everywhere." On the other are heard sneers of "Animals" and "Go home."[21] Two days later, after a state Supreme Court justice dismisses murder and manslaughter charges against the accused in the case, Sharpton cries out, "I guess what they're telling us is that to kill someone who's black is only assault at best. . . . This is Johannesburg."[22] As similar incidents plague New York City in the years to come, Sharpton remains on the forefront of the black response. In 1989, he organizes demonstrations after Yusuf Hawkins is killed by a white mob in Bensonhurst, Brooklyn, and he is stabbed protesting the Hawkins incident in 1991. Sharpton also advises Tawana Brawley, the young African American woman who in 1987 falsely accuses a group of white men of raping her in upstate New York. A lightning rod for controversy and organization, Sharpton, who metamorphoses from tracksuit appearances on local talk shows to a well-tailored national civil rights advocate and founder of the influential National Action Network, will, in some New Yorkers' minds, be permanently attached to this decade's tumultuous events.

1987

JANUARY 17, 1987 The former Southern Christian Leadership Conference (SCLC) organizer Hosea Williams, who twenty-two years earlier fronted the march to the Edmund Pettus Bridge on "Bloody Sunday" in Selma, leads a march of seventy-five to ninety people against segregation in the virtually all-white Forsyth County in Georgia. Whites attack the marchers, and Williams is hit in the head with a rock. Among those arrested is white supremacist leader

Rev. Hosea Williams, a veteran of the Selma campaign and an Atlanta City Council member (second from right), kneels in prayer in front of Dexter Avenue Memorial Church in Montgomery, Alabama, with an estimated 1,500 marchers on their way to the state capitol to protest legislative committee assignments. Rev. Dr. Martin Luther King, Jr., served as the church's pastor from 1954 to 1960.

Henry Hampton.

"Looking back, it is clear to me that history is the high ground in the battle for self," Hampton writes in his 1991 book *Voices of Freedom: An Oral History of the Civil Rights Movement from the 1950s through the 1980s*. "Without a sense of self, one's freedom is forever in the hands of others."[24] *Eyes* goes on to win six Emmy Awards.

FEBRUARY 12, 1987 Beulah Mae Donald wins a $7 million judgment against the United Klans of America, whose members lynched her nineteen-year-old son Michael six years earlier. The Southern Poverty Law Center deploys what becomes a successful strategy against white supremacist groups: suing them into bankruptcy. The United Klans of America is forced out of business, and it must turn its remaining assets over to Donald. "It could have been somebody else's child, just like it was mine," the sixty-seven-year-old mother tells Robin Toner in the March 8 *New York Times*.[25]

David Duke. A second march the following week brings twenty thousand people, including Dick Gregory, John Lewis, and Coretta Scott King. Forsyth County responds by forming a biracial panel to discuss integration. Nevertheless, segregation persists, and few notice when Williams organizes another march there in 1988.[23]

JANUARY 21, 1987 The fourteen-hour documentary series *Eyes on the Prize* premieres on PBS. Directed by Henry Hampton and narrated by Julian Bond, the series is a dramatic and necessary retelling of key moments in the civil rights movement from 1954 to 1965. (A second series premieres in 1990 and carries the story into the mid-1980s.) *Eyes* not only introduces Americans to key movement activists, it forces viewers to reckon with the violence of the past and to ponder the continued persistence of inequality.

FEBRUARY 24, 1987 At the Grammy Awards in Los Angeles, the award for Best Pop Performance by a Duo or Group goes to "That's What Friends Are For," which unites star musical talent across race and gender from Dionne Warwick and Gladys Knight to Stevie Wonder and Elton John. Warwick has collected Grammys in three different decades, beginning with 1969's "Do You Know the Way to San Jose?" and continuing in the 1970s with "I'll Never Fall in Love Again," fruits of her collaborations with songwriters Burt Bacharach and Hal David.

MARCH 23, 1987 The first annual Soul Train Music Awards, premiering live on BET from the Santa Monica Civic Auditorium, is the first TV awards ceremony exclusively dedicated to

Rita Dove stands contemplatively with Thomas Jefferson's Virginia home, Monticello, in the distance.

celebrating African Americans working in the music industry. Don Cornelius, who founded *Soul Train* on television in 1971, serves as the show's executive producer, and it is cohosted by music legends Luther Vandross and Dionne Warwick, with performances by Al Jarreau and LL Cool J, among others. Winners on the night include Janet Jackson, Anita Baker, Run-D.M.C., Al Green, and Heritage Award recipient Stevie Wonder. "The time is right for this kind of show to get on the air and stay there," Cornelius is quoted in the *Los Angeles Times* on March 25. "There's an enormous global audience for what is called 'black music' out there now, and I felt it was time they got some attention. It's appropriate now."[26]

APRIL 16, 1987 August Wilson wins the Pulitzer Prize for Drama for his 1983 play *Fences*, which also wins the Tony Award for Best Play. Wilson again captures the Pulitzer three years later for *The Piano Lesson*. In 1987, Rita Dove wins the Pulitzer in poetry for "Thomas and Beulah."

Salt-N-Pepa in concert.

Three prominent black executives: George Lewis (Phillip Morris Capital Corp.), Dr. Clifton Wharton, Jr. (TIAA-CREF), and James Avery (Exxon).

JULY 7, 1987 Rap crew Eric B. and Rakim release *Paid in Full*. With funky, innovative production from Eric B. and ingenious rapping by Rakim, the album is an instant classic. Later in the year, Salt-N-Pepa release the timeless hit "Push It," which makes them the first female rappers to have a single in the *Billboard* Top 20. "I don't like the fact that there are so few women in rap," Cheryl James ("Salt") is quoted as saying in the *Los Angeles Times* on November 26. "Rap is hard-core street music, but there are women out there who can hang with the best male rappers. What holds us back is that girls tend to rap in these high, squeaky voices. It's irritating. You've gotta rap from the *diaphragm*." The increasingly pervasive influence of rap's urban cultural styles is manifest in another of the

year's seminal hit records, Michael Jackson's *Bad*, another Quincy Jones collaboration. Its title track is translated into a music video filmed inside a New York City subway station, with Jackson transforming from a lonely, hooded street wanderer confronted by toughs into a black-leather-clad leader surrounded by his own gang of spray-paint-wielding, roller-skate-gliding backup dancers.[27]

AUGUST 9, 1987 The TLC Group, a New York investment firm chaired by Reginald Lewis, announces a leveraged buyout of the Beatrice International Food Company. The new TLC Beatrice becomes the first black-owned business to reach $1 billion in sales. Also in 1987, Clifton Wharton, Jr., the former chancellor of the State University of New York, becomes the first African American to head a Fortune 500 company when he is named CEO of the private pension fund TIAA-CREF. The assets he oversees, at $54 billion, make TIAA-CREF the largest fund of its kind in the nation. In a February 13 profile in the *Wall Street Journal*, Wharton has this to say: "When you pioneer a new position it is very important that you succeed." Within his first year, Wharton works to persuade companies operating in South Africa to pull out of the apartheid state.[28]

SEPTEMBER 13, 1987 Toni Morrison, a fifty-six-year-old former English teacher at Howard and editor at Random House, publishes her fifth novel, *Beloved*, destined to join the Western and African American literary canons as one of the finest books of the century. In her review in the *New York Times* on September 13, Margaret Atwood declares of Morrison, "If there were any doubts about her stature as a pre-eminent

Author Toni Morrison receives the Presidential Medal of Freedom from President Barack Obama.

American novelist, of her own or any other generation, *Beloved* will put them to rest." The powerful combination of reality, folklore, and the supernatural, flowing out of its main character's haunting personal memories of slavery and its impact on her choices as a mother, captures the 1988 Pulitzer Prize for Fiction. Five years later, Morrison publishes another classic, *Jazz*, and is recognized for her achievements with the 1993 Nobel Prize in Literature. The Nobel announcement declares that Morrison "delves into the language itself, a language she wants to liberate from the fetters of race. And she addresses us with the lustre of poetry." "The mode I choose is tragic," the author tells Connie Casey of the *Chicago Tribune* for an October 27 profile titled, "Pain Is the Stuff of Toni Morrison's Novels." "I don't find difficulty to be sad or bad. The reason I write is because it's hard. I'm rather bored with easy shots and fake problems." Morrison, who goes on to teach writing at Princeton University, is considered by many to be the greatest African American writer of her generation and one of the most important American writers of any age.[29]

SEPTEMBER 6, 1987 Ben Carson, the black thirty-five-year-old chief of pediatric neurosurgery at Johns Hopkins in Baltimore, and his seventy-member team complete a twenty-two-hour operation to separate seven-month-old twins conjoined at the head. "Even when I feel I'm going into a situation where there's a very high risk of mortality, I don't get nervous," Carson is quoted in the *Sun* following another harrowing surgery in March. "Getting nervous doesn't help you."[30]

SEPTEMBER 24, 1987 *A Different World*, a spin-off of *The Cosby Show*, debuts on NBC. The comedy stars Lisa Bonet (reprising her role as Denise Huxtable), Jasmine Guy, Kadeem Hardison, and

Sinbad and revolves around college students at Hillman, a fictional historically black college in Virginia. The show, which runs until 1993 (well after Bonet's departure), combines humor with serious social topics such as date rape, AIDS, and war. It also illustrates the diversity of backgrounds and experiences within the black community.

DECEMBER 1, 1987 The African American writer James Baldwin, regarded by many as the leading black author of the civil rights era, dies at sixty-three in Saint-Paul de Vence, France. His funeral is held one week later at the Cathedral of St. John the Divine in New York, the city of his birth. Among those paying tribute as speakers are Toni Morrison, Maya Angelou, and Amiri Baraka, who, in his eulogy, lauds Baldwin as the "glorious, elegant griot of our oppressed American nation . . . [making] us feel, for one thing, that we could defend ourselves or define ourselves, that we were in the world, not merely as animate slaves, but as terrifyingly sensitive measures of what is good or evil, beautiful or ugly." Baldwin leaves a host of consequential works behind him, including several taught at universities today, including *Go Tell It on the Mountain* (1953), *Notes of a Native Son* (1955), *Nobody Knows My Name* (1961), and *The Fire Next Time* (1963). A group of writers including the author Thomas Sayers Ellis, the poet Sharan Strange, and the poet-composer Janice Lowe, inspired by the experience of attending Baldwin's funeral, found the Dark Room Collective in Boston the following year. By March 1989, the collective has hosted a series of readings by contemporary black writers while nurturing a rising generation of black talent in its community, among them John Keene, Patrick Sylvain, Natasha Trethewey, and Ntozake Shange. Covering a reading by the group in Philadelphia in 1993, Samuel F. Reynolds writes: "This clear, sharp directive for Black writers to develop their writing and to gain autonomy by establishing institutions, or to enter established institutions, devoted to Black literary life points to the seriousness of this group."[31]

DECEMBER 18, 1987 *Eddie Murphy: Raw*, the profanity-filled stand-up comedy film, opens in theaters. The *New York Times* notes that "even the ushers were laughing" at the New York premiere and calls the film "hilarious, putting Mr. Murphy on a par with Mr. Pryor at his best."[32]

1988

FEBRUARY 12, 1988 Spike Lee's *School Daze* premieres. The musical comedy, set on a black college campus, explores a number of themes, including interracial relationships and the differences in skin tone among African Americans. Roger Ebert notes that *School Daze*, like Lee's debut *She's Gotta Have It*, "is the first movie in a long time where the black characters seem to be relating to one another, instead of to a hypothetical white audience." Lee follows with the Academy Award–nominated 1989 film *Do the Right Thing*, which centers on tensions between blacks and Italian Americans in the Bedford-Stuyvesant section of Brooklyn. In turn, Lee's 1992 film *Malcolm X*, starring Denzel Washington in the title role, leads to a renewed cultural emphasis on the life of the slain Black Nationalist leader who helped inspire the nascent Black Power movement.[33]

MARCH 22, 1988 The US Congress, by a vote of 73–24 in the Senate and 292–133 in the House,

Rev. Jesse Jackson with presidential candidate Michael Dukakis at the West Angeles Church of God in Christ, Los Angeles.

overrides President Regan's veto of the Civil Rights Restoration Act, designed to combat the Supreme Court's narrowing of the definition of discrimination in federally funded programs. House Speaker Jim Wright (D-Texas) says, "President Reagan may want to turn the clock back on civil rights, but the American people do not."[34]

MARCH 26, 1988 In a second run for his party's nomination for the presidency, Jesse Jackson wins the Michigan caucus, which the *Los Angeles Times* describes as "a stunning victory that gave a major boost to his presidential candidacy." Jackson goes on to finish second (to Michael Dukakis) in a crowded Democratic field, but his victories in several caucuses and primaries, netting some seven million votes, prove again that African Americans are viable candidates at the national level. In a rousing address at the Democratic National Convention in Atlanta on July 19, Jackson closes with a memorable refrain: "You must not surrender!

Washington, DC, mayor Sharon Pratt Dixon (right) and former mayor Marion Barry hold the seal of the District of Columbia at her swearing-in ceremony.

You may or may not get there but just know that you're qualified! And you hold on, and hold out! We must never surrender! America will get better and better. Keep hope alive. Keep hope alive! Keep hope alive! On tomorrow night and beyond, keep hope alive!"[35]

MAY 3, 1988 Living Colour releases the album *Vivid*. Defying racial stereotypes, the African American band fuses rock, heavy metal, funk, and jazz, storming to No. 6 on the charts on the strength of the Grammy-winning hit single and MTV favorite "Cult of Personality."

MAY 15, 1988 Eugene A. Marino becomes the first African American archbishop in the Catholic Church. The following January, the Episco-

"Fight the Power": Public Enemy's Chuck D and Flavor Flav.

pal Church ordains Barbara Harris as its first woman bishop.

JUNE 15–18, 1988 At the National Conference of Black Mayors in Philadelphia, thirteen women organize the Black Women Mayors' Caucus. By 1992, there are sixty-six black mayors in the United States, including Sharon Pratt of Washington, DC, who in 1990 becomes the first black woman elected mayor of a major American city.[36]

AUGUST 6, 1988 *Yo! MTV Raps*, hosted by Dr. Dre (New York), Ed Lover, and Fab 5 Freddy, makes its television debut. The show gives hip-hop a larger national platform than ever before. In another banner year in the genre's development, 1988 sees the group Public Enemy releasing its landmark second album, *It Takes a Nation of Millions to Hold Us Back*, which blends the musical traditions of rap and funk with lyrics deeply rooted in the African American experience and featuring calls for black leaders to step forward and represent the race. On the strength of the singles "Bring the Noise" and the incendiary "Black Steel in the Hour of Chaos," Public Enemy achieves massive acclaim for its harsh, noisy production, political lyrics from Chuck D, and slapstick entertainment from Flavor Flav. Public Enemy's popularity explodes further with the release of their single "Fight the Power" (on the *Do the Right Thing* soundtrack) in 1989 and the album *Fear of a Black Planet* in 1990. Embraced by hard-core music fans and intellectuals alike, Chuck D (born Carlton Ridenhour) roots his voice in the authenticity of his New York upbringing and takes socially conscious lyric writing to a new level, with allusions to gun violence that shock those outside of the experience and Black Nationalist evocations parallel-

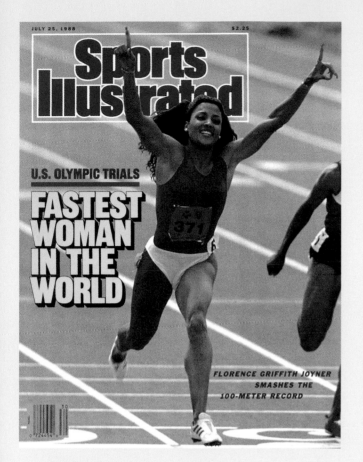

JULY 25, 1988 $2.25

Sports
Illustrated

U.S. OLYMPIC TRIALS

FASTEST
WOMAN
IN THE
WORLD

*FLORENCE GRIFFITH JOYNER
SMASHES THE
100-METER RECORD*

Florence Griffith Joyner breaks the world record at the
US Olympic track and field trials.

ing the teachings of Louis Farrakhan that inspire some and alienate others. Jon Pareles, in a July 24, 1988, article in the *New York Times*, sums up the group's brand as "Rap with a Fist in the Air."[37]

SEPTEMBER 2–OCTOBER 2, 1988 Florence Griffith Joyner, better known as Flo-Jo, wins three gold medals in track and field at the Summer Olympics in Seoul, South Korea. Carl Lewis wins two gold medals, one of which (the 100-meter) is awarded to him after Canadian Ben Johnson tests positive for steroids. Across four different Olympic games, Lewis wins a total of nine gold medals.

SEPTEMBER 21, 1988 The "Willie Horton" political ad begins to air, quickly becoming one of the most polarizing, racially charged—and devastatingly effective—commercials in presidential-election history. Lobbed like a grenade by the campaign of current vice president George H.W. Bush against his Democratic rival, Massachusetts governor Michael Dukakis, the ad attempts to link Dukakis to Willie Horton, a black inmate convicted of murder, who, while on furlough from a Massachusetts prison, raped a white woman. To drive the message home, Horton's victims lend the Bush campaign support on the campaign trail. African American groups view the ad as cynical race baiting, and its importance and infamy only grow in election-history lore when Bush closes the gap on Dukakis and eventually wins the White House in November.[38]

1988 IN EDUCATION The year 1988 marks the peak of school desegregation in the United States. Schools with a white population of 1 percent or less number 2,762; that number grows to 6,727 by 2011. In the South, the number of black students who attend majority-white schools peaks at 43.5 percent. The years witnessing mass school desegregation efforts in the US, from the early 1970s to the late 1980s, also see a narrowing of the "achievement gap" between black and white students nationwide. "In reading, for example, a 39-point gap for 13-year-olds in 1971 was reduced to an 18-point in 1988," according to a report published by the Educational Testing Service in 2010. "For 17-year-olds," the report continues, "the gap declined from 53 points to 20 points."[39]

139

1989

JANUARY 3, 1989 *The Arsenio Hall Show*, the first syndicated late-night talk show hosted by an African American, launches on television in direct competition with *The Tonight Show*, hosted by Johnny Carson. With his signature fist pumps and appeals to a crossover "MTV Generation," Hall provides a platform for African American actors and performers to exhibit their craft, from Eddie Murphy to MC Hammer and a host of rappers rarely featured on other television programs. In 1991, Hall's signature line, "Things that make you go *hmm . . .*," is adapted into a hit song by C + C Music Factory, and the show reaches a peak of cultural relevancy in 1992 when presidential contender Bill Clinton appears, playing his saxophone to the tune of "Heartbreak Hotel" with the house band the Posse, while donning a dark pair of sunglasses. Many consider it a game changer in the way candidates reach out to voters. Though *The Arsenio Hall Show* lasts only five years, it is a major landmark for African Americans in television.[40]

JANUARY 23, 1989 In *Richmond v. J.A. Croson Co.*, the US Supreme Court, in a 6–3 decision, rules against an affirmative action plan requir-

ing companies with city contracts in Richmond, Virginia, to set aside 30 percent of their contracts for minority businesses. Justice Sandra Day O'Connor writes in her majority opinion, "The

Arsenio Hall delivers his late-night monologue.

dream of a nation of equal citizens in a society where race is irrelevant to personal opportunity and achievement would be lost in a mosaic of shifting preferences based on inherently unmeasurable claims of past wrongs." The same Equal Protection Clause once cited to advance black civil rights is now being applied, with strict scrutiny by this Court, to protect white Americans from what is perceived as reverse discrimination.[41]

JANUARY 26, 1989 Colgate-Palmolive announces it will rename its Darkie toothpaste, sold in Asia and featuring a minstrel in blackface as its logo, to Darlie. "It's just offensive," says Colgate's chief executive, Reuben Mark. Later in the year, Quaker Oats redesigns its iconic Aunt Jemima character, now with pearl earrings instead of a headband, in another attempt to distance its brand from evocations of American slavery.[42]

FEBRUARY 10, 1989 Ronald Brown, a forty-seven-year-old lawyer and lobbyist who helped manage Jesse Jackson's 1988 campaign, is elected chair of the Democratic National Committee, making him the first African American to head a national political party. Brown proves instrumental in Bill Clinton's 1992 race for the White House. He dies tragically in a plane crash in 1996 while serving as Clinton's secretary of commerce.

FEBRUARY 22, 1989 At the thirty-first annual Grammy Awards in Los Angeles, DJ Jazzy Jeff and Fresh Prince Will Smith win best rap performance for their breakout hit "Parents Just Don't Understand." It is the first time this award, or any in a rap category, is given, yet the group, along with other rap artists, boycott the ceremony for its refusal to allow rappers to per-

Ron Brown, chairman of the Democratic National Committee, in his office before his first staff meeting.

form. One rap presenter at the show is Kool Moe Dee, who, according to the *New York Amsterdam News,* prefers "people to see how he carries himself, his attire, etc., in order to dispel the negative image rap has with the general public."[43]

MARCH 3, 1989 De La Soul releases its debut album, *3 Feet High and Rising,* initiating a new style of hip-hop that features adventurous, laid-back, jazzy beats; a wide variety of samples (Steely Dan, Liberace); humorous skits; socially conscious but frequently abstract lyrics; and even an appropriation of hippie imagery. De La

Soul and the like-minded crews A Tribe Called Quest and the Jungle Brothers belong to the Native Tongues, a loose confederation of rappers exploring similar lyrical and musical themes.

MARCH 3, 1989 The pop icon Madonna premieres her music video "Like a Prayer." The song already aired as part of a Pepsi commercial, but the controversy surrounding the music video convinces the soda company to end the partnership. The reason: the clip features Madonna's character falling in love with a black priest, portrayed by Leon Robinson, and reveals the consequences of that interracial relationship: white violence and burning crosses.[44]

MARCH 11, 1989 The reality television show *Cops* officially launches on the Fox network. The *New York Times* explains why many African Americans criticize the show: "The dominant image is hammered home again and again: the overwhelmingly white troops of police are the good guys; the bad guys are overwhelmingly black." *Cops* enters syndication in 1993 ahead of a massive proliferation of reality-based programming.[45]

MARCH 24, 1989 Twenty-year-old Daymond John begins selling handmade hats on the streets of Queens, New York. Three years later, John and three friends found FUBU, short for "For Us, By Us." The company is worth $350 million ten years later. The same year FUBU is founded, Def Jam's founder Russell Simmons begins production on his Phat Farm line of hip-hop streetwear.[46]

APRIL 19, 1989 A white jogger, Trisha Meili (anonymous at the time), is raped in New York City's Central Park. In the aftermath, four black males and one Hispanic male are arrested, and following sensationalistic trials, the group known as the Central Park Five is convicted and sentenced to prison, despite no serious evidence other than coerced confessions. The incident

New York City Councilman Charles Barron protests the wrongful conviction of the Central Park Five.

inspires Sapphire's 1989 poem "Wild Thing," written from the point of view of a black man who attacks a white woman. When the sexually explicit poem is published in a National Endowment of the Humanities–funded journal, conservative groups successfully call for the ouster of the organization's chairman, John Frohnmayer. The Central Park Five's prison sentences are vacated in 2002 when another man confesses to the crime. The group sues the city and in 2014 reaches a settlement worth $41 million. "Individually, these young men [boys at the time] spent six and a half to 13 years imprisoned, and collectively 40 years between them," says New York State Senator Bill Perkins, in advancing a resolution on the anniversary of the case in 2010. "Unfortunately, money can never replace what was taken from them."[47]

JULY 1989 Marlon Troy Riggs's experimental film *Tongues Untied* premieres in Los Angeles. The autobiographical film examines the ways blacks and whites discriminate against gay black men. Riggs says it is about "the vitality and significance of a community that traditionally has been silenced and ignored." Protests occur two years later when PBS announces it will air the film, and many, including the 1992 Republican presidential candidate and conservative commentator Patrick Buchanan, denounce the National Endowment for the Arts for its grant support of the film. It is the height of the "culture wars" in America. Two years later, Riggs, a Harvard alumnus and member of the faculty at the University of California, Berkeley, dies from AIDS-related complications at age thirty-seven. "He's looked upon as a hero who has probably done more for black gay visibility than anybody in the last 10 years," the director of Us Helping

Us, Ron Simmons, says of Riggs in 1992. "His films have been seen around the world. People have personally told me that after seeing his work, they feel like they've been born again."[48]

AUGUST 1989 The Centers for Disease Control announces the first hundred thousand reported cases of AIDS. Twenty-seven percent of reported AIDS cases are among blacks and 15 percent are among Hispanics, numbers that jump to 31 percent and 17 percent, respectively, by 1991. In 1989, blacks comprise half the women who have AIDS, as well as about 70 percent of babies born with the disease.[49]

SEPTEMBER 21, 1989 The US Senate unanimously confirms General Colin Powell as chairman of the Joint Chiefs of Staff. The New York–born son of Jamaican immigrants, Powell was awarded the Purple Heart and Bronze Star for his service in Vietnam, and previously worked as President Reagan's national security advisor. Nominated by President George H.W. Bush, who describes Powell as "the complete soldier," the fifty-four-year-old four-star general is the youngest and the first African American to hold the nation's highest military post. Powell calls the appointment "a special privilege." In a piece for the *Washington Post* earlier in the year, "True Black Power—Colin Powell," Juan Williams quotes the general: "To the extent that black people look at that picture of power and they gain some inspiration from seeing a black man at the table, I'm very happy about that."[50]

SEPTEMBER 22, 1989 *Family Matters*, a spin-off of the ABC sitcom *Perfect Strangers*, premieres in prime time featuring a black cast led by veteran actor Reginald VelJohnson as head of the Chicago-based Winslow family. What makes the show iconic—and a hit—is teen actor Jaleel White's performance as next-door neighbor Steve Urkel, one of the first black "nerd" characters on television, with his signature glasses, suspenders, and perpetual crush on the Winslows' daughter, Laura. There is even a Hasbro toy doll of Urkel for kids. Asked to describe the character's significance on the pop-culture scene, Harvard psychologist Dr. Alvin Poussaint says in 1991, "The fact that he's a nerd and very bright may be a step forward—accepting that a black kid can be bright and precocious and might end up in an Ivy League school." The show runs for nine seasons.[51]

OCTOBER 3, 1989 Art Shell, a forty-two-year-old former all-pro offensive tackle recently inducted into the NFL Hall of Fame, becomes the first African American head coach in the league's modern era when Al Davis, owner of the Los Angeles (now Oakland) Raiders, names Shell as the successor to Mike Shanahan in advance of a Monday-night game against the New York Jets. Shell tells the press: "It is an historic event; I understand the significance of it. . . . I'm proud of it, but I'm also a Raider. I don't believe the color of my skin entered into this decision. I was chosen because Al Davis felt I was the right person at the right time." The only previous black head coach in the league was player-coach Fritz Pollard, who helmed Indiana's Hammond Pros from 1923 to 1925.[52]

OCTOBER 15, 1989 Martin Puryear displays nine sculptures at the São Paulo Bienal in Brazil, becoming the first African American artist to represent the United States at a major international art exhibition. "I think it's very good for us as a people and for myself as an artist," he says. The following year, Puryear participates in *The Decade Show: Frameworks of Identity* in the 1980s, a collaboration between three New York City Museums: the New Museum of Contemporary Art, the Museum of Hispanic Contemporary Art, and the Studio Museum in Harlem. The *New York Times* remarks that the show "confirms that visual quality is a many-splendored thing that emanates from all sectors of America's multi-cultural society."[53]

Queen Latifah.

NOVEMBER 1989 The clothing company Benetton Group causes controversy with a racially charged advertising campaign. One ad features a white hand and black hand cuffed together; the other depicts a black woman breast-feeding a white baby. The company earned plaudits over the previous four years for its multicultural United Colors of Benetton advertisements, but Donald Polk of the National Urban League says, "Using this kind of image tends to undo the good they have tried to accomplish in the past." Four months later, Benetton unveils what its US general manger calls "a softer approach"—ads featuring a white hand holding a black baby and white and black runners participating in a relay race.[54]

NOVEMBER 7, 1989 Nineteen-year-old Queen Latifah (born Dana Owens) of East Orange, New Jersey, releases *All Hail the Queen*, a dazzling album of Afrocentric and feminist lyrics combined with beats culled from hip-hop, jazz, blues, and reggae. Explaining her nickname, and giving insight into her lyrical inspiration, Latifah says, "I feel like all black people came from a line of kings and queens that they've never really had the opportunity to know about. This is my way of giving a tribute to them." With its popular lead single "Ladies First," *All Hail the Queen* signals the emergence of Queen Latifah as a multiplatform superstar and is a watershed in the advent of black female rap artists.[55]

NOVEMBER 22, 1989 Frederick Drew Gregory, an astronaut since 1978, becomes the first African American to pilot a space shuttle when mission STS-33 of *Discovery* launches from Kennedy

Actor Morgan Freeman in uniform on the set of *Glory*.

Space Center. Gregory and his crew orbit the earth five times.[56]

DECEMBER 15, 1989 The film *Glory*, the story of one of the Civil War's first all-black regiments, premieres. Directed by Ed Zwick, *Glory* highlights the courage of black soldiers, freeborn and ex-slaves alike, and the prejudices they face in the military. Among its cast members are Morgan Freeman and Denzel Washington, who wins an Oscar for Best Supporting Actor for his portrayal of the escaped slave Trip. *New York Times* critic Vincent Canby predicts that the thirty-four-year-old Washington is "an actor clearly on his way to a major screen career." Washington, a native of Mount Vernon, New York, realizes he is in an all-too-unique position as a black actor in Hollywood. "Who else is there? Who can I say?" he tells Donna Britt for an August 25 profile in the *Washington Post*. "And you don't want to look at it along racial lines, but you have to. . . . It's not like there's six or 20 black guys who are making lots of movies and it's all okay. You know? There's nobody. There's *me*."[57]

1990–1994

Maya Angelou delivers her poem "On the Pulse of Morning" at the inauguration of President Bill Clinton in 1993.

1990

JANUARY 1, 1990 With Harry Belafonte as master of ceremonies, David Dinkins is inaugurated as the 106th mayor of New York City, the first African American to win election to that city's highest office. "I stand before you today as the elected leader of the greatest city of a great nation, to which my ancestors were brought, chained and whipped in the hold of a slave ship," the sixty-two-year-old Dinkins declares in his address outside City Hall. "We have not finished the journey toward liberty and justice, but surely we have come a long way." Two weeks later, on January 13, Douglas Wilder takes office in the Commonwealth of Virginia as the first African American elected governor in the nation's history.[1]

FEBRUARY 5, 1990 Twenty-eight-year-old Columbia University graduate Barack Obama becomes the first black president of the *Harvard Law Review* in its 104-year history. "The fact that I've been elected shows a lot of progress," he says. But, Obama warns, "You have to remember that for every one of me, there are hundreds or thousands of black students with at least equal talent who don't get a chance." During Obama's

time in Cambridge, Massachusetts, despite calls for reform, the law-school administration fails to recruit a single black female member to its faculty. In protest, Derrick Bell, Harvard's first black tenured law professor, stages a dra-

David Dinkins campaigns for the mayoralty of New York City.

Barack Obama after being named editor of the *Harvard Law Review.*

matic five-day sit-in that draws national press coverage. When the administration takes no action, Bell takes an unpaid leave, resulting in his dismissal. At a student rally on campus, Obama calls Bell "the Rosa Parks of American legal education."[2]

JUNE 7, 1990 US District Judge Jose Gonzalez rules the Miami rap group 2 Live Crew's album *As Nasty As They Wanna Be* obscene and bars its sale in three Florida counties. The next day, a record-store owner in Fort Lauderdale is arrested for selling it. On June 11, 2 Live Crew's Luther Campbell and Chris Wong Won are arrested after a performance in Hollywood, Florida. The case divides African Americans over where to draw the line when it comes to violence and misogyny in rap music. "Our cultural experience," says the NAACP's

executive director Benjamin L. Hooks, "does not include debasing our women, the glorification of violence, the promotion of deviant sexual behavior, or the tearing into shreds of our cherished mores and standards of behavior." Arguing on the other side, the literary historian Henry Louis Gates, Jr., at the time a professor at Duke University, testifies against the ban. "The failure to defend 2 Live Crew reveals the

2 Live Crew in concert.

Walter Mosley.

American member of a very exclusive club: novelists embraced by *presidents*."[4]

JUNE 20, 1990 Only four months after his release from twenty-seven years as a political prisoner in South Africa, Nelson Mandela arrives in New York City to begin an eleven-day tour of the United States to marshal support for his political party and for democracy in his home country. Mandela also seeks, in his words, "to put forth the message that sanctions must be intensified." Already a hero in the United States because of his courageous resistance to apartheid, Mandela meets fanfare everywhere he goes. As many as 750,000 people see him in New York City, where he is featured in a ticker-

ignorance of how dangerous this case is to us all," Gates says in a June 21 *Wall Street Journal* story. Gates does not excuse the misogyny in the lyrics, but he argues in a *New York Times* essay called "2 Live Crew Decoded" that the words qualify as free speech and should be viewed as a "sexual carnivalesque" in the black vernacular tradition.[3]

JUNE 17, 1990 Walter Mosley publishes *Devil in a Blue Dress*, the first of his hard-boiled Easy Rawlins mystery novels. On the campaign trail two years later, the Democratic candidate Bill Clinton declares Mosley one of his favorite authors. *Devil in a Blue Dress* is made into a film starring Denzel Washington in 1995. "To see the way it was from a black person's point of view, particularly in the '40s, '50s and '60s is very interesting," President Clinton tells the *Wall Street Journal* in 1997. "This would be interesting for all Americans." In the same article, the *Journal* describes Mosley as "the first African-

Nelson Mandela, leader of the African National Congress, addresses a Joint Session of the US Congress.

tape parade in Manhattan and presides over a sold-out rally at Yankee Stadium. He also gives a speech along the Charles River in Boston and talks with students at a majority-black high school there. In the nation's capital, Mandela meets with President Bush. "We fight for and visualize a future in which all shall, without regard to race, color, creed or sex, have the right to vote," Mandela says in a speech before Congress that receives fifteen standing ovations. The legacy of the American civil rights movement is at the forefront of the trip, as Mandela places a wreath on the grave of Rev. Dr. Martin Luther King, Jr., in Atlanta and meets Rosa Parks in Detroit. He also speaks to capacity crowds in Los Angeles, Oakland, and Miami.[5]

AUGUST 11, 1990 Operation PUSH's executive director Tyrone Crider calls for a boycott of Nike, arguing that the corporation does not use black banks or black advertising agencies and has hired no blacks for positions of power. "We've got to keep our dollar bills in our own community," Crider says. The protest is particularly significant because Nike makes the Air Jordan sneaker, inspired by Michael Jordan. One week later, Nike announces minority-hiring goals, pledging to place a non-white person on its board of directors within a year, to increase the number of non-white department heads within a year, and to name a non-white vice president within two years. When asked why Nike planned to hire non-whites rather than blacks specifically, chairman Phil Knight

The Fresh Prince of Bel-Air: (left to right) Karyn Parsons as Hilary Banks, Janet Hubert as Vivian Banks, Will Smith as William "Will" Smith, and Alfonso Ribeiro as Carlton Banks.

says of Operation PUSH, "We have a broader vision of equal opportunity than they do."[6]

SEPTEMBER 10, 1990 *The Fresh Prince of Bel-Air,* starring twenty-one-year-old rapper Will "Fresh Prince" Smith, premieres in prime time on NBC. The fish-out-of-water story of a West Philadelphia teenager sent to live with his wealthy extended Los Angeles family earns positive reviews, particularly for the performance of the hip-hop star. *Variety* says that Smith "proves to be a remarkably proficient actor, mugging mischievously for the camera with almost palpable charm but also mastering his more serious moments in the script." *The Fresh Prince of Bel-Air* runs for six seasons and still airs in syndication. The show marks the beginning of an influx of rap stars into mainstream television.[7]

OCTOBER 22, 1990 President George H.W. Bush vetoes the Civil Rights Act of 1990, designed to strengthen affirmative action programs in light of recent Supreme Court decisions. Bush argues that the act "employs a maze of legalistic language to introduce the destructive force of quotas into our national employment system." The following year, Bush signs into law the less comprehensive Civil Rights Act of 1991.[8]

NOVEMBER 27, 1990 Charles Johnson wins the National Book Award for his historical novel about the illegal nineteenth-century slave trade, *The Middle Passage,* which, Thomas Keneally, in *The New York Times Book Review,* locates "in the honorable tradition of 'Billy Budd' and 'Moby-Dick.'" Johnson, who says he has "been waiting his entire life for this," dedicates his acceptance speech to the author Ralph Ellison and predicts "in the 1990s we will see a black American fiction that will be Ellisonesque... as we as a people move from narrow complaint to broad celebration."[9]

1991

JANUARY 16, 1991 The Persian Gulf War, the United States' first war since Vietnam, commences. African Americans comprise approximately 20 percent of US troops. General Colin Powell is a key leader in the war, devising a successful ground strategy alongside General Norman Schwarzkopf. President Bush's national security advisor Brent Scowcroft describes Powell's vital role: "The military side is marked by quiet, cool efficiency, no histrionics, no visible handwringing. It has just been an extremely professional operation, which is the hallmark of Colin Powell." Powell becomes an increasingly public figure during the brief conflict, and his time in front of the news cameras earns him national attention and acclaim for his steady leadership.[10]

JANUARY 31, 1991 More than a year after the death of the historian Nathan I. Huggins, Har-

Operation Desert Shield: an African American soldier on deployment in Saudi Arabia.

vard University announces it has hired the forty-year-old literary theorist and cultural critic Henry Louis Gates, Jr., to rebuild its Afro-American Studies Department and W.E.B. Du Bois Institute. Gates overcomes his initial reluctance to leave Duke University for Harvard when he becomes convinced that the university now sees, in his words, "no conflict between traditional standards of excellence and diversity in the faculty." To attract new faculty to a department that had only one other tenured member when he arrived, Gates first recruits Kwame Anthony Appiah, a leading Ghana-born philosopher and effective administrator, to join him in Cambridge, and, by decade's end, they assemble an academic "Dream Team" consisting of other leading scholars including the sociologist William Julius Wilson, the philosopher Cornel West, and the historian Evelyn Brooks Higginbotham. "If we have taken black studies for granted as a tool for integrating higher education," Gates is quoted as saying in the *New York Times* on April 1, 1990, "we may have only begun to glimpse its potential for integrating the American mind." Following events at Yale, the history professor John Blassingame, one of Gates's mentors in New Haven, tells the *Times* in 1992, "I've always said that until Harvard has a strong program, the enterprise called African-American studies won't arrive."[11]

FEBRUARY 20, 1991 At the thirty-third annual Grammy Awards in New York City, MC Hammer (born Stanley Kirk Burrell) takes home three prizes, including one in a new category, Best Rap Solo Performance, for his crossover hit "You Can't Touch This." The album it's on, Capitol Records' *Please Hammer Don't Hurt 'Em*, becomes the first rap album ever to be certified

diamond, with more than ten million records sold. "Let's be perfectly blunt—Hammer is not a lyrical genius," Steve "Flash" Juon writes for *RapReviews*. "Hammer was the rapper your parents were okay with, which was why so many of us wound up with his tape." Also on Grammy night, the producer Quincy Jones wins six awards, including Producer of the Year, making him "the most honored pop artist in the 33-year history of the awards." Among Jones's prizes is one in another new category, Best Rap Performance by a Duo or Group, which he shares with Big Daddy Kane, Ice-T, Kool Moe Dee, Melle Mel, and Quincy Jones III for "Back on the Block."[12]

MARCH 3, 1991 After a high-speed chase, Rodney King, a twenty-four-year-old black man, is pulled over and beaten by white Los Angeles police officers Stacey Koon, Laurence M. Powell, Timothy Wind, and Ted Briseno, who hit and kick King more than fifty times and shoot him with a Taser gun. King suffers severe injuries, including skull fractures, a broken leg, and damage to his internal organs. "I was scared for my life," King will say just days after the incident. "So I laid down real calmly and took it like a man." Unbeknownst to the police, George Holliday, a bystander, tapes the assault and turns the recording over to a local television station. A horrified nation watches the video the next day. Under intense criticism, Los Angeles police chief Daryl Gates pledges that the offending officers will be punished, but he also believes the violence represents "an aberration" rather than a reflection of the LAPD. The city's African American mayor Tom Bradley, Rev. Jesse Jackson, and even the conservative columnist George Will call for Gates to step down. The four officers will face charges for the attack, with the trial begin-

Whoopi Goldberg and nuns at a party for her film *Sister Act.*

ning in the majority-white suburb of Simi Valley in 1992.[13]

MARCH 25, 1991 Actress and comedian Whoopi Goldberg, thirty-five, wins the Oscar for Best Supporting Actress for her role as Oda Mae Brown in *Ghost* at the sixty-ninth annual Academy Awards in Los Angeles. Goldberg is the first African American actress to take home an Oscar since Hattie McDaniel did it for her performance as Mammy in *Gone with the Wind* in 1940. In her acceptance speech, Goldberg, previously nominated for her role as Celie in *The Color Purple,* tells those in the Shrine Auditorium, "I come from New York. When I was a little kid, I lived in the projects. You're the people I watched; the people I wanted to be. I'm proud to be an actor." Goldberg also hosts the Oscars ceremony four times in her career, beginning in 1994. On the same night Goldberg wins for *Ghost,* thirty-eight-year-old Russell Williams II makes Oscar history by becoming the first African American to take home back-to-back awards, when he wins for Best Sound for *Dances*

with Wolves a year after claiming the same prize for *Glory.*[14]

MAY 1, 1991 Future baseball Hall of Famer Rickey Henderson of the Oakland Athletics breaks Lou Brock's all-time stolen-base record when he steals his 939th career base. With Brock by his side, Henderson says, "Lou Brock was a symbol of great base stealing, but today I am the greatest of all time."[15]

Anita Hill is sworn in to testify before the US Senate Judiciary Committee.

above: A scene from *New Jack City*: Ice-T (left) has guns pointed at him while Wesley Snipes (middle) and others watch.
right: Movie poster, *Boyz n the Hood*.

JUNE 27, 1991 Justice Thurgood Marshall, whom the *New York Times* calls "a living hero of the civil rights movement and one of the last liberal voices on the Supreme Court," announces his retirement. To fill the vacancy, President Bush taps Clarence Thomas, the former chair of the Equal Employment Opportunity Commission and a federal appeals court judge in Washington, DC, who, though African American, is as conservative as Marshall is liberal. Many black organizations, including the NAACP, oppose the nomination based on Thomas's opposition to civil rights and affirmative action legislation, but he does have the backing of the Southern Christian Leadership Conference. During the confirmation process, University of Oklahoma law professor Anita Hill accuses Thomas of sexually harassing her while she worked for him at the Department of Education and the EEOC. The sensitive, salacious nature of the testimony turns the hearings into a national spectacle that feeds a new era of 24/7 cable news. A deeply offended Thomas calls the televised hearings a "high-tech lynching," while Hill, recalling her involvement later on, says, "People think, when they think of those hearings, 'He had a race, and she had a gender.' . . . But it was really the combination. And it changed the dynamics." Thomas is narrowly confirmed by the Senate, 52–48.[16]

JULY 12, 1991 Opening in theaters is John Singleton's breakthrough film *Boyz n the Hood*, which examines the fates of childhood friends growing up amid the violence and crime of impoverished South Central Los Angeles. The *Atlanta Daily World* critic Angela E. Chamblee writes that the film "is interesting for the depiction of new kinds of African American family formations. We see a single parent father struggling to rear and guide his son, and we also see the bonds of an extended

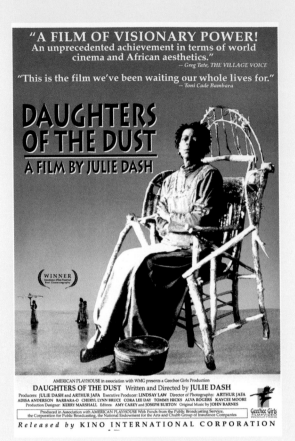

"A FILM OF VISIONARY POWER!
An unprecedented achievement in terms of world cinema and African aesthetics."
— Greg Tate, THE VILLAGE VOICE

"This is the film we've been waiting our whole lives for."
— Toni Cade Bambara

DAUGHTERS OF THE DUST
A FILM BY JULIE DASH

WINNER
Sundance Film Festival
Best Cinematography

AMERICAN PLAYHOUSE in association with WMG presents a Geechee Girls Production
DAUGHTERS OF THE DUST Written and Directed by JULIE DASH
Producers: JULIE DASH and ARTHUR JAFA Executive Producer: LINDSAY LAW Director of Photography: ARTHUR JAFA
ADISA ANDERSON BARBARA-O CHERYL LYNN BRUCE CORA LEE DAY TOMMY HICKS ALVA ROGERS KAYCEE MOORE
Production Designer: KERRY MARSHALL Editors: AMY CAREY and JOSEPH BURTON Original Music by JOHN BARNES

Produced in Association with AMERICAN PLAYHOUSE With Funds from the Public Broadcasting Service,
the Corporation for Public Broadcasting, the National Endowment for the Arts and Chubb Group of Insurance Companies

Geechee Girls
FILM+VIDEO

Released by KINO INTERNATIONAL CORPORATION

Movie poster, *Daughters of the Dust.*

family dealing with unwed, adolescent fatherhood." *New Jack City*, a New York crime film, which, like *Boyz*, stars a gangsta rapper (Ice-T in *New Jack City*; Ice Cube in *Boyz n the Hood*), is also released in 1991. But gangsta movies are not the only milestones in African American film this year. Julie Dash's *Daughters of the Dust*, released on December 27, is the first feature film directed by an African American woman to receive a widespread theatrical release.[17]

AUGUST 19, 1991 The four-day Crown Heights riot erupts in Brooklyn, New York, stemming from two incidents. First, a Hasidic man named Yosef Lifsh hits and kills an African American boy, Gavin Cato, with his car. Then, three hours later, a group of black men, including sixteen-year-old Lemrick Nelson, Jr., robs and kills the Jewish scholar Yankel Rosenbaum. Together, these two events light a powder keg of tensions,

Members of the Jewish Defense League and leaders of the African American community engage in a spirited debate outside New York City Hall after four nights of rioting in the Crown Heights section of Brooklyn.

Excavating the earliest known African American cemetery in Lower Manhattan.

festering for decades, between the neighborhood's black and Jewish residents. African Americans believe that Lifsh should have been arrested after hitting Cato. At Cato's funeral, Al Sharpton refers to Jews as "diamond dealers," while protestors shout, "Whose kid? Our kid!" Jews argue that the police do too little to protect them from black violence. Tensions flare again the following year when Nelson is acquitted.[18]

SEPTEMBER 28, 1991 The National Civil Rights Museum opens in Memphis, Tennessee, at the site of the Lorraine Motel, where Martin Luther King, Jr., was assassinated in 1968. Controversy surrounds President Bush's decision not to attend the dedication of the $10 million, ten-thousand-square-foot facility. Jesse Jackson later calls Bush "the most anti-civil-rights president of our times." The absence of Bush does nothing to blunt the emotional response of the museum's first visitors. "Lord have mercy," a teacher named Canary Williams tells the *New York Times*. "It brings back those days. It just gets to your gut. It makes you want to cry." The following month, an African burial ground, a colonial-era site where both slaves and free blacks were buried, is discovered in lower Manhattan. Archaeologists find the remains of more than four hundred blacks, and it is likely that some twenty thousand blacks are buried there. "The recovery of these remains," says State Senator David A. Paterson, "and the proper and thorough treatment, analysis and curation of them is critical to our understanding of the history of New York City. Indeed, I believe we are in the midst of rewriting that history with this find." The site is named a national monument in 2006.[19]

NOVEMBER 7, 1991 Basketball superstar Magic Johnson, the longtime point guard of the Los Angeles Lakers, stuns the world when he announces he is retiring from the game because he has contracted HIV. In an unprecedented way, Johnson uses his fame to call attention to the virus: "I think sometimes we think, well, only gay people can get it. 'It's not going to happen to me.' And here I am saying that it can happen to anybody, even me, Magic Johnson." Johnson's basketball retirement is temporary, and he becomes an international spokesman for HIV/AIDS awareness as well as a successful businessman and part team owner of the Los Angeles Dodgers.[20]

NOVEMBER 12, 1991 Twenty-year-old Tupac Shakur, born in East Harlem, New York City, bursts onto the rap scene with his debut album, *2Pacalypse Now*, a collection of raw gangsta rap with strong social and political themes. The following year, Dan Quayle calls the album "irresponsible" after the family of a police officer murdered in Texas blames Tupac's lyrics for inspiring the killer. Shakur's subsequent albums

Strictly 4 My N.I.G.G.A.Z (1993), *Me against the World* (1995), and especially *All Eyez on Me* (1996) make him one of the most popular rappers in the country and the primary symbol of West Coast gangsta rap. Unlike those born in "the inner city," those in "the outer city"—where "we're always left out"—have no "empires" to inherit, "no heirlooms" or "family crests," Shakur says in a 1992 interview. In place of such birthrights, they have to amass their empires through "culture," "dignity," and "determination," through "music." "Instead of me fulfilling my prophecy," Shakur explains, "I have to start one."[21]

NOVEMBER 17, 1991 Former Ku Klux Klan leader David Duke, who lost his bid for the US Senate a year earlier, again loses the Louisiana gubernatorial election, in large part due to an NAACP get-out-the-vote drive. The well-organized campaign utilizes radio, television, and old-fashioned door-to-door recruitment to spread the word. A record 80 percent of African American voters turn out on Election Day. "For the first time in years," the *Crisis* reports, "the NAACP was able to mobilize all segments of the African American community around a single issue."[22]

Tupac Shakur.

1992

APRIL 26, 1992 George C. Wolfe's play *Jelly's Last Jam,* based on the life of the ragtime innovator Jelly Roll Morton and starring the dancer Gregory Hines, opens on Broadway. Critic Jeremy Gerard writes in *Variety,* "If Broadway has room for another big, splashy, tuneful crowd-pleaser, here it is." Wolfe goes on to direct the critically acclaimed plays *Angels in America, Bring in da' Noise/Bring in da' Funk,* and *Top-dog/Underdog.* He also oversees the New York Public Theater from 1993 until 2004.[23]

APRIL 26, 1992 A historic truce is declared between Los Angeles's two major gangs, the Bloods and the Crips. Charles Norman, the regional director of the Community Youth Gang Services, describes to the *Los Angeles Times* how the truce is reuniting friends and families. "One young man hadn't seen a cousin who lived only a few miles away for more than 20 years, since they were both about 7 years old," he says. "Now they were walking arm-in-arm." The truce is overshadowed by the beginning of the Rodney King riots just three days later.[24]

Bring in da' Noise/ Bring in da' Funk, in performance, with Savion Glover (second from right).

Looting in Los Angeles in the wake of the exoneration of the officers accused of beating Rodney King.

APRIL 29, 1992 A jury without a single African American member acquits four officers of any wrongdoing in the 1991 beating of Rodney King in Los Angeles. Many of the city's black residents, weary from years of harsh police tactics, no longer believe the justice system works for them, and they are ready to explode. The first reported violence in what becomes known to history as the LA Riots occurs at 5:25 P.M. at the intersection of Florence and Normandie Avenues, when local child-care worker Alphonso Hawkins witnesses blacks "throwing bricks and bottles at white people." Barely an hour later, a white truck driver named Reginald Denny is pulled from his truck and beaten. Local black residents attempt

to intervene to stop the violence. Rev. Bennie Newton shields a beaten man, Fidel Lopez, while shouting, "No more! This is enough. You're going to have to kill me too." By 8:45 P.M., the violence has spread to such a degree that Mayor Tom Bradley declares a state of emergency and orders in National Guardsmen. Los Angeles grinds to a halt the next day as troops patrol the streets, and Bradley issues a citywide curfew. On May 1, Rodney King himself pleads for an end to the violence, now famously asking, "Can we all get along?" All the while, vivid scenes of violence and looting are broadcast on televisions around the country. The Koreatown neighborhood is hit particularly hard, and Jesse Jackson urges peace. All told, the three days of violence result in an estimated $1 billion in property damage and the deaths of more than fifty people. Two of the officers in the Rodney King beating are later convicted on federal civil rights violations, and in 1994 King wins a civil-suit judgment of $4 million from the city.[25]

JUNE 13, 1992 Democratic presidential candidate Bill Clinton responds to rapper Sister Souljah's statement, "If black people kill black people every day, why not have a week and kill white people?" Speaking in front of Jesse Jackson's Rainbow Coalition, Clinton says that "if you took the words *white* and *black* and you reversed them, you might think David Duke was giving that speech." This becomes known as Clinton's "Sister Souljah moment." By distancing himself from the extremes of rap music in front of an African American audience, he is seen as advancing a triangulation strategy of appealing to moderate and conservative white voters while simultaneously trying to hold on to his party's traditional liberal base, including black voters, with a broader, economically focused campaign. Instances like this one signal that Bill Clinton is what is being called a "New Democrat."[26]

JUNE 22, 1992 The US Supreme Court unanimously rules in *R.A.V. v. St. Paul* that a local hate-speech law cannot stand because "it prohibits otherwise permitted speech solely on the basis of the subjects the speech addresses." But the Rehnquist Court does not fully back away from anti-discrimination laws. In 1993's *Shaw v. Reno*, a split 5–4 Court strikes down a congressional reapportionment plan that created racially gerrymandered districts in North Carolina.[27]

top: Crips and Blood gang members express a truce that will remain in place during the uprising in South Central Los Angeles.
bottom: Gang graffiti in South Central Los Angeles.

JULY 1, 1992 *Def Comedy Jam* premieres on HBO. Produced by hip-hop mogul Russell Simmons, the show features a host of talented African American comics during its original five-year run. To critics who say the show is too raunchy, Simmons replies, "If they are not as positive as you would like them to be, you have to listen to them and understand them. It's a dose of reality."[28]

AUGUST 8, 1992 The US men's basketball "Dream Team" wins the Olympic gold medal at

The Dream Team wins Olympic gold in Barcelona: (pictured from left to right) Scottie Pippen, Michael Jordan, and Clyde Drexler.

Astronaut Mae C. Jemison.

the Barcelona games. The all-star lineup, featuring Charles Barkley, Michael Jordan, Magic Johnson, and an abundance of other NBA superstars, trounces every opponent by at least thirty points. The team is not only beloved by its home country but also by Europeans. "Europe has the fever too," writes *Washington Post* sports columnist Michael Wilbon, "and it's sicker than we imagined." Wilbon predicts the Dream Team will make basketball popular outside the United States: "Basketball is about to become the first US sport to achieve world acceptance."[29]

SEPTEMBER 12, 1992 Thirty-five-year-old astronaut Mae Carol Jemison, a Stanford graduate with a medical degree from Cornell, takes off aboard the space shuttle *Endeavor*, becoming the first African American woman in space. "Dr. Jemison's being aboard the Space Shuttle will certainly make a new statement about the participation of African-Americans in the life of this nation," says Benjamin Hooks of the NAACP.[30]

US senator-elect Carol Moseley Brown declares victory in Chicago.

woman and only the fourth African American of either gender to win election to the United States Senate. "You have shown what we can do when we come together," she tells her cheering supporters, "when we stop them from dividing us along race lines and gender lines and geography, when we come together."[32]

OCTOBER 8, 1992 Saint Lucian poet and playwright Derek Walcott is awarded the Nobel Prize in Literature. The prize committee notes that his inspiration derives from his "three loyalties": "the Caribbean where he lives, the English language, and his African origin." The recognition of black literary achievements will reach another milestone in 1993 when the Pulitzer Prize–winning poet Rita Dove is named Poet Laureate.[31]

NOVEMBER 3, 1992 Illinois Democrat Carol Moseley Braun, a forty-five-year-old former prosecutor, becomes the first African American

NOVEMBER 6, 1992 President-elect Bill Clinton names Vernon Jordan, an attorney, lobbyist, and former executive director of the Urban League, as co-chair of his transition team. Jordan remains a close adviser throughout Clinton's presidency, standing by him during his most trying moments. In 1996, Bryant Gumbel of NBC's *Today* show describes their relationship this way: "Just as surely as Hillary Clinton is the first lady, Vernon Jordan is the first friend."[33]

NOVEMBER 17, 1992 The Grammy-winning *Bodyguard* soundtrack is released. Featuring the

The Clinton-Gore transition team: (pictured from left to right) Warren Christopher, Bill Clinton, Al Gore, and chairman Vernon Jordan.

Boyz II Men in concert.

1992 IN MUSIC Ice-T's thrash-metal side project Body Count releases its debut self-titled album, featuring the song "Cop Killer." President Bush calls the song "sick," and protesters call for a boycott of Body Count's record label, Time Warner, which rereleases the album without the song. In other music news in 1992, Boyz II Men's "End of the Road" spends thirteen weeks at No. 1, and former N.W.A member Dr. Dre releases his first solo album, *The Chronic*. The "g-funk" record, which introduces Snoop Dogg (Calvin Broadus) to rap fans, is an artistic and commercial success, selling more than five million copies. Also in 1992, Mary J. Blige releases her classic debut *What's the 411?*, a winning combination of hip-hop and soul.[35]

megahit cover of Dolly Parton's "I Will Always Love You" by Whitney Houston (who also stars in the film alongside Kevin Costner), the soundtrack sells more than a million copies in its first week. The album tops the *Billboard* charts for twenty weeks, and the single remains at No. 1 for fourteen weeks. According to a retrospective in *Billboard* magazine, "On March 13, 1993, the set made Houston the first female artist to place three songs in the Billboard Hot 100's top 20 simultaneously: 'I Will Always Love You,' 'I'm Every Woman' and 'I Have Nothing.'"[34]

Snoop Dogg.

1993

JANUARY 3, 1993 Avery Brooks premieres in the starring role of Commander Benjamin Sisko on the newest *Star Trek* television franchise, *Deep Space Nine.* Brooks's Sisko, following in the footsteps of Captains Kirk and Picard, is the first African American to command a *Star Trek* ship. "If there are still Africans in the world or the universe 400 years hence," Brooks is quoted saying in the *Washington Post* on January 3, "there will still be a relationship with the Divine and with spirituality." Also quoted in the article is show cocreator and executive producer Rick Berman, who says, "I think the role model he can establish is a wonderful thing. It's been a long time since an African-American male was cast in the lead of an hour-long dramatic series. But were we specifically looking for a black actor? No." Berman explains, "Avery was simply the best." *Star Trek: Deep Space Nine* remains on TV until 1999.[36]

JANUARY 20, 1993 Maya Angelou reads her poem "On the Pulse of the Morning" at President Bill Clinton's inauguration ceremony in Washington, DC. Leading up to the banner day, Angelou toiled away at her iconic work while engaged in rehearsals for a revival staging of her 1976 play *And Still*

I Rise (also the name of her most celebrated poem). Asked about her process, Angelou says in the Washington Post on January 16, "While I operate in the familiar—I take showers, say hello, greet people—I am not really there. . . . I am up

Dr. Joycelyn Elders, Clinton nominee for US surgeon general, testifies during her confirmation hearings in 1993. Elders is the first African American to hold the post. According to the Office of the Surgeon General website, "Elders argued the case for universal health coverage, and was a spokesperson for President Clinton's health care reform effort. She was a strong advocate for comprehensive health education, including sex education, in schools. She was outspoken in her views, and was forced to resign after only 15 months in the position as a result of a controversial remark about sex education."[37]

in that place where the poem is." As the nation's forty-second president, Clinton names a number of African Americans to top posts in his administration, including four cabinet secretaries in his first term: Jesse Brown, Veterans Affairs; Ron Brown, Commerce; Mike Espy, Agriculture; and Hazel O'Leary, Energy. Clinton's "Drug Czar" (director, Office National Drug Control Policy) is Lee Brown, and his pick for Surgeon General is Dr. Joycelyn Elders. One nominee who doesn't make it through the appointments process is University of Pennsylvania law professor Lani Guinier, who conservatives accuse of taking radical positions in her support of affirmative action and political allocations for blacks. With the media zeroing in on Guinier's writings, Clinton withdraws her

The cast of *Living Single:* (from left to right) Erika Alexander, Queen Latifah, Kim Fields, and Kim Coles.

nomination to the civil rights division of the Justice Department, saying, "Had I read them before I nominated her, I would not have done so." In 1998, Guinier will become the first black woman tenured at Harvard Law School.[38]

FEBRUARY 6, 1993 The fifty-nine-year-old tennis great Arthur Ashe dies of AIDS-related complications. In the aftermath, debates flare in Richmond, Virginia, over whether to include a monument to the hometown star on Monument Row, which memorializes white Confederates of the Lost Cause, including Stonewall Jackson and Robert E. Lee. Finally unveiled on July 10, 1996, Ashe's statue is smaller than the others and is the only one whose back faces the city.[39]

AUGUST 22, 1993 *Living Single* premieres on the Fox network. Breaking new ground for highlighting black women, the show stars Queen Latifah, Kim Coles, Erika Alexander, and Kim Fields and becomes one of the most popular programs

Keenan Ivory Wayans, creator of the hit sketch-comedy series *In Living Color*.

Noche Diaz (center) rallies with supporters against mass incarceration and police stop-and-frisk procedures outside Manhattan Criminal Court.

of the 1990s. It airs alongside a number of African American–oriented shows on Fox, including *Martin, Roc,* and the hit sketch-comedy series *In Living Color,* which makes the Wayans brothers household names.[40]

NOVEMBER 3, 1993 Defeating the incumbent mayor David Dinkins, Rudy Giuliani is elected to lead New York City with his calls for a new "zero tolerance" policy on crime. Giuliani's policies are based on the 1982 article "Broken Windows" by George L. Kelling and James Q. Wilson, which argues that even small instances of vandalism, crime, or decline, such as broken windows, must be resolved immediately in order to create a general environment of lawful, orderly behavior. Giuliani and his police commissioner, William Bratton, will institute the stop-and-frisk policy to reach these ends. Over time, crime rates fall, but black people are disproportionately targeted and arrested, and

numerous African Americans accuse the police of discrimination and brutality.[41]

NOVEMBER 9, 1993 The Wu-Tang Clan releases *Enter the Wu-Tang (36 Chambers).* With its intriguing personalities (Method Man, Ol' Dirty Bastard, and Ghostface Killah among them), hard-hitting beats courtesy of the production mastermind the RZA, and samples and themes that testify to African Americans' long-standing interest in the martial arts, the album influences a generation of hip-hop fans.

The Wu-Tang Clan celebrates the twentieth anniversary of their debut album, *Enter the Wu-Tang Clan.*

1994

JANUARY 3, 1994 *The Tom Joyner Morning Show* enters syndication, making Joyner the first African American to host a national radio program. The event is a milestone for urban radio and the man known as the "fly jock," a nickname Joyner earns for his incredible travel itinerary: from 1985 until 1993, Joyner hosted the morning drive radio show in Dallas and then would fly to Chicago to host an afternoon show there.[42]

FEBRUARY 5, 1994 In a third and final trial, white supremacist Byron De La Beckwith is convicted and sentenced to life in prison for the 1963 murder of the civil rights leader Medgar Evers. Darrell Evers, who was nine years old when his father was murdered, makes a point of attending the trial, explaining that De La Beckwith "never saw my father's face. All he saw was his back. I wanted him to see the face, to see the

Tom Joyner (left), host of the syndicated *Tom Joyner Morning Show*, with broadcaster Tavis Smiley.

State troopers escort Byron De La Beckwith and his wife to court during the white supremacist's third trial for the 1963 murder of civil rights leader Medgar Evers.

ghost of my father come back to haunt him." *Ghosts of Mississippi*, a film about the murder starring Whoopi Goldberg as Evers's widow, Myrlie Evers-Williams, is released the following year. In February 1995, Evers-Williams becomes the first woman elected chair of the NAACP.[43]

FEBRUARY 23, 1994 The Senate begins hearings, chaired by Carol Moseley Braun, on gangsta rap. African Americans testify in favor of and in opposition to the genre. C. Delores Tucker of the National Political Congress of Black Women says, "It is an unavoidable conclusion that gangsta rap is negatively influencing our youth," while Democratic representative Maxine Waters of Los Angeles argues that people must listen more critically to what gangsta rappers are trying to say.[44]

APRIL 13, 1994 *New York Times* Chicago bureau chief Isabel Wilkerson becomes the first African American woman to win the Pulitzer Prize for Journalism. Fifteen years later, she publishes a landmark book, *The Warmth of Other Suns*, about the Great Migration of the early to middle twentieth century, in which close to six million African Americans left the rural South for the urban centers of the Northeast, the Midwest, and the West.

MAY 16, 1994 Harvard literary scholar and West Virginia native Henry Louis Gates, Jr., publishes his coming-of-age memoir *Colored People*, about growing up in the segregated, then desegregating, South. In his review in the *New York Times* on May 16, Christopher Lehmann-Haupt writes: "What distinguishes 'Colored People' most is its great good humor. That and its irrepressible sense of life." Gates, in his journey from Piedmont to New Haven, "overcame handicaps both trivial and daunting," "yet what he cap-

Isabel Wilkerson.

top: Cornel West.
bottom: Members of the Piedmont, West Virginia, community, hometown of Professor Henry Louis Gates, Jr., and subject of his bestselling memoir, *Colored People.*

can come together for dialogue" on race, including forging new models of black leadership. In the same year, historian David Levering Lewis wins the Pulitzer Prize for the first volume of his groundbreaking study of the life and times of W.E.B. Du Bois, *Biography of a Race, 1868–1919.* The second volume, *The Fight for Equality and the American Century, 1919–1963,* takes the Pulitzer in 2001.[45]

JUNE 17, 1994 The football Hall of Famer and actor O.J. Simpson leads police on a low-speed chase through Los Angeles as television cameras roll from helicopters following overhead. Simpson is fleeing arrest on charges that he murdered his ex-wife Nicole Brown Simpson and her friend Ronald Goldman five days earlier. Both victims were white. The unprecedented media frenzy only increases once Simpson's trial begins on

tures most vividly in this memoir is the world that was lost when desegregation arrived: the world of the segregated school and church, and in particular the last annual colored mill pic-a-nic, as he calls it." Also in 1994, the Princeton philosopher (en route to Harvard to join Gates) Cornel West publishes his manifesto *Race Matters,* which, West hopes, will "establish a framework within which we

At the O.J. Simpson Trial (from left to right): defense attorneys Johnnie Cochran and Robert Shapiro with their client O.J. Simpson.

January 24, 1995, with millions of Americans watching the proceedings on the new Court TV channel, among other outlets. The courtroom spectacle features a number of personalities and stories that become ingrained in America's consciousness, including the racial epithets used by detective Mark Fuhrman and Simpson's legal "dream team" headed by Johnnie Cochran, who, in exposing the LAPD's bungling of the evidence, coins the oft-repeated line "If it doesn't fit, you must acquit" in reference to a pair of bloody gloves, one found on Brown Simpson's property and the other at Simpson's home. The case becomes a symbol of racial tension in the country, with blacks in Los Angeles (where the trial is held) still looking for redemption from the beating of Rodney King and the riots that followed in 1992 and whites outraged by the case's turn away from the victims at the center of the crime. Simpson is eventually acquitted of murder on October 3, 1995, a verdict celebrated by many African Americans who believed blacks could not get a fair shake in the judicial process. As exhausted as the country is from the proceedings, few forget where they are when the verdict is announced. Two years later, however, at a civil trial, Simpson, in a life that continues to spiral downward, is found liable in a wrongful-death suit and is ordered to pay $8.5 million in damages.[46]

SEPTEMBER 1994 Richard J. Herrnstein and Charles Murray publish *The Bell Curve: Intelligence and Class Structure in American Life.* The authors present pseudoscientific evidence of inherited intelligence and the supposed inferiority of African Americans' mental capacities. Henry Louis Gates, Jr., of Harvard, takes the authors to task for their argument "that the gap between *black* haves and have-nots is a reflection of natural variations within the group, and is not a function of the cutbacks in the very federal programs that helped create the black middle class in the first place."[47]

SEPTEMBER 13, 1994 Weeks before his first midterm elections, when Republicans will seize control of the House of Representatives campaigning on a new, more conservative "Contract with America," President Bill Clinton signs the Violent Crime Control and Law Enforcement Act of 1994, aimed at stemming gun violence and what appears to be a spiraling epidemic of gang and drug-related crimes in the country. "The Violent Crime Control and Law Enforcement Act of 1994 represents the bipartisan product of six years of hard work," the U.S. Justice Departments notes in a fact sheet released on October 24. "It is the largest crime bill in the history of the country and will provide for 100,000 new police officers, $9.7 billion in funding for prisons and $6.1 billion in funding for prevention programs which were designed with significant input from experienced police officers." In explaining the law, Clinton tells those gathered at the signing in Washington, "Gangs and drugs have taken over our streets and undermined our schools . . . Every day, we read about somebody else who has literally gotten away with murder." While the law leads to a dramatic reduction in crime nationwide over the next eight years, it also contributes to a criminal justice system in which tougher sentences are meted out and prison populations soar, such that by 2015, with more than 2.2 million people locked up across the nation, Clinton, long since having left the White House, expresses alarm and regret that the bill he signed helped pave the way for a mass incarceration era that has taken a particular toll on young black and Hispanic men. "I signed a bill that made the problem worse . . . And I want to admit it," the former President confesses at the 106th NAACP Annual Convention in Philadelphia on July 15, 2015. "The good news is we had the biggest drop in crime history and the first eight-year decline in crime in history . . . The bad news is we had a lot of people who were essentially locked up who were minor actors for way too long."[48]

SEPTEMBER 13, 1994 Also on this date New York rapper the Notorious B.I.G. (Christopher Wal-

Notorious B.I.G. (left) with producer Sean Combs.

lace) releases his debut album, *Ready to Die*, featuring the hit singles "Juicy" and "Big Poppa." The *Source* magazine gives the album 4.5 mics and writes, "Whether the street essence is your reality or whether you just feel like hitting hard through someone else's stories, Biggie will captivate you with his 'machine gun funk.'" *Ready to Die* is a commercial breakthrough for Sean "Puff Daddy" Combs's new label, Bad Boy Records, founded in 1993, which releases a string of hits and becomes known for its mix of gangsta rap and commercial beats. The only album to get the full five-mic rating from the *Source* that year is Nas's debut *Illmatic*, another New York masterpiece that sets a new bar for innovative rhyming and gritty beats. Down South, the Atlanta-based group TLC releases its second album, *CrazySexyCool*, with its single "Waterfalls" becoming an inescapable hit; the album sells more than twenty-three million copies worldwide.[49]

OCTOBER 14, 1994 The release of Quentin Tarantino's cult classic *Pulp Fiction*, laced with noir themes and a carefully curated soundtrack, features veteran black actor Samuel L. Jackson in the role of a lifetime: the righteous, scripture-citing hit man in a dark suit and Jheri curl, Jules Winnfield. Jackson, born in 1948, is no stranger to the screen, having appeared in numerous films, including as the crack addict Gator in Spike Lee's *Jungle Fever*, for which he was honored at the Cannes Film Festival. Yet it is Jackson's turn in *Pulp Fiction* that earns him an Oscar nomination (as well as a BAFTA win) and a place in film history. In the years that follow, Jackson remains a regular in Tarantino's films, from *Jackie Brown* to the critically important slave revenge fantasy *Django Unchained*,

Congressman J.C. Watts (right) speaks with reporters.

while crossing over into other genres, from blockbuster action hits like *Die Hard with a Vengeance* and *Snakes on a Plane* to the courtroom drama *A Time to Kill* to such prestige tentpole franchises as *Star Wars* and Marvel's *The Avengers*. In 2011, Jackson makes his Broadway debut as Rev. Dr. Martin Luther King, Jr., in the stage drama *The Mountaintop*—especially poignant since Jackson attended King's alma mater, Morehouse College, in Atlanta and served as an usher at his funeral. "Before Jules [Winnfield in *Pulp Fiction*]," Jackson tells Pat Jordan of the *New York Times Magazine* in 2012, "my characters were just 'The Negro' who died on Page 30. Every script I read, 'The Negro' died on Page 30. . . . After Jules, I became the coolest [expletive] on the planet. Why? I have no clue. I'm not like Jules. It's called being an actor." Fittingly, the title of Jordan's article is "How Samuel L. Jackson Became His Own Genre."[50]

NOVEMBER 8, 1994 With his election to the US Congress, J.C. Watts is the first black Republican elected to the House from south of the Mason-Dixon line since Reconstruction. Watts is part of the Republican triumph in the midterm elections, as conservatives find success running on their Contract with America platform in opposition to the policies of President Clinton, especially his push for national health insurance. Watts is the first black congressman to pass on joining the Congressional Black Caucus. Three years later, he makes headlines when he calls unnamed civil rights leaders "race-hustling poverty pimps."[51]

NOVEMBER 10, 1994 The exhibition *Black Male* opens at New York's Whitney Museum of American Art. Curated by Thelma Golden, the exploration of black masculinity inspires controversy and praise, with *New York* magazine saying it "courageously subverts the stereotype of what black art should be like." The year 1994 is a standout for African Americans in the visual arts. Kara Walker makes an impression on the art world with her controversial silhouettes displayed at New York City's Drawing Center; the artist Howardena Pindell says Walker's art "seems to be catering to the bestial fantasies about blacks created by white supremacy and racism." Glenn Ligon's installation *To Disembark*, inspired by slavery, also debuts at the Hirshhorn Museum in Washington, DC.[52]

Sports Illustrated

The New Master
Tiger Woods

1995–1999

U.S. $4.50 CAN.

Tiger Woods.

1995

FEBRUARY 1995 Eighty-seven-year-old Dorothy West, the last surviving artist of the Harlem Renaissance, publishes her second novel, *The Wedding*. The *New York Times* heaps praise on the book, saying, "You have only to read the first page to know that you are in the hands of a writer, pure and simple." Oprah Winfrey produces a two-part television miniseries based on the novel two years later.[1]

FEBRUARY 1, 1995 Richard Parsons becomes president of the media giant Time Warner, Inc. The protégé of Nelson Rockefeller and a former White House lawyer in the Nixon and Ford administrations, Parsons entered the business world in 1988 as the COO of the Dime Savings Bank of New York. He was named CEO and chairman two years later. Though he takes over a company suffering from what the *Wall Street Journal* calls "growing pains," Parsons experiences a similar rise at Time Warner, gaining promotion to co-CEO in 1999, CEO in 2001, and chairman of the board in 2003.[2]

MAY 2, 1995 Shirley Ann Jackson, a physicist and the first black woman to earn a PhD from MIT, is sworn in as chair of the US Nuclear Regulatory Committee, a post she holds for four years before becoming the first black president of New York's Rensselaer Polytechnic Institute.[3]

Dorothy West, author of *The Wedding* and the last living member of the Harlem Renaissance.

Richard Parsons, CEO of Time Warner, and host D.L. Hughley at the Trumpet Awards.

JUNE 12, 1995 In a 5–4 decision, the US Supreme Court deals another blow to affirmative action in the case *Adarand Constructors v. Pena*, involving a construction company that files suit after losing a contract, despite having the lowest bid, because it is not certified as a minority business.

The Court rules that racial classifications "must serve a compelling government interest, and must be narrowly tailored to further that interest." More pointedly, Justice Clarence Thomas writes that strict racial classifications "ultimately have a destructive impact on the individual and our society." In the fallout from the decision, President Clinton defends affirmative action the following month, saying famously, "We should have a simple slogan: Mend it, but don't end it."[4]

JULY 18, 1995 Chicago-based attorney and law-school lecturer Barack Obama publishes his memoir, *Dreams from My Father: A Story of Race and Inheritance,* recounting his upbringing as the child of an African father and white American mother in Hawaii; his education at Occidental College, Columbia, and Harvard; and his experiences as a community organizer

Thousands march in Paris for the release of Mumia Abu-Jamal.

The Million Man March gathering on the mall with the Washington Monument in the distance.

in his adopted home of Chicago. The *New York Times* critic Paul Watkins writes, "Whether Mr. Obama has at last made peace with himself remains unclear, but he has at least stepped out of the paternal shadow." The same year, an altogether different memoir garners attention as Mumia Abu-Jamal, a MOVE activist sentenced to death for killing a Philadelphia police officer, publishes *Live from Death Row*. A sampling of Abu-Jamal's prison writings, the book spurs a national debate over whether Abu-Jamal was wrongfully convicted and inspires the HBO documentary *Mumia Abu-Jamal: A Case for Reasonable Doubt?* In 2001, Abu-Jamal's sentence is commuted to life imprisonment without parole.[5]

OCTOBER 15, 1995 The Million Man March takes place in Washington, DC, becoming the most widely known and covered march among black males coming of age in the last decades of the twentieth century. Organized and led by the Nation of Islam leader Louis Farrakhan, the march is billed as "a day of atonement" in which African American men can address their own personal responsibility as they protest discrimination, disenfranchisement, police brutality, and the disproportionate incarceration of blacks. The impressive list of speakers gathered includes Rosa Parks, Maya Angelou, Cornel West, and Stevie Wonder. The march does not go without criticism, however: much of it is directed at Farrakhan, who angers a number of Americans with his past statements about Jews, gays, and whites. At the same time, many African American women, among them Angela Davis, oppose the male focus of the march. (A Million Woman March takes place two years later.) Even the estimated attendance proves controversial, as Farrakhan and other organizers put the number north of one million, while the National Park Service estimates four hundred thousand. "By concentrating on Farrakhan and the 'controversy' his leadership caused, the media elevated him to a status he might not actually deserve (although it would be foolhardy to dismiss him out of hand)," Harry Amana writes in *Black Issues in Higher Education* on November 2. "In the process, they also missed the real story: the complexity of pride, pain, frustration, determination, love and the will to survive of African-American men and women everywhere in this country." A year later, Spike Lee releases *Get on the Bus*, a film following a group of African American men, across generations, on their way to the march; in the cast is actor Ossie Davis, who attended the historic March on Washington in 1963.[6]

NOVEMBER 8, 1995 Retired general Colin Powell declares he will not run for president in 1996. "To offer

myself as a candidate for president," he says, "requires a commitment and a passion to run the race and to succeed in the quest; the kind of passion and the kind of commitment that I felt every day of my 35 years as a soldier. A passion and commitment that, despite my every effort, I do not yet have for political life, because such a life requires a calling that I do not yet hear." Powell is the first African American in history to be considered as a "serious" candidate for the Republican ticket.[7]

Retired army general Colin Powell addresses the Republican National Convention, where Senator Bob Dole is nominated to run against incumbent Democratic president Bill Clinton.

1996

FEBRUARY 1996 *The Boondocks* comic strip debuts on the website Hitlist. The artist and University of Maryland student Aaron McGruder draws sharp and witty black characters who critique discrimination, capitalism, politics, and television. He also satirizes mainstream black

A cutout of Huey Freeman of the animated cartoon *The Boondocks.*

media, such as BET. The comic initially has difficulty securing syndication because of its blunt treatment of racial issues. "What am I supposed to do," McGruder says in a 1997 interview with the *Washington Post*, "when I get letters that say, 'I love your drawings. I love your characters. Don't change a thing. Sorry, we can't run it'?" After United Press Syndicate finally picks up *The Boondocks* for syndication, it debuts on April 19, 1999, and in 2005 it premieres as an animated series on the Cartoon Network.[8]

FEBRUARY 12, 1996 After a pair of unsuccessful campaigns for Senate in 1988 and 1992, forty-five-year-old Alan Keyes, a former assistant secretary of state for international organization affairs under President Reagan, officially launches his run for the Republican nomination for president with a sixth-place finish (7 percent) in the Iowa caucus. The conservative Keyes campaigns on social issues, telling a crowd in the Hawkeye State, "We can go on talking about the budget and the flat tax like they really matter. And our children can go on going astray, dying in our streets, and our families can go on dissolving, and we can go on pretending that money can

The Fugees: (left to right) Wyclef Jean, Lauryn Hill, and Pras Michel.

solve problems that can only be solved if we return to the right principles." Keyes finishes fifth overall in the primaries and runs for president twice more.[9]

FEBRUARY 13, 1996 In music, the Fugees release their second album, *The Score*. With hits like "Ready or Not" and "Killing Me Softly" (a cover of the song that went No. 1 for Roberta Flack in 1973), the trio's record catapults the singer-songwriter Lauryn Hill and the Haitian rapper Wyclef Jean to popular and critical acclaim. In particular, the group looks to take hip-hop in an alternative direction. "There are kids into hip-hop who want to do something creative," Hill says. "Whether the record industry wants to support them is another question." Wyclef agrees, saying, "Hip-hop is whatever you are; it doesn't have to mean walking around looking as mean as you can and grabbing yourself." *The Score* is an instant classic, and in 2011 *Rolling Stone* ranks it at number forty-four on its list of the hundred best albums of the 1990s.[10]

FEBRUARY 28, 1996 At the thirty-eighth annual Grammy Awards in Los Angeles, a new category is announced, Best Rap Album, which, when the envelope is opened, goes to Naughty by Nature for their fourth album, *Poverty's Paradise*. Coolio's "Gangster's Paradise" competes for Song of the Year, which ends up going to Seal for "Kiss from a Rose."[11]

MARCH 18, 1996 In *Hopwood v. Texas*, the Fifth Circuit US Court of Appeals rules that the admissions

Students demanding the repeal of Proposition 209 in California carry signs outside the Ninth Circuit US Court of Appeals in San Francisco.

policy of the University of Texas Law School, which includes race as a factor, discriminates against white applicants. The ground shakes again in November, when Proposition 209 passes in California, destroying affirmative action by forbidding the use of race, gender, or ethnicity as factors in hiring decisions or admission to public colleges and universities. Ward Connerly, an African American, leads the campaign. "Nobody ever gave me any race or sex preferences when I came into the cold world 56 years ago," Connerly says. "If I could make it, anybody can, because the playing field is a lot closer to level now. The truth is that preferences at this point are not just reverse discrimination, they're degrading to people who accept them."[12]

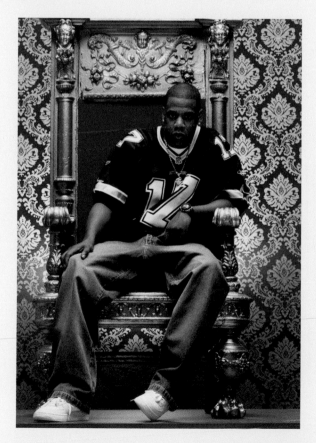

Jay Z.

APRIL 9, 1996 The classical composer and pianist George Walker wins the Pulitzer Prize for Music for "Lilacs," a vocal and orchestral piece based on a Walt Whitman poem. In announcing the award, the *New York Times* calls Walker an "overnight success of 60 years."[13]

JUNE 26, 1996 Jay Z (aka Shawn Carter), a former drug dealer turned rapper born in Brooklyn in 1969 and raised in the Marcy Projects, releases his debut album, *Reasonable Doubt*, on his own label, Roc-a-Fella Records. The gangsta rap classic marks the beginning of an incredible multifaceted career that proceeds with a number of critically and commercially successful albums, notably *The Blueprint* (2001) and *The Black Album* (2004). Jay Z also becomes an entrepreneur and mogul, starting his own fashion line in 1999, becoming head of Def Jam Records and purchasing a share of the New Jersey Nets basketball team in 2004, founding the entertainment company Roc Nation in 2008, and starting the sports agency Roc Nation Sports in 2013. "Although my album has already gone gold, it will be my last one," Jay Z tells *Billboard* magazine for an end-of-year piece in 1996. "From this point, it's all about the business."[14]

JULY 19, 1996 In one of the most poignant moments in the history of the Olympic Games, Muhammad Ali, shaking from Parkinson's disease, lights the Olympic torch in Atlanta. George Vecsey summarizes the scene in the *New York Times*: "Muhammad Ali floats above the Summer Games, no longer an elusive butterfly but a great glowing icon as large as a spaceship."[15]

AUGUST 22, 1996 President Clinton signs the Personal Responsibility and Work Opportunity

Oprah Winfrey with Toni Morrison (left), whose work is selected for Oprah's Book Club.

in the passenger seat. Shakur dies after six days in a medically induced coma. No one is charged with his murder. The following March 9, Shakur's rap rival, the Notorious B.I.G., is shot and killed in Los Angeles; no one is charged in his murder either. In the aftermath of these killings, rappers call for an end to the East Coast–West Coast feud.[17]

Act after vetoing two other, more severe bills. Commonly called "welfare reform," the act, which Clinton claims will "end welfare as we know it," cuts Aid to Families with Dependent Children, puts a term limit of five years on benefits, and requires head-of-household recipients of assistance to obtain a job within two years. Reflecting on the law ten years later in an editorial he writes for the *New York Times,* President Clinton writes, "I was widely criticized by liberals who thought the work requirements too harsh and conservatives who thought the work incentives too generous. Three members of my administration ultimately resigned in protest. Thankfully, a majority of both Democrats and Republicans voted for the bill because they thought we shouldn't be satisfied with a system that had led to intergenerational dependency."[16]

SEPTEMBER 7, 1996 Tupac Shakur is shot four times in his car in Las Vegas, Nevada, after a Mike Tyson fight at the MGM Grand. Shakur's Death Row Records label boss, Suge Knight, sits

SEPTEMBER 17, 1996 Oprah Winfrey's Book Club makes its first selection: Jacquelyn Mitchard's *The Deep End of the Ocean.* The club almost immediately evolves into a tastemaker, with Winfrey choosing a diverse mix of books, from relatively unknown novelists like Mitchard and David Wroblewski to well-regarded authors like Joyce Carol Oates, William Faulkner, and Toni Morrison. In 2003, Winfrey selects James Frey's *Five Easy Pieces*, a memoir that becomes controversial when parts are revealed to be fabricated. The national debate over Frey's book illustrates the singular place of Winfrey in the entertainment world.[18]

NOVEMBER 5, 1996 Incumbent President Bill Clinton cruises to victory over Republican candidate Bob Dole, becoming the first Democrat to win two White House terms since Franklin Delano Roosevelt. On Election Day, 84 percent of African American voters cast their ballots for

Clinton, compared to his 44 percent support among white voters and 49 percent of the popular vote overall. While the Clinton crime bill and welfare reform law, among other policies, raise serious questions for some about his record, the Clinton years also are remembered by many as an era of progress, with economic growth front and center. This includes African Americans, the administration itself points out in a report it issues at the end of its eight-year run. Titled "The Clinton Presidency: Building One America" (January 2001), the report notes that President Clinton guided a surging economy in which blacks saw household incomes rise while "the unemployment rate for African Americans fell from 14.2 percent in 1992 to 7.3 percent today and the African-American poverty rate has dropped from 33.1 percent to 26.1 percent in 1998—the lowest level recorded, and the largest five-year drop in African-American poverty since 1967–1972." In his second term, President Clinton appoints three additional black cabinet secretaries, bringing the total for his first administration to seven. They are: Alexis M.

Herman, Labor; Rodney E. Slater, Transportation; and Togo D. West, Veterans Affairs. Also of note, President Clinton taps Franklin Raines to serve as director of the Office of Management and Budget while naming Eric Holder Deputy US Attorney General. "The President has appointed more African Americans to federal judgeships than were appointed during the last sixteen years combined," the report "Building One America" states, "and 14 percent of all Clinton Administration appointees are African American, twice as many as in any previous Administration." In sum, the report claims, President Clinton has convened "the most diverse cabinet in history."[19]

NOVEMBER 5, 1996 Also on this date, New York Yankees shortstop Derek Jeter, the twenty-two-year-old New Jersey–born son of a white mother and black father, is unanimously voted Major League Baseball's Rookie of the Year after leading the Yankees to the World Series title. The championship is the first of five that the future Yankees captain wins before retiring as a Yankee in 2014.

NOVEMBER 15, 1996 Texaco agrees to pay more than $140 million to settle a racial discrimination lawsuit brought by its employees. The lawsuit has been in the courts for two years, but the record-breaking settlement comes quickly after the *New York Times* reveals the existence of recordings of Texaco officials denigrating minority employees and discussing the destruction of incriminating documents. NAACP president Kweisi Mfume praises the settlement but adds, "I caution this is only a first step on a long path toward racial reconciliation."[20]

Derek Jeter, American League winner of the Jackie Robinson Rookie of the Year award.

Financial analyst Bari-Ellen Roberts, lead plaintiff in the class-action discrimination lawsuit *Roberts v. Texaco*.

DECEMBER 18, 1996 Oakland, California, schools adopt a resolution making Ebonics an official language of African American students. Criticism emerges from multiple sources. Many African Americans feel black children should be taught standard English. "I understand the attempt to reach out to those children," Jesse Jackson says on NBC's *Meet the Press*, "but this is an unacceptable surrender, borderlining on disgrace." Other opponents accuse Oakland school officials of pandering for federal bilingual education money. "The administration's policy," says President Clinton's Department of Education secretary Richard Riley, "is that 'Ebonics' is a nonstandard form of English and not a foreign language." The resolution also leads to racist commentary on black vernacular in general. Congressional hearings on Ebonics commence the following year.[22]

NOVEMBER 21, 1996 Thirty-nine-year-old evangelical minister T.D. Jakes, a West Virginia native, hosts his three-day Manpower 4 Conference in Los Angeles, with an expected audience of forty thousand. Also in 1996, Jakes opens his Potter's House megachurch in a $3.2 million, five-thousand-seat building in Dallas, Texas. The Potter's House has eight thousand members by year's end and grows even bigger after Jakes baptizes four Dallas Cowboys on October 19, 1997. Jakes's media reach is enormous, including through his BET program *Get Ready with T.D. Jakes*. In 2001, Jakes appears on the cover of *Time* magazine under the headline "Is This Man the Next Billy Graham?"[21]

Pastor T.D. Jakes.

1997

JANURY 15, 1997 On Martin Luther King's birthday, Jesse Jackson and Operation PUSH announce the Wall Street Project, with a goal of convincing major finance and corporate organizations to invest in black and poor communities, to make loans and capital available to minority-owned businesses, and to place more minorities in corporate positions of power. By the turn of the century, African Americans join the boards of many major companies, including Seagram Company, the Goldman Sachs Group, and MCI/Worldcom.[23]

The tenth annual Rainbow Push Wall Street Project Summit: (left to right) Rev. Jesse Jackson, US Senator Hillary Clinton, Rev. Al Sharpton, and Earvin "Magic" Johnson.

Chris Rock on the set of *The Chris Rock Show.*

FEBRUARY 7, 1997 *The Chris Rock Show* premieres on HBO. The first late-night talk show hosted by an African American since *The Arsenio Hall Show*, it features a mix of sketch comedy, music, and celebrity and political guests. The show wins an Emmy for Outstanding Writing of a Variety or Music Program in 1999. The thirty-two-year-old Rock was a regular cast member on *Saturday Night Live* earlier in the decade but hits his stride on cable. "There are like 900 channels on television and they have to be filled up so that has a lot to do with it," Rock tells Cherry Bañez of the *Philadelphia Tribune* on June 27, 1997. "TV just needs people now. And they're just like, forget racism, whoever's good, let's get them, let's lock them up. That's a big thing. Def Jam Comedy, as wild as it was, definitely opened up a lot of doors. I wouldn't know who Chris Tucker was if it wasn't for Def Jam. I wouldn't know who Bernie Mac was. I wouldn't know who Bill Bellamy was." Rock adds: "I hope guys make the most of the opportunities and don't just get happy just 'cause you have a show. . . . Try to do a good show."[24]

MARCH 24, 1997 At the sixty-ninth annual Academy Awards in Los Angeles, twenty-eight-year-old Cuba Gooding, Jr., wins the Oscar for Best Supporting Actor for his performance as the football player Rod Tidwell in *Jerry Maguire*, in which he immortalizes the line "Show me the money!"[25]

APRIL 13, 1997 Twenty-one-year-old Tiger Woods wins the Masters golf tournament, dominating the field and claiming victory by a record-breaking twelve strokes. Woods's father, Earl Woods, encouraged Tiger's interest in golf at an early age, and Tiger won a number of amateur championships and the 1996 NCAA men's golf championship during his sophomore year at Stanford University before turning pro. *Sports Illustrated* calls the event "the week everything changed in golf" and notes the significance of a black man winning a tournament whose founder said in 1933, "As long as I'm alive, golfers will be white, and caddies will be black." Woods himself prefers not to focus on his race and, after his Masters victory, emphasizes that he is not only black but rather what he terms "Cablinasian," a mix of Caucasian, black, American Indian, and Asian (Thai and Chinese). Woods goes on to win fourteen major championships (and counting). Few doubt the singular impact Woods has on the game of golf and its appeal as a sport both to watch and play.[26]

APRIL 15, 1997 On the fiftieth anniversary of the late Jackie Robinson's major league debut breaking the color line, Major League Baseball retires his number 42 throughout the league. Robinson is the only player in history to receive such an honor, because the sacrifices he made as a Brooklyn Dodger in 1947 paved the way for every black player on every professional team that followed. The initiative is driven by the Jackie Robinson Foundation, which the Hall of Famer's widow, Rachel Robinson, founded in his honor. "The impact of Jackie Robinson's breakthrough was so profound that Americans began to see themselves, and their favorite sport, in a new light," the chair of the Foundation, Leonard Coleman, Jr. (also president of the National League at the time), says on the occasion. "Jackie's ascendancy foreshadowed the greatest civil movement in America in the 20th century. His contributions on the playing field and as a civil rights leader led to barriers being broken in business, education, politics, and sports."[27]

MAY 16, 1997 President Clinton apologizes for the Tuskegee Syphilis Study, during which the US Public Health Service withheld treatment,

over a forty-year period, from six hundred African American men in Alabama, two thirds of whom were infected with syphilis, and the following month creates a new race-relations panel, the Advisory Board of the President's Initiative on Race. Clinton names the eighty-two-year-old distinguished historian John Hope Franklin as its chair.[28]

JULY 15, 1997 Missy "Misdemeanor" Elliott releases *Supa Dupa Fly*, which introduces Elliott and her producer Timbaland to the hip-hop world. *Supa Dupa Fly* is a platinum seller, and the video for its lead single, "The Rain," dominates MTV.

Abner Louima on the cover of New York's *Daily News.*

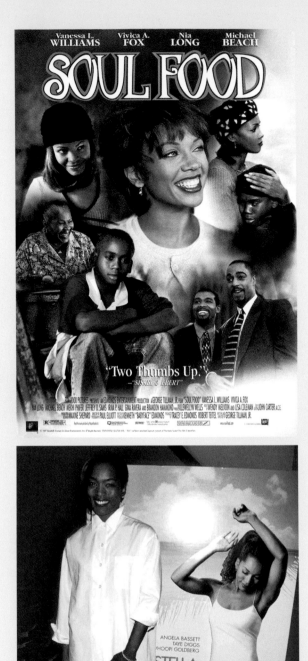

AUGUST 9, 1997 New York police arrest Haitian immigrant Abner Louima outside a Brooklyn nightclub. On the way to the police station, the officers beat Louima and, once there, sodomize him with a broken plunger handle. Louima suffers a ruptured colon and bladder and broken teeth, and stays in the hospital for two months after the attack. The case makes national news as a particularly gruesome example of police brutality, with Al Sharpton leading protests in response. Two of the officers, Justin Volpe and Charles Schwarz, receive prison sentences for the crime, and Louima successfully sues the city for $8.7 million. Ten years later, Sharpton argues, "Louima is to police-community relations what Selma was to the voter rights movement."[29]

SEPTEMBER 26, 1997 *Soul Food*, starring Vanessa L. Williams and Vivica A. Fox, is released. It is one of numerous films starring black women during the second half of the 1990s. Other highlights include *Waiting to Exhale* (1995), *Set It Off* (1996), and *How Stella Got Her Groove Back* (1998).

NOVEMBER 1997 In an interview in *Management Review*, Geoffrey Canada, a forty-five-year-old Harvard Business School graduate in charge of the Rheedlen Centers for Children and Families, discusses his vision for a new collaboration in upper Manhattan with the NYC Fund and NYC Housing Partnership called the Harlem Children's Zone. The Harlem Children's Zone is a seven-year plan that, Canada says, will focus on "eight square blocks of Central Harlem

top: Movie poster, *Soul Food*.
bottom: Angela Bassett at the premiere of *How Stella Got Her Groove Back*.

Geoffrey Canada of the Harlem Children's Zone.

providing an array of support services, working with the schools and performing a building-by-building, block-by-block effort to create a safer, better place for families." By the time Canada retires as CEO in 2014, the Harlem Children's Zone has expanded to nearly one hundred city blocks and reaches more than twenty-four thousand adults and children each year. As Sophia Hollander writes in the *Wall Street Journal*, it is "one of the country's most ambitious experiments in combating poverty and improving educational outcomes for disadvantaged students." Among the acclaimed programs run by the Harlem Children's Zone is the Baby College, a parenting initiative it launches in 2000, and its Promise Academy Charter School, opening in 2004. Canada, who grew up in the South Bronx, is quoted in the *Journal* as saying, "The idea of the old culture was that it was a rite of passage for boys to go to reform schools, end up going to prison—we want that over. . . . This is about working hard, focusing on college, being responsible, delaying pregnancy and childbearing until you're a professional." That same year, *Fortune* magazine ranks Canada among the world's fifty greatest leaders.[30]

DECEMBER 25, 1997 Steven Spielberg's *Amistad*, the unflinching tale of the 1839 Joseph Cinque–led slave-ship mutiny and subsequent trial, is released. Film critic Roger Ebert praises *Amistad* for "the way it provides faces and names for its African characters, whom the movies so often make into faceless victims." *Amistad* earns four Oscar nominations as well as a Golden Globe nomination for the actor who portrays Cinque, Djimon Hounsou, who was born in Benin before migrating to France and the United States.[31]

1998

MARCH 24, 1998 On a visit to Uganda, President Bill Clinton expresses regret for the United States' role in the transatlantic slave trade. "Going back to the time before we were even a nation," he says, "European-Americans received the fruits of the slave trade and we were wrong in that." In October, the Nobel Prize–winning author Toni Morrison compares conservative ad hominem attacks on Clinton during the Whitewater and Monica Lewinsky scandals to the routine character assassinations of African Americans, famously writing in the *New Yorker*, "white skin notwithstanding, this is our first black President." Clinton, Morrison explains, is "blacker than any actual black person who could ever be elected in our children's lifetime. After all, Clinton displays almost every trope of blackness: single-parent household, born poor, working-class, saxophone-playing, McDonald's-and-junk-food-loving boy from Arkansas. And when virtually all the African-American Clinton appointees began, one by one, to disappear, when the President's body, his privacy, his unpoliced sexuality became the focus of the persecution, when he was metaphorically seized and body-searched, who could gainsay these black men who knew whereof they spoke?"[32]

JUNE 7, 1998 In rural Jasper, Texas, three white supporters of the Ku Klux Klan murder an African American man, James Byrd, Jr., by beating

Spray paint marks the horrific scene of the murder of James Byrd, Jr., in Texas.

him, chaining him to the back of their pickup truck, and dragging him behind them for three miles, tearing him to pieces. They leave what remains of his body in front of a black cemetery before heading to a barbecue. "It is our hope that the perpetrators of this crime receive a quick and speedy trial and that justice, in this case, is both swift and deliberate," NAACP president and CEO Kweisi Mfume responds. Two of the killers, John King and Lawrence Brewer, receive death sentences, and the third, Shawn Berry, receives life in prison for the brutal hate crime. In 2009, Congress passes and President Barack Obama signs the Matthew Shepard and James Byrd, Jr., Hate Crimes Prevention Act.[33]

JUNE 19–21, 1998 More than two thousand people attend the inaugural meeting of the Black Radical Congress in Chicago. The organization, announced three months earlier by an impressive group of black activists, artists, and intellectuals including Angela Davis, Amiri Baraka, Sonia Sanchez, Manning Marable, and Cornel West, calls for "a revival of the militant spirit of resistance that our people have always possessed" and argues, "Now is the time to rebuild a strong, uncompromising movement for human rights, full employment and self-determination." The BRC targets not only racism but also sexism, homophobia, and class exploitation.[34]

JULY 1, 1998 French corporation L'Oréal agrees to purchase SoftSheen Products, the Chicago company founded by Edward and Bettiann Gardner in 1964. Also in 1998, Carson, Inc., a black-owned firm, purchases Johnson Products; two years later, it, too, is acquired by L'Oréal, giving the company control of the top two black-owned beauty companies. The American Health

and Beauty Aids Institute (AHBAI) reports that L'Oréal now controls 62 percent of the hair-color market and just over half of the women's relaxer market. "The combination of L'Oréal's massive marketing power plus the acquired brands of SoftSheen and Carson," warns Alfred Washington of the AHBAI, "will work to squeeze black manufacturers from the retail shelf."[35]

SEPTEMBER 18, 1998 South African president Nelson Mandela becomes only the third person, following George Washington and Winston Churchill, to receive an honorary degree from Harvard at a special ceremony outside of the university's annual commencement exercises. Arriving in Cambridge, Massachusetts, Mandela is greeted by the Harvard Afro-American Studies Department and W.E.B. Du Bois Insti-

Stylist Johnny Wright attends a SoftSheen-Carson Optimum Care Salon event at the Hoodie Awards in Las Vegas.

South African president Nelson Mandela hoists his honorary degree at Harvard's Tercentenary Theatre.

NOVEMBER 5, 1998 After two centuries of rumors, a team of researchers led by Eugene A. Foster publishes in the journal *Nature* DNA results indicating that Thomas Jefferson fathered a child with his mulatto slave Sally Hemings. "The case," Brent Staples writes in the *New York Times*, "shows that Jefferson lied about sex in the last century just as much as William Jefferson Clinton did in this one." Two years later, a research committee convened by the Thomas Jefferson Foundation concludes that Jefferson "most likely was the father of all six of Sally Hemings's children appearing in Jefferson's records." The news once again lays bare the contradiction between the Founding Fathers' talk of liberty and freedom and their simultaneous commitment to slavery. It also reveals the increasing importance of DNA research in uncovering African Americans' genealogical roots.[37]

tute's faculty, led by Henry Louis Gates, Jr., and Kwame Anthony Appiah. "On the morning you were released, Mr. Mandela," Gates says, "my wife and I woke our daughters early just to watch you walk out of prison, back straight, head unbowed. There walked the Negro—as my father might have put it—there walked the whole of the African people, regal as a king." In a statement, Harvard University president Neil Rudenstine adds, Mandela "embodies not only the example of courage and determination under the harshest conceivable circumstances, but—something even more rare—the very spirit of reconciliation in his own nation and throughout the world."[36]

NOVEMBER 5, 1998 At age forty-eight, Henry Louis Gates, Jr., chair of the Afro-American Studies Department and director of the W. E. B. Du Bois Institute at Harvard, becomes the first African American scholar to receive a National Humanities Medal, conferred at a White House ceremony by President Bill Clinton. The award, dating back to 1984, honors "virtuosity in the humanities in a variety of ways—through writing and teaching, scholarship and literary creation, and public outreach and philanthropy," William R. Ferris, chair of the National Endowment for the Humanities, is quoted as saying in the *New York Times* when the announcement is made on October 28.[38]

1999

JANUARY 21, 1999 Ninety years after W. E. B. Du Bois first conceived of a comprehensive encyclopedia of the black experience, coeditors Henry Louis Gates, Jr., and Kwame Anthony Appiah of Harvard release *Encarta Africana*, a CD-ROM comprising some 2.5 million words, as well as maps, graphics, and even video clips, cataloguing three-thousand-plus entries backed by four hundred scholars. The project, developed in partnership with Microsoft, "weaves historical threads into a tapestry with thousands of sounds and images," writes Michel Marriott of the *New York Times.* As part of the rollout, Microsoft, Marriott notes, will donate eight thousand copies of *Encarta Africana* to educational institutions around the country, including two thousand to "urban schools." In response, Gates and Appiah receive the following note from Du Bois's son, David G. Du Bois: "Anthony Appiah and Henry Louis Gates, Jr., inspired by Father's original idea, have made a magnificent, state-of-the-art contribution to African and African American studies and humanities with Encarta Africana." A five-volume print version, *Africana: The Encyclopedia of the African and African-American Experience*, follows in the fall, and in September 2000, Time Warner, Inc., acquires the Web-based startup company Gates and Appiah create to promote their encyclopedia project, Africana.com, Inc.[39]

FEBRUARY 4, 1999 Amadou Diallo, an immigrant from Guinea, is killed by police in the doorway of his Bronx apartment building in New York. The four officers—Kenneth Boss, Scan Carroll, Edward McMellon, and Richard Murphy—fire forty-one shots, nineteen of which hit Diallo. The police claim they thought Diallo was reaching for a gun, when, in fact, he was reaching for his wallet. The number of bullets fired marks the killing a case of police brutality. As in the aftermath of the 1997 Abner Louima assault, protests erupt in New York and across the nation. At a February 20 rally led by Al Sharpton and O. J. Simpson's attorney Johnnie Cochran, US representative José E. Serrano summarizes the thoughts of many New York blacks: "I am worried more now about the local police than I am about the local mugger." Unlike in the Louima case, this time the officers are acquitted of all charges. Diallo's father, Saikou, refers to the verdict as the "second killing" of his son.[40]

FEBRUARY 24, 1999 At the forty-first annual Grammy Awards in Los Angeles, *The Miseducation of Lauryn Hill* becomes the first hip-hop album to win Album of the Year. "This is crazy because this is hip-hop music," the twenty-three-year-old Hill says, holding a copy of the Bible in her acceptance speech. In recognition of her breakthrough solo effort, the Fugees' lead singer receives five awards in all on the night. Despite his choice to boycott the ceremony due to a lack of recognition for rap artists overall, Jay Z wins Best Rap Album of the year for his monumental *Vol. 2 . . . Hard Knock Life*. "Hip hop culture has overtaken the American landscape. Evidenced by the fact that Lauryn Hill was not only nominated for the most Grammy Awards ever, but won the most of any female artist also," Lee Hubbard writes in a March 4 *Los Angeles Sentinel* piece titled "Hip Hop Is Here to Stay, America." "Couple that with the fact that her face adorned the cover of *Time* magazine for the Feb. 8 issue as the juggernaut publication celebrated 20 years of rap," Hubbard adds, "there is no denying it—rap has blanketed American society."[41]

MARCH 28, 1999 Carolyn Peck becomes the first black female coach to win an NCAA Women's Basketball Championship when she leads Purdue to a dominating 62–45 victory over Duke in the tournament final in San Jose, California. Peck is also the first black woman to win the New York Athletic Club's Winged Foot Award. The following year she takes over as head coach of the WNBA's Orlando Miracle.[42]

MARCH 31, 1999 Laurence Fishburne captivates film audiences when the first installment of the blockbuster trilogy *The Matrix* premieres in theaters. Having appeared in Francis Ford Coppola's war epic *Apocalypse Now* when he was a teenager in 1979, Fishburne, as Morpheus in *The Matrix* series, is the fierce leader of a rebel group fighting to save humanity from being taken over by mind-controlling machines. In this role and many others, Fishburne establishes himself as one of the leading African American actors of his generation, and his versatility extends from playing Othello, Thurgood Marshall, and August Wilson's characters onstage (Fishburne earned a Tony Award in 1992 for his performance in Wilson's *Two Trains Running*) to indelible screen turns as father Furious Styles in *Boyz n the Hood*, Ike Turner in *What's Love Got to Do with It*, and Dr. Larabee in *Akeelah and the Bee*. Fishburne goes on to headline the hit television crime drama *CSI* on the CBS network before starring as Pops in the ABC family comedy *Black-ish*.

APRIL 6, 1999 Sean "Puff Daddy" Combs launches his own clothing line, Sean Jean sportswear, at Bloomingdale's in New York City, signaling the rise of the rap star as mainstream fashion mogul. "We call it urban high fashion," Combs says. "It's not a Hiphop line . . . anybody can wear [it], any race, religion, or creed." That same year, rap artist Jay Z and Damon Dash establish Roc-a-Wear clothing. Dash expresses surprise at the company's quick success, saying, "We always knew that people would like it, but we did not expect it to grow so fast." Also in 1999, Russell Simmons, who arguably started this trend when he founded Phat Farm in 1992, creates Baby Phat, a new line of women's and girls' clothing.[43]

APRIL 14, 1999 A settlement is reached in *Pigford v. Glickman*, a class-action lawsuit filed by black farmers against the US Department of

Lucias Abrams, a plaintiff in the class-action lawsuit filed by black farmers against the USDA, *Pigford v. Glickman*.

Agriculture for denying African Americans loans and assistance from 1981 to 1996. The government agrees to pay out over $1 billion to more than fifteen thousand black farmers. Despite the victory, farmers run into bureaucratic difficulty when trying to claim money, and other black and minority farmers file additional lawsuits against the USDA.[44]

JUNE 19, 1999 *Juneteenth*, Ralph Ellison's second novel, is published posthumously, some forty-seven years after the debut of his canonical work, *Invisible Man*, widely regarded as the greatest African American novel of the twentieth century. Originally a manuscript of more than two thousand pages, *Juneteenth* is trimmed to 365 pages by the Ellison estate's literary executor, John F. Callahan. Michiko Kakutani writes in the *New York Times* that "there are bravura passages of writing in the volume—dazzling riffs that remake the American vernacular tradition by juxtaposing old-time Bible-Belt sermons with fire-breathing political rants, call-and-response exchanges with Joycean stream-of-consciousness lines."[45]

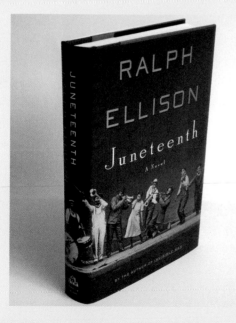

Ralph Ellison's posthumous novel, *Juneteenth*.

JULY 12, 1999 At the organization's annual convention, NAACP president Kweisi Mfume criticizes the nation's major television networks for the lack of minority characters in prime-time shows. "This glaring omission is an outrage and a shameful display by network executives who are either clueless, careless, or both," Mfume says. During the fall, whites make up 86 percent of the characters on prime-time ABC, NBC, and Fox programs. Shows on the Fox network, which saw an increase in black programming in the early 1990s, now feature African Americans in just 6.5 percent of roles.[46]

Venus and Serena Williams celebrate Olympic gold at the Sydney Games.

SEPTEMBER 11, 1999 At Arthur Ashe Stadium in New York, seventeen-year-old tennis phenomenon Serena Williams bests Martina Hingis to win the US Open championship, becoming only the second African American woman, after Althea Gibson, to win a major tennis championship. The following year, Serena's older sister, Venus Williams, captures the Wimbledon crown. The accolades for the sisters only increase from there. At the 2000 Sydney Olympics, the Williams sisters win the doubles gold medal, and Venus wins the singles gold. The following year, the sisters meet in the finals of the US Open, with Venus coming out on top. In 2002, however, Serena defeats Venus in the Wimbledon and US Open finals. The Williams sisters parlay their tennis success into new ventures such as acting, interior design, and the reality show *Venus and Serena: For Real.* Coached from young ages by their father, Richard, in the hardscrabble neighborhood of Compton, California, the Williams sisters defy the odds of becoming international superstars and, in turn, inspire legions of African American girls to take up tennis. Upon winning her first US Open title, Serena Williams exclaims, "It's really amazing for me just to have the opportunity to be compared to someone as great as Althea Gibson." By the time Serena Williams wins her sixth Wimbledon championship on July 11, 2015, she will have twenty-one Grand Slam titles, placing her third all-time among women's singles players and four wins away from passing Margaret Smith Court for the top spot, in a career that shows no signs of slowing down. Williams "has transcended her sport and staked a claim as arguably the greatest American athlete of her era," Matt Schiavenza of *The Atlantic* writes the day "Serena Slam" captivates the Wimbledon crowd. "We aren't just watching the greatest women's tennis player of all time. We're watching one whose greatest accomplishments, improbably, may be yet to come.[47]

Maria Magda Campos-Pons. *The Calling.* 2003.

2000–2004

2000

FEBRUARY 15, 2000 By a unanimous vote, the Harvard faculty agrees to the creation of a full-fledged doctoral program in African American studies, joining four other universities in the country, including Temple University, which in 1987 became the first to offer a PhD in the field. Professor Henry Louis Gates, Jr., who heads Harvard's department, is quoted as saying in the

Atlanta Daily World: "The study of the African-American experience is as vital to a university education in the 21st century as it was a century ago, when the great W. E. B. Du Bois foresaw prophetically that the problem of the 20th century is the problem of the color line." Doctoral classes in African American studies commence in fall 2001 at Harvard, and two years later, the department expands its mission to include African studies in addition to African American studies.[1]

JULY 1, 2000 South Carolina removes the Confederate flag from its state capitol building, where it has flown since 1962. "Now all of South Carolina can be a part of a great day, of a great coming together of our citizens," says State Senator Robert Ford of Charleston. In 1999, the NAACP, which protested the flag for years, announced a tourism boycott of the state, putting the issue center stage. Even after the Palmetto State removes the rebel flag from the capitol building, the government places it atop a nearby monument to Confederate soldiers, eliciting ire from Representative Joseph H. Neal, who explains, "That flag represents the Confederacy that enslaved, exploited, murdered, raped and killed

Confederate flags fly in protest of South Carolina's decision to remove the emblem from its capitol building in Columbia. It will take the mass murder of nine African Americans at the Emanuel A.M.E. Church in Charleston, South Carolina, in 2015 to prompt lawmakers to remove the Confederate flag from the statehouse grounds.

our people for over 300 years." The NAACP boycott continues, with the group's president, Kweisi Mfume, calling the new location of the flag a "slap in the face."[2] It will take the mass murder of nine African Americans at the Emanuel A.M.E. Chruch in Charleston, South Carolina, in 2015 to prompt lawmaker to remove the flag from the statehouse grounds.

AUGUST 18, 2000 *The Original Kings of Comedy*, a film capturing the live stand-up performances of four influential black comedians, hits theaters. Directed by Spike Lee, the "kings" include Cedric the Entertainer, Steve Harvey, D.L. Hughley, and Bernie Mac. "Created by Walter Latham in 1997, the 'Kings of Comedy' tour went on to become the most successful comedy tour of all time, with ticket sales exceeding $37 million," writes Steve Holsey of the *Michigan Chronicle* on August 23. "But even so, there remained a lack of awareness on the part of most of the public, specifically the non-Black sector." Lee's film raises that awareness. On an estimated budget of $3 million, *The Original Kings of Comedy* grosses over $38 million, according to the Internet Movie Database.[3]

OCTOBER 31, 2000 The Atlanta rap duo OutKast releases their hit album *Stankonia*, which earns a full five-mic rating from the *Source*. *Rolling Stone* calls it "one of the best albums of the year." "OutKast," writes *Rolling Stone* reviewer Nathan Brackett, "are on the brink of pulling off something that other hip-hop progressives like De La Soul haven't been able to do for any amount of time: Get played on the radio, keep it real, but also keep it right." OutKast—along with Houston's UGK, Atlanta's Ludacris, Goodie Mob, and Lil' Jon, and the rappers on the No Limit and Cash Money labels in New Orleans—prove that the "Dirty South" now must be considered as important a rap center as New York or Los Angeles.[4]

NOVEMBER 7, 2000 Election night ends without a clear winner in the race for president between Democrat Al Gore, the nation's sitting vice president, and the Republican governor of Texas, George W. Bush, son of the forty-first president, George H.W. Bush. In the fallout, African American voters, ninety percent of whom cast ballots for Gore nationwide, levy accusations of voter suppression, with many believing that black votes, particularly in Florida, have gone uncounted in order to give an advantage to Bush, who is eventually declared the winner after a series of recounts and a US Supreme Court decision handed down on December 12. The following June, the US Commission on Civil Rights reports serious violations of the Voting Rights Act: "Potential voters confronted inexperienced poll workers, antiquated machin-

OutKast's André Benjamin (a.k.a. Andre 3000) and Antwan Patton (a.k.a. Big Boi) perform at Z100 Zootopia, 2002.

Supporters on either side of the 2000 "recount" election make their voices heard outside the US Supreme Court in Washington, DC.

employees who charge that African Americans averaged $26,000 per year less in earnings than their white coworkers. The soda giant agrees to pay a record-breaking $156 million and to allow an independent panel to monitor its progress on black hiring, pay, and promotion. "There's going to be fundamental change at the Coca-Cola Company," says the plaintiff Kimberly Gray Orton, who has worked for Coca-Cola for more than a decade. Jesse Jackson agrees. "It sets a new standard for corporate settlements," he says. "The internal cultures of companies have been built on patterns of exclusion based on gender and race. This is a step in the right direction."[6]

ery, inaccessible polling locations, and other barriers to being able to exercise their right to vote. The Commission's findings make one thing clear: widespread voter disenfranchisement—not the dead-heat contest—was the extraordinary feature in the Florida election."[5]

NOVEMBER 16, 2000 Coca-Cola settles a federal racial discrimination lawsuit brought by black

In Tallahassee, Florida, a supporter of Vice President Al Gore ties ribbons dedicated to voters whose ballots were not counted in the 2000 election.

2001

JANUARY 20, 2001 Colin Powell becomes the first African American US secretary of state after a unanimous confirmation in the Senate. When President-elect Bush first announces the appointment, Powell promises the American people that the government will take a tough stand on terrorists: "We will meet them, we will match them, we will contend with them." Regarding the new president, Powell says, "He will be a president for all the people, all the time. I know that is the deepest emotion in his heart."[7]

JANUARY 24, 2001 A major business deal reaches completion, as Robert Johnson sells Black Entertainment Television and BET Holdings to Viacom for more than $2 billion in stock, making him Viacom's second largest shareholder; he also remains vice chairman of BET.

A pair of CEOs takes in a New York Knicks game: Kenneth Chenault of American Express and Richard Parsons of Time Warner.

Johnson says the sale is "an opportunity for the black community to receive more information, entertainment and relevant news because of our partnership and relationship." Johnson later becomes the first African American majority owner of an NBA team when he buys the Charlotte Hornets. Johnson is not the only African American businessperson making waves in 2001. In the same year, Kenneth Chenault becomes CEO of American Express and Pamela Thomas-Graham becomes president and CEO of the CNBC television network.[8]

APRIL 28, 2001 *Freestyle,* an art exhibition curated by Thelma Golden, opens at the Studio Museum in Harlem. Golden writes that the twenty-eight artists—men and women from the African diaspora—who participate in the exhibit specialize in "post-black art," meaning they are "adamant about not being labeled 'black' artists, though their work was steeped, in fact deeply interested, in redefining complex notions of blackness." The *New York Times* reviewer Holland Carter writes that *Freestyle,* which defies easy categorizations and technologies, "suggests recasting the notion of what 'black art' means in a country, a neighborhood, even an art world where racial balances are shifting. In the process, it rethinks, but doesn't abandon, the identity politics that drove much of the advanced art of the past 20 years."[9]

JUNE 1, 2001 The Oklahoma state legislature passes the 1921 Tulsa Race Riot Reconciliation Act, accepting "moral responsibility on behalf of the state and its citizens" for the violence that, eighty years before, claimed anywhere from seventy-five to three hundred lives, the vast majority of them black, and destroyed

Veneice Dunn Simms, a survivor of the Tulsa Race Riots, stands outside the Vernon AME Church, which was burned down during the riot.

more than a thousand homes in the section of the city once known as the "Black Wall Street." The state in 2001 does not accept a legislative commission's recommendation to pay reparations to the survivors and descendants, however. As a result, more than two hundred people, led by Harvard Law School professor Charles J. Ogletree, Jr., sue the state for reparations, but the case is thrown out three years later because the statute of limitations has passed. Also making the case for reparations in 2001 is Randall Robinson, founder of the TransAfrica lobby and author of the bestselling book *The Debt: What America Owes to Blacks.* "The damage done over a 346-year period is both economic and social," Robinson says in a November interview with *Blacks in Higher Education.* "To strip a people of the story of themselves is to do enormous and devastating psychological damage to the victims. African Americans have been damaged in a way they can't quantify."[10]

JUNE 12, 2001 The first meeting of the Hip-Hop Summit Action Network begins in New York.

Russell Simmons addresses the Hip-Hop Summit to raise Awareness on the Rockefeller Drug Laws.

Founded by Russell Simmons, the organization calls for "the progressive transformation of American society into a Nu America as a result of organizing and mobilizing the energy, activism and resources of the hip-hop community at the grassroots level throughout the United States." It adopts a broad agenda focused on racial and gender discrimination, economic inequality, equal education, the elimination of mandatory minimum prison sentences, and HIV/AIDS awareness.[11]

AUGUST 25, 2001 The multiplatinum singer Aaliyah dies in a plane crash in the Bahamas. She is just twenty-two years old. *Vibe* magazine editor Emil Wilbekin sums up the loss: "I think Aaliyah was the next Jennifer Lopez, the next Whitney Houston, the next Madonna, the next Janet Jackson."[12]

SEPTEMBER 11, 2001 The terrorist attacks on the World Trade Center kill nearly three thousand people, more than two hundred of whom are black. The attacks lead to an increase in racial profiling of blacks and Hispanics in New York City and nationwide. In addition, Muslims and people of Middle Eastern descent face further police scrutiny as the US embarks on its War on Terror. The racial politics of 9/11 extend into memorials as well, with the twelve black firefighters and twelve Hispanic firefighters killed in the attacks rarely depicted in 9/11 commemorations.[13]

OCTOBER 5, 2001 Thirty-seven-year-old San Francisco Giants slugger Barry Bonds hits his seventy-first home run, breaking Mark

Young fans of R&B singer Aaliyah sign a record-store mural following her death.

Barry Bonds.

"There is no question that many of the assets that underwrote the University's creation and growth derived, directly and indirectly, from slavery and the slave trade," the committee reports. In 2014, Brown opens its Center for the Study of Slavery and Justice. On the occasion of her inauguration in 2001, Simmons, one of twelve children born to Texas sharecroppers in the Jim Crow era, is quoted in the *New Pittsburgh Courier* as saying, "When I think about what the Founding Fathers had in mind when they created this place, and then I think about who I am and where I came from, it's jarring." One of the themes of her inaugural address is the important role universities must play in training the next generation of teachers. In the same year, *Time* magazine names Simmons America's best college president.[15]

McGwire's single-season home run record. Six years later, Bonds passes Hank Aaron to become the career home run leader. However, Bonds's link to BALCO, a Bay Area steroid manufacturer and distributor, calls his accomplishments into doubt and has to this point kept him out of the Baseball Hall of Fame. Bonds admits to using performance-enhancing drugs but says he did so unknowingly.[14]

OCTOBER 14, 2001 Fifty-six-year-old Dr. Ruth J. Simmons, a specialist in Romance languages and literature who previously served as the president of Smith College, is sworn in as the eighteenth president of Brown University, making her the first African American president of any Ivy League school. Two years later, Simmons creates a steering committee to research the school's roots in slavery and the slave trade.

Dr. Ruth J. Simmons.

2002

JANUARY 7, 2002 When Shirley Clarke Franklin is inaugurated as the next mayor of Atlanta, at fifty-six, she becomes the first black woman to lead a major southern city. Supporting her campaign on Election Day is Atlanta's first black mayor, Maynard Jackson, in whose administration she once worked. "I proudly represent all of the women who have toiled in the fields, worked in the kitchens, fought for our rights, and challenged our society," Franklin says.[16]

Atlanta mayor Shirley Clarke Franklin.

JANUARY 7, 2002 *The Tavis Smiley Show* premieres on National Public Radio with Cornel West as its first guest. The thirty-seven-year-old Smiley, a former *BET Tonight* host and a commentator on *The Tom Joyner Show,* quickly becomes one of black America's most widely heard voices. In 2004, he adds a television talk show on PBS, but he also leaves NPR, criticizing its outreach to minority listeners. "In the most multicultural, multiethnic and multiracial America ever," he says, "I believe that NPR can and must do better in the future." He takes his show to Public Radio International. In 2006, Smiley publishes the book *The Covenant with Black America,* which the *New York Times* calls "the surprise hit of the year" written by "a cultural phenomenon." He and West, whom Smiley calls "Doc," set out by bus on an eleven-state Poverty Tour in 2011 and never shrink from criticizing the nation's leaders, including President

Barack Obama, for not doing more to solve the inequality gap.[17]

JANUARY 8, 2002 President Bush signs the No Child Left Behind Act, a broad set of education reforms with the stated goal of closing the "achievement gap" between white and non-white schools. The plan faces criticism for its emphasis on standardized testing and the fact that it glosses over the hurdles involved in choosing a different school to avoid an "underperforming" one.[18]

MARCH 24, 2002 History is made in Hollywood at the seventy-fourth Academy Awards, when a pair of African American stars claims the top two acting prizes. The first to the Kodak Theatre stage is Halle Berry, 35, who becomes the first black woman to win the Academy Award for Best Actress for her performance as Leticia Musgrove in *Monster's Ball*. In an emotional speech, Berry thanks past, present, and future black actresses and points to the future: "This moment is so much bigger than me. This moment is for Dorothy Dandridge, Lena Horne, Diahann Carroll. It's for the women that stand beside me, Jada Pinkett, Angela Bassett, Vivica Fox. And it's for every nameless, faceless woman of color that now has a chance because this door tonight has been opened." On the same stage, Denzel Washington, 47, wins Best Actor for his role in *Training Day;* it is Washington's second career Oscar and his first in a leading role. Making the moment all the more poignant is the fact that earlier in the broadcast, Washington presented an honorary award to Sidney Poitier, 75, the first black actor to win Oscar gold in the same category in 1964. In his remarks, Poitier, looking back on his career, revealed, "I arrived in Hollywood at the age of

Best Actor Denzel Washington and Best Actress Halle Berry at the Academy Awards in Los Angeles.

twenty-two in a time different than today's, a time in which the odds against my standing here tonight fifty-three years later would not have fallen in my favor. Back then, no route had been established for where I was hoping to go, no pathway left in evidence for me to trace, no custom for me to follow. . . . I accept this award in memory of all the African-American actors and actresses who went before me in the difficult years, on whose shoulders I was privileged to stand to see where I might go." Now, with Poitier looking on from the balcony, Washington, holding his Oscar, tells the audience: "Forty years I've been chasing Sidney [Poitier], they finally give it to me, what'd they do? They give it to him the same night. I'll always be chasing you, Sidney. I'll always be following in your footsteps. There's nothing I would

Original title page from the mid-nineteenth-century manuscript *The Bondswoman's Narrative.*

rather do, sir. Nothing I would rather do. God bless you."[19]

APRIL 1, 2002 *The Bondwoman's Narrative*, the first discovered fugitive-slave novel written by a woman, is published. Uncovered by Henry Louis Gates, Jr., at an auction in 2001, the novel was written around 1855 by a fugitive slave who signed it Hannah Crafts. "The most important thing," Gates tells the *Harvard Crimson*, "is that now, 150 years after she lived, a female slave is finally having her day." In 2013, the literature professor Gregg Hecimovich determines that the author's true name is Hannah Bond.[20]

APRIL 8, 2002 Thirty-eight-year-old Suzan-Lori Parks becomes the first African American woman to win the Pulitzer Prize for Drama for her breakthrough play, *Topdog/Underdog*, which features the actor Jeffrey Wright and the hip-hop artist Mos Def playing rival brothers locked in a card game in their apartment. Parks, awarded a MacArthur Fellowship the year before, is quoted in the *New York Times* on her Pulitzer win: "I wish I were the 101st.... You open the door but it's everybody's responsibility to walk through."[21]

JUNE 2, 2002 *The Wire*, an in-depth, novelistic examination of the city of Baltimore's drug trade, debuts on HBO. Its creator is David Simon, a former journalist also behind the television show *Homicide: Life on the Streets* and the HBO miniseries *The Corner*. "I wanted to present a vision of the war on drugs as an institutionalized disaster," Simon says. To that end, the show delves deep into the problematic nature of the city's schools, police department, government, and media in order to examine the myriad ways they fail Baltimore's black and poor population. With a cast of black actors that includes Wendell Pierce, Michael Kenneth Williams, and Idris Elba, *The Wire* earns rave reviews and a Peabody Award (among others) for its novelistic storytelling and realistic depiction of urban catastrophe. By the time its five-season, sixty-episode run is complete, it is not only a cultural touchstone, it becomes source material for college courses across the country, including at Duke, Middlebury, and Harvard. "It's easy to think of *The Wire* as a show about drug dealers or cops," one Duke student enrolled in such a class observes, "but we've gotten past that pretty quickly."[22]

JUNE 12, 2002 The Los Angeles Lakers, led by the duo of Kobe Bryant and Shaquille O'Neal, close out a sweep of the New Jersey Nets to win

top: Native Baltimorean Felicia Pearson, aka Snoop, of the Stanfield Crew on HBO's *The Wire.*
bottom: Michael Kenneth Williams, Jamie Hector, and Gbenga Akinnagbe, cast members of the award-winning HBO television series *The Wire,* during their appearance at MTV's "Sucker Free" event in New York, 2006.

the first of three consecutive NBA championships. O'Neal, thirty, is considered one of the most dominant centers to play the game, while many see the twenty-three-year-old Bryant as heir to another player with whom head coach Phil Jackson journeyed to the finals, Michael Jordan.[23]

NOVEMBER 8, 2002 Laila Ali, the daughter of Muhammad Ali, defeats Valerie Mahfood to unify the three women's super-middleweight boxing championships. Channeling her father,

Ali says to Mahfood prior to the fight, "There are different levels of beat-down, and you're going to get the highest level." The *New York Times* declares, "Ali has answered the doubters who thought she was just trading on her father's name."[24]

DECEMBER 5, 2002 Republican Senate majority leader Trent Lott of Mississippi outrages Americans when he says the nation would have turned out better had the segregationist senator Strom Thurmond won the presidency in 1948.

"I want to say this about my state," Lott says at Thurmond's hundredth birthday party. "When Strom Thurmond ran for president, we voted for him. We're proud of it. And if the rest of the country had followed our lead, we wouldn't have had all these problems over all these years, either." Amid the controversy that follows, Lott is forced to step down as Senate majority leader on December 20. The following year, just months after Thurmond's death, Essie Mae Washington-Williams comes forward as the mixed-race child of Thurmond and an African American woman. She says she kept the story private until now because "I never wanted to do anything to harm him."[25]

Laila Ali receives her boxing trophy belt after defeating Valerie Mahfood.

Essie Mae Washington-Williams (center), daughter of the late US senator Strom Thurmond.

2003

JANUARY 22, 2003 *Chappelle's Show*, starring the twenty-nine-year-old comic Dave Chappelle, debuts on Comedy Central. The sketch-comedy show offers a satirical take on race (stereotypes in particular), politics, and celebrity culture, and becomes a national sensation. Chappelle,

Dave Chappelle.

a Washington, DC, native once booed off the stage at the Apollo Theater in Harlem, is noted for his unique brand of humor, which leaves no topic off the table, including slave reparations. When asked about it, Chappelle, who describes his show as "a hip-hop *Masterpiece Theatre*," tells the *New Pittsburgh Courier*, "Reparations is topical, but it's been topical for 100 years now." Two years later, Chappelle shocks the entertainment world when he quits the show and walks away from a $50 million contract.[26]

FEBRUARY 6, 2003 50 Cent, a twenty-seven-year-old underground rapper and former drug dealer once shot nine times, releases his debut album, *Get Rich or Die Tryin'*, which features guest spots from Dr. Dre and Eminem. The hit record is nominated for a Grammy, and *Rolling Stone* calls 50 Cent, born Curtis James Jackson III in Queens, New York, "the new king of hardcore hip hop." He founds his own label, G-Unit Records, the same year.[27]

FEBRUARY 28, 2003 Oprah Winfrey becomes the first black woman to appear on *Forbes* magazine's list of billionaires. Winfrey mobilizes her

top: Eminem, 50 Cent, and Dr. Dre launch Shade 45, a new satellite radio station, at the Roseland Ballroom in New York City.
bottom: 50 Cent and Snoop Dogg perform at the MTV Music Awards in New York City.

fame and fortune for a number of global philanthropic efforts. As she later tells *Forbes*, "I realized that the only way to create long-term improvement and empowerment, and literally change the trajectory of somebody's life, is through education." Among her most prominent efforts are the Oprah Winfrey Foundation, founded to provide education for women and children without means, and the Oprah Winfrey Leadership Academy for Girls in South Africa. In 2013, she gives $12 million to the National Museum of African American History and Culture.[28]

Students prepare for the inaugural graduation of the Oprah Winfrey Leadership Academy for Girls in South Africa.

MARCH 1, 2003 Kweisi Mfume of the NAACP and the Cuban leader Fidel Castro announce that the Cuban government will purchase more than $15 million worth of agricultural goods from the National Black Farmers Association's NBFA Foods, which pledges to distribute money back to the farmers. NBFA president John Boyd says the deal will allow black farmers to avoid white discrimination in the marketplace: "It gives us the opportunity to offer a fair price to black farmers. Historically, we have taken our products to the market, and they'd get docked."[29]

MARCH 20, 2003 After months of furious debate, the Iraq War begins when US and allied forces invade the country in an attempt to topple its ruling dictator, Saddam Hussein. Barack Obama, by then a state senator in Illinois, opposes the war, calling it in October 2002 "A dumb war. A rash war. A war based not on reason but on passion, not on principle but on politics." In a now-controversial address to the United Nations in February 2003, Secretary of State Colin Powell alleges that Hussein and his government are ignoring UN weapons inspectors and "concealing their efforts to produce more weapons of mass destruction." African Americans make up roughly one fifth of the invasion force, and 40 percent of the Army's women soldiers are black. But by 2004, the vast majority of African Americans believe the war is a mistake. A Gallup poll reveals that only 18 percent of blacks believe the war is worth it, compared to 56 percent of whites. By 2008, black enlistment drops substantially.[30]

JUNE 20, 2003 Twenty-one-year-old Beyoncé Knowles releases her debut solo album, *Dangerously in Love*. A native of Houston, Texas,

Beyoncé rises to fame in the late 1990s as part of the group Destiny's Child, which wins an NAACP Image Award in 2000, the year they split up. Yet even that success will pale in comparison to Beyoncé's solo career. As *Dangerously in Love* wins four Grammys, she begins her ascent to almost unprecedented superstardom. Affectionately known as Queen Bey by her legions of fans worldwide, Beyoncé releases four more bestselling albums, *B'Day* (2006), *I Am . . . Sasha Fierce* (2008), *4* (2011), and *Beyoncé* (2013), which causes a stir with its surprise drop

Beyoncé Knowles performs "Dangerously in Love 2" at the Grammys.

on iTunes. At the same time, Beyoncé establishes herself as an actress with major roles in *Austin Powers in Goldmember* (2002), *The Pink Panther* (2006), a star turn *in Dreamgirls* (2006), and *Cadillac Records* (2008), in which she plays the music legend Etta James. In 2008, Beyoncé marries the rapper Jay Z, creating hip-hop's ultimate power couple. She even performs at a presidential inaugural ball in 2008 and at the inauguration itself in 2012, with President Obama saying, "Beyoncé could not be a better role model for my girls because she carries herself with such class and poise and has so much talent."[31]

JUNE 23, 2003 In a pair of cases decided on the same day, the Supreme Court sends a mixed message on affirmative action in higher education. In *Gratz v. Bollinger,* the Court rules that the University of Michigan's undergraduate admissions policy violates the Equal Protec-

tion Clause of the Fourteenth Amendment "because the University's use of race in its current freshman admissions policy is not narrowly tailored to achieve respondents' asserted compelling interest in diversity." But in *Grutter v. Bollinger*, the Court rules that the University of Michigan Law School's use of race as a criterion for admission passes constitutional muster, because "race-based action to further a compelling governmental interest does not violate the Equal Protection Clause so long as it is narrowly tailored to further that interest." As legal scholars parse the decisions, much is made of the sunset provision charted by Justice Sandra Day O'Connor in her majority opinion in *Grutter*: "race-conscious admissions policies must be limited in time. . . . The Court expects that 25 years from now, the use of racial preferences will no longer be necessary to further the interest approved today." Suddenly, the future year 2028 takes on special significance as the national

Advocates of affirmative action evoke *Brown v. Board of Education* outside the US Supreme Court as the justices weigh *Grutter v. Bollinger* inside.

"King" LeBron James in flight.

OCTOBER 29, 2003 Eighteen-year-old LeBron James of Akron, Ohio, debuts with the Cleveland Cavaliers, beginning a basketball career that somehow will live up to the incredible expectations captured in his nickname, King James. A high school phenomenon, James is drafted first overall by Cleveland without playing any college ball. Nevertheless, he wins Rookie of the Year and follows up with four MVP awards and two NBA titles. James's quest for those titles is marred in the eyes of some fans by *The Decision*, a 2010 ESPN special in which he reveals in dramatic fashion that he has left his home-state Cavs to join Dwyane Wade and Chris Bosh as the "Big Three" of the Miami Heat. When James returns to Cleveland in 2014, he opts for an understated announcement in *Sports Illustrated,* writing, "Before anyone ever cared where I would play basketball, I was a kid from Northeast Ohio. It's where I walked. It's where I ran. It's where I cried. It's where I bled. . . . People there have seen me grow up. I sometimes feel like I'm their son. Their passion can be overwhelming. But it drives me." James has become one of the most popular players of all time, his popularity bolstered by his presence on social media and in the wider culture.[33]

debate over affirmative action continues to boil. In his partial dissent, partial concurrence in *Grutter,* Justice Clarence Thomas leaves no doubt about where he stands: "The Constitution abhors classifications based on race, not only because those classifications can harm favored races or are based on illegitimate motives, but also because every time the government places citizens on racial registers and makes race relevant to the provision of burdens or benefits, it demeans us all."[32]

2004

FEBRUARY 10, 2004 Twenty-six-year-old Kanye West, a Chicago rapper best known for his production work for Jay Z, releases his debut album, *The College Dropout*, which scores with the hit singles "Through the Wire" and "All Falls Down." "I'm the rap version of Dave Chappelle," West says in an April 29 *Rolling Stone* profile. "I'm not sayin' I'm nearly as talented as Chappelle when it comes to political and social commentary, but like him, I'm laughing to keep from crying." West's subsequent albums—*Late Registration* (2005), *Graduation* (2007), *808s and Heartbreak* (2008), *My Beautiful Dark Twisted Fantasy* (2010), and *Yeezus* (2013)— all achieve the rare mix of commercial and critical acclaim. His brash personality elevates him to pop-culture superstardom, particularly after he interrupts Taylor Swift's 2009 MTV Video Music Award acceptance speech to argue that Beyoncé should have won the prize. (He repeats this performance when Beck wins the Grammy for Album of the Year six years later.) West's 2013 marriage to reality star Kim Kardashian keeps him in the tabloids, though not at the expense of his musical output, or burgeoning career as a fashion designer.[34]

MARCH 23, 2004 At age twenty-five, Usher releases the album *Confessions*. Featuring the hit single "Yeah!," the album sells 1.1 million copies in its first week and makes Usher (full name Usher Terry Raymond IV) one of the most successful recording artists of the decade.[35]

Kanye West performs from *The College Dropout.*

APRIL 5, 2004 Edward Jones wins the Pulitzer Prize for Fiction for *The Known World*, a complex, beautifully written novel that revolves around a freed slave who purchases slaves of his own.

MAY 17, 2004 At an NAACP event marking the fiftieth anniversary of the *Brown v. Board of Education* decision, Bill Cosby criticizes incarcerated blacks and prison activists who allege that the criminal justice system targets African Americans. "These are people going around stealing Coca-Cola," he says. "People getting shot in the back of the head over a piece of pound cake." More broadly, Cosby blames black parents for not providing their children proper guidance and giving them "names like Shaniqua, Shaligua, Mohammed, all that crap." The speech inspires major debate on black cultural conservatism. The playwright August Wilson castigates Cosby as "a billionaire attacking poor people for being poor," and Ta-Nehisi Coates accuses him of "[playing] one ugly role that his activist friends like to ignore—patron saint of black elitists." Cosby's reputation is more gravely challenged a decade later, when allegations about his life off stage, specifically accusations of disturbing sexual conduct reported by dozens of women outside of his marriage, ignite a media firestorm prompting an array of institutions to wrestle with re-evaluating his legacy and, in some cases, severing ties.[36]

JUNE 16, 2004 The four-day National Hip-Hop Political Convention, which the *New York Times* calls "a political convention, with beats," begins in Newark, New Jersey. More than 2,500 people attend, including the rappers Busta Rhymes, Wyclef Jean, MC Lyte, and Chuck D. The delegates seek to inspire political activism among

Usher introduces *Confessions* at New York's Webster Hall.

hip-hop fans, and they single out education, criminal justice, economic justice, and human rights as key issues.[37]

JULY 27, 2004 In a year in which Carol Moseley Braun and Al Sharpton enter the Democratic primary, the US Senate candidate Barack Obama of Chicago, Illinois, captures headlines with his keynote speech at the Democratic National Convention in Boston, where the party nominates Senator John Kerry to take on the incumbent president, George W. Bush, in the fall campaign. Candidate Obama tells the crowd, "There's not a liberal America and a conservative America; there's the United States of America. There's not a black America and white America and Latino America and Asian America; there's the United States of America." When Gwen Ifill of PBS asks his opinion of the speech, Michael Duffy of *Time*

US Senate candidate Barack Obama addresses the Democratic National Convention in Boston.

at New York's Frederick P. Rose Hall, with stunning views overlooking Manhattan's Columbus Circle. The event is led by Wynton Marsalis, the Pulitzer Prize–winning trumpet player who has held the position of artistic director since the Jazz at Lincoln Center program began in 1987. In a statement, Marsalis writes, "Jazz is not merely music. Jazz is America—relationships, communication, and negotiations."[39]

NOVEMBER 2, 2004 President George W. Bush wins reelection in another contest marred by charges of voter suppression in Ohio and Florida. Democrats on the House Judiciary Committee report that in Ohio, "The misallocation of voting machines led to unprecedented long lines that disenfranchised scores, if not hundreds of thousands, of predominantly minority and Democratic voters." In Florida, the ACLU alleges that the state delayed sending out absentee ballots until it was too late for voters to return them. Nationally on Election Day, President Bush earns eleven percent of black votes cast, with eighty-eight percent breaking for his opponent in the race, Massachusetts Senator John Kerry.[40]

magazine says, "A star is born," while the *Washington Post* scribe David Broder says, "His future is just unlimited now." Despite John Kerry's defeat at the top of the ticket in November, Obama wins his senatorial race against his Republican opponent, Alan Keyes, a conservative African American who previously ran for president in the GOP primaries of 1996 and 2000.[38]

OCTOBER 18, 2004 Jazz at Lincoln Center has its opening-night gala at its new $128 million home

Wynton Marsalis (right) leads a New Orleans–style procession from Lincoln Center to the Time Warner building in New York's Columbus Circle in celebration of the opening of *Jazz at Lincoln Center.*

2005–2009

President Barack Obama looks on as Eric Holder is sworn in as US Attorney General.

2005

JANUARY 26, 2005 Fifty-year-old Condoleezza Rice is confirmed as the first black woman to serve as US secretary of state, succeeding Colin Powell after a four-year tour as President George W. Bush's national security advisor. Rice grew up in segregated Birmingham, Alabama, before entering college at age fifteen. She began her professional life in academia, eventually rising to the position of provost of Stanford University. At her Senate confirmation hearing on January 18, 2005, Rice opens with a statement paying tribute to the history and values that brought her to this day: "I personally am indebted to those who fought and sacrificed in the civil rights movement so that I could be here today. For me, this is a time to remember other heroes as well. I grew up in Birmingham, Alabama, the old Birmingham of Bull Connor and church bombings and voter intimidation, the Birmingham where Dr. King was thrown in jail for demonstrating without a permit. Yet, there was another Birmingham, the city where my parents, John and Angelena Rice, and their friends built a thriving community in the midst of terrible segregation. It would have been so easy for them to give in to despair and to send that message of hopelessness to their children. . . . But they refused to allow the limits and injustices of their time to limit our horizons. My friends and I were raised to believe that we could do or become anything; that the only limits to our aspirations came from within. We were taught not to listen to those who said, 'No, you can't.'"[1]

US secretary of state Condoleezza Rice.

FEBRUARY 27, 2005 In Los Angeles, at the seventy-seventh annual Academy Awards, hosted by Chris Rock, history is made when a pair of black actors become the first to take home both male acting prizes: sixty-seven-year-old Morgan Freeman is the year's Best Supporting Actor for his role as the ex-boxer Eddie Dupris in *Million Dollar Baby*, and thirty-seven-year-old Jamie Foxx is chosen as Best Actor for his turn as the music legend Ray Charles in *Ray*. Freeman, who receives a standing ovation when his name is announced, tells the press afterward: "It means Hollywood is continuing to make history. Life goes on. Things change. They never stay the same. We are evolving with the rest of the world." "In our music, our everyday life—why not have something positive," Foxx says, "and stamp it with blackness."[2]

JUNE 21, 2005 On the forty-first anniversary of the murder of three civil rights workers—James Chaney, Andrew Goodman, and Michael Schwerner—during Freedom Summer in Philadelphia, Mississippi, the former pastor Edgar Ray Killen is convicted of manslaughter for heading the conspiracy that led to their deaths. Killen, eighty, receives the maximum sentence of sixty years in prison. Marcus Gordon, the seventy-three-year-old judge who sentences Killen, expresses his hope that the sentence will repair the reputation of Neshoba County, where both he and Killen grew up: "That was not the act of Neshoba County," he says of the killings. "That was the act of a small, howling mob."[3]

AUGUST 23–31, 2005 Hurricane Katrina devastates the nation's Gulf Coast, killing more than 1,800 people and displacing more than a million others. The worst-hit city is New Orleans, and the worst-hit part of New Orleans is the predom-

In Katrina's wake: the displaced line up outside the Houston Astrodome.

inantly black Ninth Ward, where the breaking of the levees causes mass damage. In the ghastly aftermath, thousands of residents are relocated to a temporary shelter in the Reliant Astrodome in Houston. Delays in the government's response to the crisis, which disproportionately affects communities of color, lead to charges of racism. The most blatant of these charges comes from the rapper Kanye West, who, at a concert to raise money for hurricane survivors, bluntly asserts that President Bush "doesn't care about black people." In September, Bush's FEMA chief Michael Brown resigns as a result of the controversy, while Congress approves a $10.5 billion aid package to rebuild the Crescent City. The official death toll of Hurricane Katrina is 1,833, with 1,577 of those deaths occurring in Louisiana. The storm also causes more than $80 billion of damage, making it the costliest in American history.[4] While most New Orleans residents will return after Katrina, thanks to public and private rebuilding efforts—including Musicians' Village, launched by city natives and jazz greats Harry Connick, Jr., and Branford Marsalis (along with Habitat for Humanity)—the city's population, and particularly its black population, remains lower than it was before the storm. According to census figures, the population of New Orleans in 2013 is 378,715, marking a 21.9 percent decline from its 2000 population of 484, 674.[5]

OCTOBER 27, 2005 Sheryl Swoopes, a three-time MVP and WNBA champion as well as an Olympic gold medalist in basketball, announces that she is in a lesbian relationship. In doing so, she becomes one of the first openly gay African American athletes in any sport. "My reason for coming out isn't to be some sort of hero," the Houston Comets star tells *ESPN: The Magazine.* "I'm just at a point in my life where I'm tired of having to pretend to be somebody I'm not. I'm tired of having to hide my feelings about the person I care about, about the person I love."[6]

OCTOBER 24, 2005 The Montgomery bus boycott icon Rosa Parks dies at the age of ninety-two. Before her funeral, her casket is flown to Washington, DC, where she lies in state in the rotunda of the US Capitol. Martin Luther King's daughter, Rev. Bernice King, eulogizes Parks on behalf of her ailing mother, Coretta. "She sparked a prairie

A mourner in Detroit stands in front of the Montgomery, Alabama, bus on which Rosa Parks refused to yield her seat in 1954.

fire that continues to blaze brightly in the hearts of freedom-loving people in all nations, and the nonviolent revolution she set in motion continues to reverberate in nation after nation as an inspiration to human liberation movements everywhere." Just over three months later, on January 30, 2006, the country loses another figure of the civil rights movement when Coretta Scott King dies at age seventy-eight. While Parks's funeral was largely a celebration of her legacy, speeches at King's memorial include pointed remarks critical of President Bush, who is in attendance. In particular, Rev. Joseph Lowery cites the administration's failure to find evidence of weapons of mass destruction in Iraq, while former president Jimmy Carter notes that the Kings were the targets of government wiretapping in an analogy to contemporary government surveillance programs. In 2015, at the end of the era covered in this chronology, FBI director James Comey acknowledges the FBI's role in wiretapping Martin Luther King, Jr., in a broader speech he delivers at Georgetown University discussing racial bias in law enforcement and other "hard truths" aimed at addressing the alarming, and too frequently violent, disconnects between police and African Americans in communities they are sworn to protect. "There is a reason that I require all new agents and analysts to study the FBI's interaction with Dr. Martin Luther King, Jr., and to visit his memorial in Washington as part of their training," Comey reveals. "And there is a reason I keep on my desk a copy of Attorney General Robert Kennedy's approval of J. Edgar Hoover's request to wiretap Dr. King. It is a single page. The entire application is five sentences long, it is without fact or substance, and is predicated on the naked assertion that there is 'communist influence in the racial situation.' The reason I do those things is to ensure that we remember our mistakes and that we learn from them."[7]

2006

FEBRUARY 18, 2006 Speed skater Shani Davis becomes the first black athlete to win an individual gold medal in a Winter Olympics sport when he clinches the men's 1,000-meter event at the games in Turin, Italy. Four years later, Davis becomes the first man to win back-to-back gold medals in the event at the Vancouver games.

MAY 9, 2006 Cory Booker, a former Rhodes Scholar and alumnus of Stanford University and Yale Law School, is elected mayor of Newark, replacing five-term mayor Sharpe James. The passing of the torch from James to the thirty-seven-year-old Booker is seen as a sign of the advent of a new generation of African American leaders who came of age after the civil rights era. "Newark, New Jersey, has spoken with clarity, spoken with faith, spoken with honor, spoken with love and spoken with courage," Booker says during his acceptance speech. "This is the beginning of a new chapter in the life of our city."[8]

MAY 19, 2006 Sophia Danenberg becomes the first African American and the first black woman to reach the top of Mount Everest. "There aren't a lot of African Americans—or black people from

Mayor-elect Cory Booker celebrates his electoral sweep in Newark, New Jersey.

Veteran mountain climber Sophia Danenberg sits atop Mt. Everest.

anywhere, American or otherwise—in high-altitude mountaineering," Danenberg notes. In fact, she says, she has never seen another black person on a major climb.[9]

MARCH 2006 Signaling a reverse "Great Migration" of African Americans from the North back to the South, William H. Frey of the Brookings Institution reports that Atlanta has added more than 180,000 black residents between 2000 and 2004. The city now trails only New York and Chicago in black population. Frey reports that the black population of the South as a whole grew by more than one million during the same period, while none of the other three regions saw growth of more than two hundred thousand.[10]

DECEMBER 4, 2006 Six black teenagers in Jena, Louisiana, are arrested for beating a white classmate unconscious. Initially, five of the six, all aged sixteen or seventeen years old, are charged as adults with attempted murder in the second degree. Seen by many as excessive, the charges, which come on the heels of a racially charged incident in which white students hung a noose from a tree at Jena High School, are eventually downgraded. The largest demonstration in support of the Jena Six, organized by Jesse Jackson, draws more than ten thousand people. "We will not stop marching," Jackson promises, "until justice runs down like waters."[11]

2007

FEBRUARY 4, 2007 Indianapolis Colts head coach Tony Dungy becomes the first African American head coach to guide his team to a Super Bowl ring. The milestone is all the

Tony Dungy, head coach of the Indianapolis Colts, celebrates his team's Super Bowl victory.

more significant because of a history of under-representation of black head coaches in the NFL. Five years earlier, in 2002, a study showed that black coaches were more likely than white coaches to be fired and less likely to be hired despite having a better average record. The firing of Dungy, then the head coach of the Tampa Bay Buccaneers, who finished the 2001 season with a winning record, was one of the incidents that motivated the study. As a result of the paper, the NFL passed the so-called Rooney Rule, named after Pittsburgh Steelers owner Dan Rooney, who chaired the NFL's diversity committee. To increase diversity in the league, it is now mandated that teams interview minority candidates for head coaching positions.[12]

FEBRUARY 10, 2007 US Senator Barack Obama formally announces his candidacy for the Democratic nomination for president. Despite his captivating address at the 2004 Democratic National Convention, many within his party believe the junior senator lacks the experience to defeat the presumed front-runner, Hillary Clinton. Obama makes his announcement standing in front of the Old State Capitol

Don Imus appears on Rev. Al Sharpton's radio show to address the comments he made about the Rutgers women's basketball team.

building in Springfield, Illinois, the same place where Abraham Lincoln delivered his "A House Divided" speech. Obama's address on the occasion emphasizes themes of hope and change that will define his campaign: "It was here, in Springfield, where North, South, East, and West come together that I was reminded of the essential decency of the American people—where I came to believe that through this decency, we can build a more hopeful America."[13]

FEBRUARY 25, 2007 At the seventy-ninth annual Academy Awards in Los Angeles, forty-five-year-old Forest Whitaker wins the Best Actor Oscar for his performance as Idi Amin in *The Last King of Scotland*, and twenty-five-year-old Jennifer Hudson takes home the statue for Best Supporting Actress for her role as Effie White in the screen adaptation of the Broadway musical *Dreamgirls*. Joining them as nominees in the night's top categories are three other black performers, an Oscar record: Will Smith, for *The Pursuit of Happyness*; Eddie Murphy, for *Dreamgirls*; and Djimon Hounsou, for *Blood Diamond*.[14]

APRIL 4, 2007 Radio host Don Imus refers to the mostly African American members of the Rutgers women's basketball team as "nappy-headed hos" during a broadcast of his long-running show *Imus in the Morning*. Coach C. Vivian Stringer responds by focusing on the many accomplishments of her players. "Before you," she points out, "are valedictorians of their class, future doctors, musical prodigies, and yes, even Girl Scouts. They are young ladies of class, distinction. They are articulate, they are brilliant, they are gifted. They are God's representatives in every sense of the word."[15] *Imus* is soon canceled, although its host will return to the radio later that year and to a new TV slot on the Fox Business Channel.

JUNE 28, 2007 In *Parents Involved in Community Schools v. Seattle School District Number 1*, the Supreme Court rules 5–4 that the desegregation policies used by two school districts to achieve racial balance are unconstitutional, and only narrowly affirms the state's compelling interest in achieving diversity. The decision curtails, but

top: In 1944, the NAACP hosted a symbolic funeral for "Jim Crow."
bottom: In 2007, the NAACP convened a similar funeral for the "N-Word."

the black community and to criticize attempts by black youth to reclaim the term with their own casual use of it, especially in rap and hip-hop songs. "Die, N-word," says Detroit mayor Kwame Kilpatrick. "We don't want to see you around here no more."[17]

SEPTEMBER 4, 2007 Edwidge Danticat's memoir, *Brother, I'm Dying*, is published by Random House. The book, which earns the National Book Critics Circle Award and is short-listed for the National Book Award, reveals the increasing influence of a growing population of black immigrants to the US from the Caribbean (Danticat is Haitian), Latin America, and Africa. Fast-forward to 2013, when, as further proof, the National Book Critics Circle Award goes to *Americanah* by Chimamanda Ngozi Adichie, a Nigerian who received her university education in North America and divides her time between Nigeria and the United States. A review of the book in the *Guardian* begins, "There are some novels that tell a great story and others that make you change the way you look at the world. Chimamanda Ngozi Adichie's *Americanah* is a book that manages to do both."[18]

does not end, the ability of school districts to consider diversity in assigning students to public schools. Writing for the plurality of justices opposed to recognizing affirmative action as a compelling interest, Chief Justice John Roberts maintains, "The way to stop discrimination on the basis of race is to stop discriminating on the basis of race."[16]

JULY 9, 2007 The NAACP holds a symbolic funeral for the "N-word" at its annual convention at Detroit. The act, modeled after a similar "burial" of Jim Crow at the 1944 convention, is intended to put to rest a slur used against

SEPTEMBER 25, 2007 BET airs the first in a three-part series, *Hip-Hop vs. America*, that

Chimamanda Ngozi Adichie reads at the *Between the Lines* series at the Schomburg Center for Research in Black Culture in New York.

examines hip-hop culture and its relationship to corporate America, law enforcement, and violence against women. While some participants are sharply critical of the violent and misogynistic language often found in hip-hop lyrics, some of the artists defend the content of their music as a way of reaching audiences. "If I have to throw some 'B's' and 'H's' in there to educate people," says the rapper T.I., "then so be it."[19]

DECEMBER 2007 This month is considered the official start of the economic downturn that will come to be known as the Great Recession,

lasting through June 2009. Conditions include a dramatic fall in the stock market, rising unemployment, and mass foreclosures on homes purchased with so-called sub-prime mortgages. Black Americans are hit particularly hard: according to a 2014 Pew study, the net-worth disparity between white and black Americans increases from just over 10–1 to nearly 13–1 between 2007 and 2013. The median net worth of a white household in 2013 is $141,900, while that of a black household is only $11,000.[20]

DECEMBER 10, 2007 In a 7–2 decision, *Kimbrough v. United States*, the nation's Supreme Court rules that, in drug cases, sentencing

Padlocked door on a foreclosed home in Liberty City, Florida.

judges thenceforth will have discretion to correct disparities in the Federal Sentencing Guidelines between higher sentences for crimes involving crack cocaine and lower sentences for crimes involving powdered cocaine. Citing a Sentencing Commission report, Justice Ruth Bader Ginsburg, for the majority, writes, "The Commission stated that the crack/powder sentencing differential 'fosters disrespect for and lack of confidence in the criminal justice system' because of a 'widely held perception' that it 'promotes unwarranted disparity based on race.' . . . Approximately 85 percent of defendants convicted of crack offenses in federal court are black; thus the severe sentences required by the 100-to-1 ratio are imposed 'primarily upon black offenders.'" While the thorny issue of mandatory minimum sentences remains in place in the federal system, Ray Miller, a state senator in Ohio, hails the Court's decision in a December 19 article in the Cleveland *Call and Post*: "I know that this puts race front and center, but there's no question about it that many of the decisions turn on the issue of one's race. . . . I'm pleased with the court's decision, and the most important thing is that we have equality in sentencing."[21]

2007 IN DANCE The twenty-four-year-old dancer Misty Copeland becomes only the third African American soloist ever to dance for the American Ballet Theatre, changing perceptions of the traditionally white art form. Copeland says she hopes to inspire other black dancers: "I think it's so important for young dancers of color to have someone who looks like them as an example— someone they can touch. . . . I tell them to be true to themselves." Copeland sets another example on June 30, 2015, when she is named a principal dancer of the American Ballet Theatre, the first African American woman to hold that exalted position since the company's founding in 1940.[22]

2008

JANUARY 3, 2008   Barack Obama upsets Hillary Clinton to win the Iowa Democratic caucus, the first race in the nominating season, but then loses narrowly to her in the following week's New Hampshire primary. Although New Hampshire is, like Iowa, a state with few African American voters, exit polls show much greater support for Obama among younger whites with university degrees, while Clinton's greatest support comes from older, working-class whites, a pattern that

Presidential hopeful Barack Obama holds his daughter Sasha while his wife, Michelle, hugs their daughter Malia on the night he wins the Iowa Democratic caucus.

continues throughout the campaign. The critical contest, however, is the January 28 primary fight in South Carolina, a state with a large black population, where Obama wins 55 percent of the vote against Clinton's 27 percent, and, crucially, 78 percent of the African American vote against Clinton's 19 percent. While Clinton maintains her staunch support from black congressional leaders like John Lewis of Georgia and Charles Rangel of New York, momentum for Obama begins to build as the campaign raises $37 million in the month of January alone, compared to Clinton's $20 million.[23]

JANUARY 28, 2008 Donald E. Graham, CEO of the Washington Post Company, and Harvard's Henry Louis Gates, Jr., launch *The Root.com*, an African American opinion, news, and culture website unofficially known as "the Black Huffington Post." *The Root* itself is a manifestation of a growing black Web presence that includes significant churn on the social networking service Twitter. According to a 2013 Pew survey, 26 percent of black non-Hispanic Americans have Twitter accounts as of late 2012, compared to 14 percent of white non-Hispanics. Beyond serving as a virtual community for African Americans, "Black Twitter" as a distinct networked cultural identity becomes a forum for expressing opinions about and calling attention to issues affecting the black community.[24]

FEBRUARY 5, 2008 On Super Tuesday, Barack Obama wins thirteen out of twenty-two primary contests. By now he has netted endorsements from several major figures in the Democratic Party, including the party's elder statesman, Massachusetts senator Ted Kennedy. Early in the campaign, Obama's most prominent sup-

Henry Louis Gates, Jr., speaks at the Museum of Television and Radio in New York City prior to the launch of his **PBS** series *Looking for Lincoln.*

porters are celebrities who help drive a wave of popular enthusiasm for the candidate. Many of them, including the singer John Legend, the NBA great Kareem Abdul-Jabbar, the actress Scarlett Johansson, and the rapper Common, appear in will.i.am's "Yes We Can" video, released on February 2. The song, whose lyrics are composed entirely of quotations from Obama speeches, helps solidify "Yes We Can" as a slogan and rallying cry for the upstart campaign.

MARCH 18, 2008 Now the front-runner in the race for the Democratic nomination, Barack Obama responds to mounting controversy involving statements made by his former Chicago pastor, Jeremiah Wright, who, in a recording from 2003, is seen and heard claiming the US government created AIDS as a form of biological warfare against the black community and blaming US policies for the 9/11 attacks. The heated passage gets heavy play in the media, particularly on the conservative airwaves: "The government gives them the drugs, builds bigger prisons, passes a three-strike law and then wants us to sing 'God Bless America.' No, no, no, not 'God *bless* America,' God *damn* America—that's in the Bible for killing innocent people. God *damn* America for treating our citizens as less than human. God *damn* America as long as she tries to act like she is God and she is supreme." To address the swirling controversy that threatens to torpedo his campaign, the candidate Obama delivers what many believe is the finest speech of the contest; it is certainly the most consequential on the issue of race, inarguably defining his pioneering run for the White House. At the National Constitution Center in Philadelphia, Pennsylvania, a bellwether state whose upcoming primary is viewed as pivotal and where Hillary Clinton is a narrow favorite, Obama delivers the speech titled "A More Perfect Union." In it, he categorically rejects his former pastor's comments while eloquently acknowledging the painful racial legacy that gave rise to the anger of Wright and others, suggesting that Americans must work to continue repairing their fractured racial past: "The profound mistake of Reverend Wright's sermons is not that he spoke about racism in our society. It's that he spoke as if our society was static; as if no progress has been made; as if this country . . . is still irrevocably bound to a tragic past. But what we know—what we have seen—is that America can change. That

is the true genius of this nation. What we have already achieved gives us hope—the audacity to hope—for what we can and must achieve tomorrow." Obama will go on to lose Pennsylvania to Clinton by nine points, largely on the strength of traditional white working-class Democrats' support for her candidacy and opposition to Obama. Although the loss is a blow to the Obama campaign, the key metric in the race continues to be the scramble for delegates, a clear advantage for the Illinois senator.[25]

APRIL 4, 2008 R&B star Beyoncé and the rapper Jay Z marry, becoming music's top power couple. The development of their music since their marriage is seen as representative of a new, "grown-

Democratic presidential candidate Barack Obama delivers his address "A More Perfect Union" in Philadelphia.

Blue Ivy Carter with her parents, Jay Z and Beyoncé, at the MTV Video Music Awards in California.

up wing" of hip-hop that embraces emotion and commitment to family. After the birth of the couple's daughter, Blue Ivy, in 2012, Jay Z, who previously wrote songs like "Money, Cash, Hoes" and "Big Pimpin'," now adds doting songs like "Glory" to his repertoire in her honor. Combined, Beyoncé and Jay Z have sold more than three hundred million albums and lend support to a number of political and philanthropic causes.[26]

JUNE 3, 2008 At the formal end of the primary season, Obama becomes the presumptive Democratic nominee. Although both candidates have amassed more than eighteen million votes each, Obama leads Clinton by only 125 pledged delegates from primaries and caucuses. That margin is later inflated to three hundred with the addition of super-delegates, including many of the Congressional Black Caucus elders who originally supported Clinton.

JUNE 12, 2008 The Obama campaign releases a copy of the candidate's short-form Hawaiian birth certificate to try to stem rumors that he

was born in his father's native Kenya, which would render him ineligible to serve as president. In spite of the written proof, doubters in some quarters continue to speculate that Obama is not native born, and even his decision in 2011 to release his long-form birth certificate does not entirely satisfy "birthers." Many Obama supporters suggest that the root of these claims, as well as other conspiracy theories espousing that he is a covert Muslim, is discomfort with his race. One of the president's most vociferous critics, however, is the prominent black conservative Alan Keyes, who brings forward a lawsuit challenging Obama's status as a "natural-born citizen." The suit is later dismissed.[27]

JULY 29, 2008 The US House of Representatives passes H.Res 194, a resolution formally apologizing for slavery and Jim Crow. A similar bill passes in the Senate in June of 2009, but with a stipulation that the symbolic acknowledgment of responsibility does not entitle the descendants of slaves to reparations. As a result, though each house of Congress has apologized for slavery, the US government as a whole, unlike a number of other countries involved in the slave trade, has never made an unconditional apology for slavery. The reason, at least in part, is political expediency: according to a 2014 poll, only 28 percent of Americans support such a resolution. The issue of redressing

The New York Public Library's Annual Library Lions Gala, with Annette Gordon-Reed, Jessye Norman, and Anna Deavere Smith.

the consequences of history is revived in June 2014, when Ta-Nehisi Coates, a writer for *The Atlantic,* pens his prize-winning cover story, "The Case for Reparations," with the subheading, "Two hundred fifty years of slavery. Ninety years of Jim Crow. Sixty years of separate but equal. Thirty-five years of racist housing policy. Until we reckon with our compounding moral debts, America will never be whole."[28]

AUGUST 28, 2008 On the forty-fifth anniversary of Martin Luther King's "I Have a Dream" speech, Barack Obama accepts the Democratic nomination at the 2008 Democratic National Convention in Denver. One of the convention speakers is Representative John R. Lewis (D-Ga.), the last survivor of the "Big Six" leaders of the civil rights movement and organizers of the March on Washington who spoke to the two-hundred-thousand-strong crowd on the day of King's speech. "With the nomination of Senator Barack Obama tonight," says Lewis, "the man who will lead the Democratic Party in its march toward the White House, we are making a down payment on the fulfillment of [King's] dream."[29]

SEPTEMBER 17, 2008 Legal scholar Annette Gordon-Reed releases her groundbreaking study *The Hemingses of Monticello: An American Family,* a story of several generations of the family of Sally Hemings, Thomas Jefferson's slave and the mother of six children who most historians believe were fathered by him. Gordon-Reed becomes the first African American to be awarded a Pulitzer Prize for History for her work; the book also wins the National Book Award.

NOVEMBER 4, 2008 With nearly 53 percent of the popular vote, Barack Obama defeats his Republican opponent, Senator John McCain, to become the first African American elected to the nation's highest office: president of the United States. Core to Obama's election-day coalition is

Election night in Grant Park, Chicago.

there is anyone out there who still doubts that America is a place where all things are possible, who still wonders if the dream of our founders is alive in our time, who still questions the power of our democracy, tonight is your answer."

2008—THE DAWN OF A NEW "POST-RACIAL AMERICA"? As the long election season comes to a close, Obama's victory generates widespread discussion of whether or not America has entered a "post-racial" era in which the end of racial discrimination has rendered color a comparatively unimportant aspect of social and political identity. To test this, sociologists Lawrence Bobo and Alicia Simmons conduct a poll shortly after the election asking whether America has achieved racial equality: 53 percent of African American respondents answer yes, a markedly lower sampling than the 80 percent of whites who give the same answer.[30] Political scientist Cathy Cohen polls young people a few months later, asking whether racism is still a major problem in the United States. Among young African Americans, 69 percent respond yes, compared to 32 percent of young whites. Cohen later publishes her findings as part of a larger argument challenging the notion that the election of Obama, whose mixed-race background gave him access and exposure to traditionally white culture and institutions that he would otherwise not have had, indicates the advent of "post-racial" America.[31]

the massive support he receives from voters in the 18–29 age group; more dramatically, 96 percent of African American voters vote for Obama, compared to 43 percent of white voters. In a poignant speech before a sea of nearly a quarter of a million people in Chicago's Grant Park that night (among them Oprah Winfrey and Jesse Jackson), Obama tells his supporters, "If

2009

JANUARY 20, 2009 Barack Obama is inaugurated as the forty-fourth president of the United States. His inaugural theme, "A New Birth of Freedom," takes its title from Lincoln's Gettysburg Address. In keeping with the theme, pre-inauguration events include a train tour that reenacts Lincoln's own post-election journey from Illinois to Washington, DC, and a free concert at the Lincoln Memorial with performers such as Pete Seeger and Bruce Springsteen. Obama's speech, delivered at a time of great economic uncertainty (unemployment stands between 7 and 8 percent), focuses on America's capacity to meet the challenges ahead: "Let it be said by our children's children that when we were tested we refused to let this journey end, that we did not turn back nor did we falter; and with eyes fixed on the horizon and God's grace upon us,

left: Barack H. Obama is sworn in as the forty-fourth US president at the Capitol in Washington, DC. First Lady Michelle Obama holds the Bible upon which his hand is placed. Daughters Malia and Sasha look on as family and national history is made.
right: The Obamas take their inauguration-day walk down Pennsylvania Avenue.

Michael Steele, the first African American Chairman of the Republican National Committee.

we carried forth that great gift of freedom and delivered it safely to future generations." Aside from the obvious political milestone, the arrival of Barack and Michelle Obama, along with their daughters, Malia and Sasha—then ten and seven years old, respectively—at the White House, puts a nuclear black family at the forefront of public consciousness.[32]

JANUARY 31, 2009 Michael Steele is chosen to be the first African American chair of the Republican National Committee. His selection is seen as an attempt by the party to counteract perceptions of Republican racial bias in the wake of the election of the nation's first black president. This issue only intensifies after one of the candidates for chairman resigns after a leaked email reveals that he circulated copies of a satirical song called "Barack the Magic Negro." Steele, raised by a widowed mother from a family of sharecroppers, resists the suggestion that race influenced his election: "I am a Republican who happens to be African-American."[33]

FEBRUARY 2, 2009 Fifty-eight-year-old lawyer Eric Holder, a New York native and Columbia University alumnus and former trustee, becomes the first black attorney general in the nation's history. Before long, Holder finds himself embroiled in two controversies involving his handling of racial issues. During a Justice Department event celebrating Black History Month, Holder says

A couple arrives for the groundbreaking ceremony for the Smithsonian National Museum of African American History and Culture, scheduled to open on the Mall in Washington in 2016.

America continues to be a "nation of cowards" when it comes to discussions of race.[34] And in May, Holder faces criticism after dropping a voter-intimidation charge against members of the New Black Panther Party who allegedly stood outside a Philadelphia polling place during the 2008 presidential election wearing uniforms and holding nightsticks. Some in Holder's own department charge that he is unwilling to use civil rights laws originally intended to protect minorities to prosecute African Americans, prompting an investigation by the US Commission on Civil Rights.[35]

Michael Jackson's star on the Hollywood Walk of Fame becomes a makeshift memorial following his death.

MAY 12, 2009 Congress passes the Civil Rights History Project Act of 2009, which "direct[s] the Librarian of Congress and the Secretary of the Smithsonian Institution to carry out a joint project at the Library of Congress and the National Museum of African American History and Culture to collect video and audio recordings of personal histories and testimonials of individuals who participated in the civil rights movement, and for other purposes." Between 2010 and 2013, interviews are conducted with 139 participants in major events of the movement.[36]

MAY 28, 2009 Lynn Nottage wins the Pulitzer Prize for her stage drama *Ruined.* Nottage is one of a group of acclaimed twenty-first-century African American playwrights that includes Marcus Gardley, Katori Hall, Tarell McCraney, Lydia Diamond, and Suzan-Lori Parks. In the fall of 2011, works by three of these playwrights— Hall, Diamond, and Parks—appear on Broadway, unusual in a theater scene in which it is often difficult for plays by black artists to get attention. As Hall reveals, "I've had frank conversations with theaters who say, 'We love your play,

but we've already done a play by another black person this year,' or 'I don't think the kind of people you write about are the ones our audience wants to see.'"[37]

JUNE 25, 2009 Michael Jackson, the King of Pop, dies at age fifty of cardiac arrest brought on by an accidental overdose on prescription medications, including an anesthetic generally used only during surgery. Jackson's personal physician, Conrad Murray, is later found guilty of involuntary manslaughter for improperly administering the drugs. While Jackson became a controversial figure in the black community over concerns that he was deliberately trying to shed his racial identity through plastic surgery and alleged skin lightening, the memorial service following his death in Los Angeles, which features presentations by Al Sharpton and Martin Luther King III and performances by Smokey Robinson, Stevie Wonder, and a number of other prominent black artists, indicates a posthumous embrace by the community. Sharpton in particular credits Jackson with raising the profile of African American artists, saying he "broke down the color curtain where now our videos are shown and magazines put us on the cover."[38]

JUNE 29, 2009 In *Ricci v. DeStefano*, the US Supreme Court rules 5–4 in favor of a group of white firefighters suing the city of New Haven under the Civil Rights Act of 1964. The men passed a qualifying test to become officers, but the city threw out the exam because no African American firefighters scored high enough to qualify. City officials claimed they were attempting to avoid a lawsuit for administering a test that had a "disparate impact" on minority applicants.[39]

JULY 16, 2009 Upon returning to Cambridge, Massachusetts, from China, where he was filming his PBS genealogy series *Faces of America*, Harvard University professor Henry Louis Gates, Jr., is mistaken by a passerby for an intruder when he is spotted entering his own home. Following a dispute with Cambridge City Police sergeant James Crowley, who asks him

to produce identification, Gates is arrested and spends four hours in jail on a disorderly conduct charge. A photo of the fifty-eight-year-old Harvard professor in handcuffs, as he is escorted off his front steps, soon goes viral. At a July 22 White House press conference focused on healthcare, President Barack Obama is asked to comment, and says, extemporaneously, "I don't know, not having been there and not seeing all the facts, what role race played. . . . But I think it's fair to say, number one, any of us would be pretty angry; number two, that the Cambridge police acted stupidly in arresting somebody when there was already proof that they were in their own home; and number three, what I think we know separate and apart from this incident is that there's a long history in this country of African Americans and Latinos being stopped by law enforcement disproportionately. That's just a fact." The president also quips that if the same thing were to happen to him upon entering his current home, the White House, "I would be shot." His extemporaneous response ignites a

The "Beer Summit"— President Obama and Vice President Joe Biden meet with Professor Henry Louis Gates, Jr., and Sergeant James Crowley at the White House.

Fortune's senior editor at large Pattie Sellers (left) interviews Ursula Burns, chair and CEO of Xerox, at the magazine's *Most Powerful Women Dinner* in New York City.

firestorm of controversy, and President Obama forges a "teachable moment" out of the affair by inviting Gates and Crowley to a "Beer Summit" in the White House Rose Garden on July 31. "Even before we sat down for the beer," President Obama says in a statement after the meeting, "I learned that the two gentlemen spent some time together listening to one another, which is a testament to them. I have always believed that what brings us together is stronger than what pulls us apart." This incident apparently serves as a "teachable moment" for the president as well, one in which he learns that, despite his historic role as the nation's first black commander in chief, and perhaps because of it, he will need to be more circumspect in weighing in on race matters in the country. The following year, Gates's attorney and Harvard colleague Charles Ogletree publishes a bestselling book contextualizing the event, *The Presumption of Guilt: The Arrest of Henry Louis Gates, Jr., and Race, Class and Crime in America.*[40]

JULY 23, 2009 E. Lynn Harris, the pioneering novelist of the African American gay experience, dies at age fifty-four. A former computer salesman (full name Everette Lynn Harris), he self-published his first book, *Invisible Life*, in 1991, selling copies from his car until the manuscript was picked up by Random House and reissued for mass distribution in 1994. In Harris's *New York Times* obituary, Bruce Weber writes: "Mr. Harris, who was openly gay but who lived for many years in denial or shame or both over that fact, was able to draw on his own experiences to make credible the emotional conflicts of his characters, and his readers, many of them women, were drawn to his books because they addressed issues that were often surreptitiously pertinent to their own lives."[41]

JULY 1, 2009 Fifty-year-old Ursula Burns takes command as CEO of the Xerox Corporation, becoming the first African American woman to serve as CEO of a Fortune 500 company. Burns adds to her title in May 2010 when she is named

President Barack Obama, winner of the Nobel Peace Prize, stands with prize committee chairman Thorbjoern Jagland after delivering his Nobel lecture in Oslo, Norway.

chairwoman as well. She attributes her success to her mother, who encouraged her children to pursue dreams beyond the poor inner-city world in which they lived: "Where you are today," she told them, "is not who you are."[42]

OCTOBER 9, 2009 President Obama is awarded the Nobel Peace Prize for his "extraordinary efforts to strengthen international diplomacy and cooperation between peoples." Some commentators question the decision to award the prize to a president at the beginning of his term, especially given the US's continued military engagements in Iraq and Afghanistan. Obama himself says he does not "feel that I deserve to be in the company of so many of the transformative figures who have been honored by this prize," but that he will "accept this award as a call to action, a call for all nations to confront the challenges of the 21st century."[43]

OCTOBER 20, 2009 The singer-songwriter Alicia Keys and the rap artist Jay Z release their collab-

oration "Empire State of Mind." With its fusion of R&B and hip-hop styles, the song fits and is embraced by a new generation of New Yorkers, standing beside "New York, New York" as a new signature anthem for the city. Its popularity soars when Keys and Jay Z perform it live before the second game of the World Series, which the Yankees win to clinch their twenty-seventh title.[44]

OCTOBER 28, 2009 President Obama signs into law the Matthew Shepard and James Byrd, Jr., Hate Crimes Prevention Act, expanding existing hate-crime laws to include sexual orientation and gender identity. The law also gives the federal government broader authority to prosecute and investigate suspected hate crimes of all kinds. It is named in honor of Matthew Shepard, a gay college student beaten to death in Wyoming in a crime motivated in part by his sexuality, and James Byrd, Jr., a black man who died after being dragged behind a pickup truck for three miles by white supremacists in Texas.

Anika Noni Rose at the premiere of Disney's *The Princess and the Frog.*

In his remarks at the White House, Obama says: "It's hard for any of us to imagine the mind-set of someone who would kidnap a young man and beat him to within an inch of his life, tie him to a fence, and leave him for dead. It's hard for any of us to imagine the twisted mentality of those who'd offer a neighbor a ride home, attack him, chain him to the back of a truck, and drag him for miles until he finally died. . . . But we sense where such cruelty begins: the moment we fail to see in another our common humanity—the very moment when we fail to recognize in a person the same fears and hopes, the same passions and imperfections, the same dreams that we all share."[45]

NOVEMBER 25, 2009 Disney's *The Princess and the Frog* is released, featuring the Tony Award–winning actress Anika Noni Rose as the voice of Tiana, the first black Disney princess. "Finally," says one mother interviewed at a screening of the movie, "there's a princess that looks like my little girls." While many viewers praise Disney for making an effort to diversify their movies, some criticize the film for its perceived use of racial stereotypes and failure to pair Tiana with an identifiably African American prince, noting that all previous Disney princesses, with the exception of Pocahontas (whose marriage to the white John Rolfe is inspired by fact), ended up romantically attached to men of their own race.[46]

Confirmation hearing of Loretta
Lynch as US Attorney General.

2010-2015

Hon. Loretta Lynch

2010

JANUARY 12, 2010 A devastating earthquake rocks Haiti, leaving hundreds of thousands dead and many more homeless in a humanitarian crisis that sets the western hemisphere's poorest nation back years. In response, the Obama administration pledges $100 million in aid and relief support to the Caribbean nation, declaring, "Haiti will not be forgotten," and tasking former presidents Bill Clinton and George W. Bush with leading the nation's effort. People of Haitian ancestry in the US number more than 830,000, up from 290,000 in 1990, and they play a central role in publicizing and organizing the relief. Still, progress in the rebuilding effort comes slow and frustrates many in Haiti who point to a disconnect between monies raised and tangible improvements on the ground.[1]

FEBRUARY 14, 2010 The New Press publishes Michelle Alexander's book *The New Jim Crow: Mass Incarceration in the Age of Colorblindness* which earns a place on the *New York Times* bestseller list for ten months. In it, Alexander argues that the disproportionate enforcement of harsh drug laws against black men has created a permanent urban underclass that repli-

cates the more formal disenfranchisement of minorities under Jim Crow. The United States, with only 5 percent of the world's population, holds 25 percent of its prisoners, nearly 40 percent of whom are African American. Alexander opens the book with a striking example in support of her central claim: "Jarvious Cotton cannot vote. Like his father, grandfather, great-grandfather, and great-great-grandfather, he has been denied the right to participate in our electoral democracy. . . . Cotton's great-great-

Attendees at the fiftieth anniversary of the *March on Washington for Jobs and Freedom* in 2013 look back and toward the challenges ahead.

Gabourey Sidibe (left) and Mo'Nique in a scene from *Precious*.

grandfather could not vote as a slave. His great-grandfather was beaten to death by the Ku Klux Klan for attempting to vote. His grandfather was prevented from voting by Klan intimidation. His father was barred from voting by poll taxes and literacy tests. Today, Jarvious Cotton cannot vote because he, like many black men in the United States, has been labeled a felon and is currently on parole."[2]

MARCH 7, 2010 Lee Daniels's film *Precious*, based on the Sapphire novel *Push*, earns six Oscar nominations, including for Best Picture and Best Director. The forty-two-year-old actress Mo'Nique takes home the statue for Best Supporting Actress for her role as the brutal Mary Lee Johnston, the mother of Precious Jones, played by Gabourey Sidibe, who is nominated for Best Actress. *Precious* is an unflinching account of sexual abuse, teen pregnancy, and the deprivations of urban life in New York City. "I want to thank Miss Hattie McDaniel for enduring all that she had to, so that I would not have to," Mo'Nique says in her acceptance

speech, paying homage to the first African American actor to win an Oscar.[3]

MARCH 23, 2010 President Obama signs into law his signature domestic policy initiative, the Patient Protection and Affordable Care Act, known in shorthand as Obamacare. Although the act falls short of the single-payer national health service supported by Representative John Conyers (D-Mich.) and thirty-three of the forty-two members of the Congressional Black Caucus, it is the first successful enactment of comprehensive healthcare reform, a goal that Democrats from Harry Truman to Bill Clinton, hoped but failed to secure. The law aims to increase the affordability of healthcare, increasing eligibility for Medicaid, requiring more employers to provide coverage, offering lower-cost plans through public health exchanges, and mandating that individuals above a certain income level purchase health insurance. Obama, in his second year as president, continues to be a lightning rod in the nation on this issue, with criticism focusing on the constitutionality of the individual mandate, the cancellation of old plans that didn't meet ACA standards, the economic burden placed on employers, and whether or not the plan's offers are truly affordable for lower-income Americans. On June 28, 2012, the US Supreme Court upholds the constitutionality of the act in a 5–4 decision, *National Federation of Independent Business v. Sebelius.* As of January 2015, 9.5 million Americans have signed up for plans under the exchanges; overall, the percentage of uninsured Americans has dropped by the end of the fourth quarter of 2014 to 12.9 percent, the lowest number since Gallup began tracking the statistic in early 2008, and a decline of the uninsured population by 4.2 percent from the previous year.[4]

President Barack Obama signs the *Affordable Health Care Act* at a ceremony in the East Room of the White House.

APRIL 26, 2010 A revival of August Wilson's Tony Award–winning play *Fences* opens at the Cort Theatre on Broadway in New York, fueled by the collaboration of the African American director Kenny Leon and Denzel Washington in the lead role of Troy Maxson, a combustible former Negro League slugger confronting his mortality as a sanitation worker in Pittsburgh. Like James Earl Jones, who originated the role in 1987, Washington wins the Tony for Best Performance by a Leading Actor in a Play, along with his costar, Viola Davis, who snags the Tony for Leading Actress for her performance as Troy's wife, Rose. The production also wins the Tony for Best Revival of a Play. In 2014, Leon and Washington team up again for a revival of Lorraine Hansberry's 1959 play *A Raisin in the Sun,* which earns Tony Awards for Leon's direction as well as for Best Revival; also, Sophie Okonedo, who plays Ruth Younger to Washington's Walter, wins Best Performance by a Featured Actress in a Play. That same year, Leon directs a musical adaptation of the hip-hop oeuvre of Tupac Shakur, *Holler If Ya Hear Me.*[5]

AUGUST 3, 2010 President Obama signs into law the Fair Sentencing Act, which reduces the disparity between the amount of powdered cocaine and the amount of crack cocaine a person needs to trigger mandatory minimum sentences from 100-to-1 to 18-to-1. This is the culmination of years of effort and goes further than previous actions taken to make the penalties more equitable.[6]

SEPTEMBER 24, 2010 The documentary film *Waiting for Superman* is released, exploring the failures of the American public education system, particularly in inner-city neighborhoods. The film focuses particular attention on the Harlem Children's Zone president and CEO Geoffrey Canada, who advocates improving urban education through family support services, early childhood intervention, and the establishment of charter schools in areas where traditional schools are inadequate. "Education is the only billion-dollar industry that tolerates abject failure. Any other business that failed so spectacularly for fifty years, it would be out of business," says Canada. As one might expect, some charter schools show dramatic results in their students' performances; for others, the jury is still out on their success, since test scores and other measures have shown less improvement in student outcomes than many initially hoped. Other education advocates continue to be focused on finding ways to improve the country's public schools, with state testing and Common Core standards the subjects of fierce national debate.[7]

NOVEMBER 2, 2010 In the congressional midterm elections, Republicans gain six seats in the Senate and sixty-three seats in the House of Representatives to win back control of the lower chamber from the Democrats. The returns are judged to be a repudiation of President Obama's first two years in office by those who turn out to vote. Of particular significance is the success of Republican candidates, associated with or endorsed by the Tea Party Movement, who win thirty-nine seats in the House and five in the Senate. Begun as a grassroots political movement in 2009, the Tea Party, which does not have a formal platform or party infrastructure, advocates for limited government and fiscal restraint; the group is especially exercised by the president's health insurance law and spending measures, including his bailout of US auto manufacturers teetering on bankruptcy in Detroit. While these reflect traditional conservative and libertarian beliefs, the predominantly white base of support for the Tea Party, its opposition to funding for social welfare programs, and, by 2014, its resistance to any form of "amnesty" for undocumented immigrants have led to charges of racism. Others maintain that racial animus and anxiety are not primary motivations among Tea Party supporters.[8]

A politically motivated caricature of Barack Obama set up outside a house in rural Virginia.

2011

FEBRUARY 13, 2011 At the fifty-third annual Grammy Awards in Los Angeles, the Carolina Chocolate Drops win for Best Traditional Folk Album with their creation *Genuine Negro Jig*. The group, based in Durham, North Carolina, formed in 2005 at the first black Banjo Gathering held at Appalachian State University in Boone, North Carolina. Influenced by the traditional black string bands of the southern Piedmont, jug bands, and the blues, the Drops also adapt con-temporary R&B hits like Blu Cantrell's "Hit 'Em Up Style (Oops!)," a song about a spurned lover's credit card revenge described by one reviewer as a "joyous slab of hillbilly hip-hop." The band's main vocalist, fiddle player, and banjoist, Rhiannon Giddens, traveled to Gambia in 2006 to study with master musicians of the West African stringed instrument called the akonting, a close relative of the banjo, and the band is featured on the 2007 soundtrack of *The Great Debaters*, a

Cast members of OWN's *Love Thy Neighbor* at a screening in New York City: (left to right) Jonathan Chase, Andre Hall, Patrice Lovely, Darmirra Brunson, Kendra C. Johnson, and Palmer Williams.

film starring Denzel Washington as Melvin Tolson, the 1930s debate coach at the historically black Wiley College in Texas.[9]

MAY 25, 2011 *The Oprah Winfrey Show* airs its final episode after twenty-five years in syndication. This follows the launch on January 1, 2011, of Winfrey's Oprah Winfrey Network (OWN). As part of her goodbye, Winfrey tells her audience to go out and find their own ways of making a difference in the world: "Your being alive makes worthiness your birthright. You alone are enough. . . . [My platform] is a stage in a studio. Yours is wherever you are, with your own reach."[10]

JULY 2, 2011 Twenty-four year-old rapper Kendrick Lamar, of Compton, California, drops his album *Studio.80* on iTunes and is soon seen by many, including hip-hop legend Snoop Dogg, as the torchbearer of the West Coast style. Lamar's next album, 2012's *good kid, m.A.A.d city* (this time for the Top Dawg label) exceeds a million copies sold, with the young MC garnering seven Grammy nominations in 2014. "We have long looked to gifted hip-hop artists to paint an authentic portrait of what it's like to be young and black in America," Lizzy Goodman of the *New York Times Magazine* writes that year. "Lamar has done this without retreading familiar ground. 'We've been in Compton before,' points out Eminem, with whom Lamar has collaborated in the studio and toured. 'But the way that Kendrick did it was so different. . . . The album is crafted from front to back, the way each song ties into each other—to me that's genius.'" In 2015, after the release of Lamar's third album, *To Pimp a Butterfly*, which notches a new record for the most number of streams in a single day on Spotify (9.6 million worldwide), California state senator Isadore Hall III designates Lamar his district's "Generational Icon" both because of his musical accomplishments and his charitable work in his native Compton. "Mr. Lamar has not only given voice to a new generation of urban youth," Hall declares, "he is demonstrating the best of what it means to work hard, do well and give back to his community."[11]

SEPTEMBER 2011 *Forbes* names the writer, director, and actor Tyler Perry the highest-paid male entertainer of the year, with a whopping $130 million netted between May 2010 and May 2011. The box-office success of the forty-two-year-old Perry's films, which include the popular *Madea* franchise, demonstrate the market for movies set in urban, African American communities. Surveying his career in *Film Comment*, Wesley Morris writes: "Tyler Perry saw and filled a void. . . . His movies speak to a range of black life, and they do so without a Hollywood-studio subsidy. . . . They all bear his stamp of what I called 'department-store moviemaking': sermon on this floor, drama up the escalator, romance at the perfume counter, farce in the basement near the restrooms. His movies do more in 20 minutes than most do in two hours. Mostly set in Atlanta, they take you to church, to cookouts, to mansions, to the projects, to the Rockies, to court, the hospital, and jail." Perry is the first African American to own his own major television and film studio, the Atlanta-based Tyler Perry Studios, beginning in 2006. "I saw a need for positive, inspiring entertainment . . . especially in the African-American community," he tells Felicia Lee of the *New York Times* in 2007.[12]

SEPTEMBER 17, 2011 Several hundred protesters at Zuccotti Park on the edge of New York City's financial district begin what becomes the Occupy Wall Street movement. Occupy spawns similar protests in other American and European cities, reflecting an emerging organized opposition to the concentration of money and power in the hands of an elite "1 percent" of citizens, at the expense of the remaining "99 percent." Although African Americans are largely among that 99 percent, the overwhelmingly white Occupy movement is criticized both for failing to engage with black Americans who have been in similar economic straits for many years and for the group's historically inexact and racist depictions of twenty-first-century class inequality as "slavery." Although the academic Cornel West, the hip-hop mogul Russell Simmons, Representative John Lewis, and other African Americans endorse the broad goals of Occupy, the protests fizzle out by the end of 2011. Occupy's failure speaks to the longstanding inability of Americans to construct a popular movement to challenge racial and economic inequality simultaneously.[13]

A profile view of the Martin Luther King, Jr., Memorial on the National Mall in Washington, DC.

OCTOBER 16, 2011 A Martin Luther King, Jr., Memorial is formally dedicated in a ceremony in Washington, DC. It is the first monument in the area of the National Mall to memorialize an African American and only the fourth to honor someone other than a US president. President Obama, speaking at the event, takes the opportunity to call Americans to action in King's name: "Our work is not done. And so on this day, in which we celebrate a man and a movement that did so much for this country, let us draw strength from those earlier struggles."[14]

2012

JANUARY 31, 2012 Keegan-Michael Key and Jordan Peele debut as the stars of *Key & Peele*, an original sketch comedy show. The duo's sketches frequently deal with racial issues, drawing on the comedians' own experience as biracial Americans. Recurring characters include Luther, the president's "anger translator," who expresses candid thoughts his carefully controlled public persona cannot articulate; Mr. Garvey, a former inner-city teacher now working as a substitute in the suburbs; and the Black Republicans, who claim to be "outside-of-the-box" thinkers but parrot precisely the same phrases.[15]

FEBRUARY 16, 2012 A newly released Pew study finds that the rate of interracial marriages in the United States has more than doubled in the past twenty years, from 3.2 percent in 1980 to 8.4 percent in 2010, suggesting a decline in historical taboos against racial mixing and reflecting the increasingly complex nature of racial identity in America.[16]

FEBRUARY 26, 2012 Trayvon Martin, age seventeen, is killed by George Zimmerman, a "neighborhood watchman," while walking home from a convenience store during a visit to his father's home in Sanford, Florida. There had been several recent burglaries in the neighborhood, and the armed Zimmerman followed Martin despite being advised by police that it was not neces-

Sketch comedians Key & Peele.

A New York City sidewalk message and drawing after a jury in Florida finds George Zimmerman was justified in the murder of Trayvon Martin.

sary to do so. By the time police arrive, Martin lies dead of a gunshot wound, with Zimmerman claiming he shot Martin in self-defense after Martin attacked him. Law enforcement initially declines to press charges, but after a public outcry, Zimmerman is charged with second-degree murder. The killing and Zimmerman's eventual acquittal in July 2013 inspire a national debate over racial profiling generally and, in particular, Florida's controversial "Stand Your Ground" law, which lowers the standard for justifying the use of a firearm in self-defense. Calling for an investigation into the case, President Obama draws an analogy between Trayvon Martin and his own children: "When I think about this boy, I think about my own kids. . . . If I had a son, he would look like Trayvon."[17]

FEBRUARY 26, 2012 In Los Angeles, at the eighty-fourth annual Academy Awards, the African American actress Octavia Spencer wins the Oscar for Best Supporting Actress for her performance as the black domestic Minny Jackson in the film *The Help*. "I hope that in some way I can be some sort of beacon of hope, particularly because I'm not the typical Hollywood beauty,"

the thirty-nine-year-old Spencer says upon receiving her award.[18]

APRIL 15, 2012 Shonda Rhimes's latest network drama, *Scandal*, starring Kerry Washington, debuts on ABC. For the first time in more than thirty years, a black woman has been cast as the lead in a drama series. So far, Washington has been twice nominated for an Emmy for Best Actress in a Drama for her role in the show. By the fall of 2014, the entire ABC prime-time Thursday lineup will be devoted to shows produced by Rhimes's Shondaland production company, with *Scandal* sandwiched between the long-running *Grey's Anatomy* and Rhimes's new series, *How to Get Away with Murder*, starring Viola Davis.

MAY 9, 2012 In an interview on ABC's *Good Morning America*, President Obama becomes the first US president to support same-sex marriage publicly and officially: "It is important for me to go ahead and affirm that I think same-sex couples should be able to get married," Obama tells the show's host, Robin Roberts. Ten days later, at their quarterly meeting, the NAACP's board of directors, led by president and CEO Benjamin Todd Jealous, votes 62–2 to endorse same-sex marriage as a civil right. In 2015, the US Supreme Court rules that the right to marry is fundamental under the Constitution, thus legalizing same-sex marriage nationwide. Voting with the majority are the two justices President

A still from season one of Shonda Rhimes's hit television series *Scandal*, with Kerry Washington (as Olivia Pope) and Tony Goldwyn (as fictional president Fitzgerald Thomas Grant III).

Obama nominated to the court: Sonia Sotomayor and Elena Kagan.[19]

MAY 17, 2012 New census figures reveal that non-white births in the country have, for the first time, surpassed white births, at 50.4 percent. Whites still make up the plurality of all births. The study suggests the changing face of America and anticipates a time in which the majority of Americans will be non-white.[20]

JUNE 19, 2012 Fred Luter, Jr., becomes the first African American president of the Southern Baptist Convention, the nation's largest Protestant body. The election of Luter, who rebuilt his thousands-strong New Orleans congregation after Hurricane Katrina, is a sign of increasing diversity in a movement once known for its support of slavery and segregation. While Baptist officials hope Luter's elevation will broaden the appeal of the church to minority groups, they also praise his powerful preaching and post-storm humanitarian efforts: "[Luter] would likely be a candidate for sainthood one day if he were a Catholic," says David Crosby, the pastor who nominated him, going on to call Luter "the fire-breathing, miracle-working pastor of Franklin Avenue Baptist Church."[21]

JULY 1, 2012 Forty-nine-year-old Donald Thompson is named the first black president of the McDonald's Corporation. Raised in inner-city Chicago, Thompson joined McDonald's in 1990 as an electrical engineer before beginning his rise up the corporate ladder. While Thompson earned his start as an engineer, he was naturally business-minded even as a child, and recalls printing out business cards at age eleven and passing them out to elderly people who might want to hire someone to do chores. Thompson remains at the top spot at the popular fast-food giant until his retirement in 2015.[22]

JULY–AUGUST 2012 Galvanized by the acquittal of George Zimmerman in the killing of Trayvon Martin, a group of young protesters calling themselves the "Dream Defenders" stage a thirty-one-day sit-in at the office of Florida governor Rick Scott. Their demands include a repeal of the "Stand Your Ground" law, the end of racial profiling, and the closing of the so-called school-to-prison pipeline. Although Scott does not agree to meet the group's demands, the Florida legislature modifies Stand Your Ground that fall. Since then, the Dream Defenders, whose Florida campaign attracted support from civil rights leaders Jesse Jackson and Julian Bond, have continued to encourage activism on racial and human rights issues throughout the nation.[23]

AUGUST 2, 2012 Sixteen-year-old Gabby Douglas becomes the first black female to win the individual all-around gold medal in women's gymnastics at the Summer Games in London. Douglas, nicknamed the Flying Squirrel, goes on to win a second gold medal in the team competition.

SEPTEMBER 19, 2012 The Civil Rights Project at UCLA releases a study on segregation in American schools, finding that, while the percentage of minority students attending public schools has sharply increased from 1970, levels of segregation have worsened. Nationally, 43 percent of Latino and 38 percent of black students attend "intensely segregated" schools where whites represent less than 10 percent of the student body; at the same time, the report reveals, 15 percent of black students and 14 percent of Hispanic students attend so-called apartheid schools in which whites make up less

than 1 percent of the study body. The concentration of these schools is particularly intense in urban areas, with about half of all black students in Chicago and one third in New York attending apartheid schools. At the same time, in the American South, the number of black students attending majority-white schools has fallen from a peak of 43.5 percent in 1988 to 23.2 percent in 2011. This retreat from what was a concentrated desegregation effort nationally is accompanied by a slow-down in narrowing the 'achievement gap' between black and white students. "If we had kept going, when we had cut it by half [between 1971 and 1988], I don't know that we would have eliminated it totally, because there's a long history here, but you could see where we would have been so close to eliminating it," journalist Nikole Hannah-Jones reports in an episode of *This American Life* on NPR in 2015. "But instead, since 1988, we have started to re-segregate, and it is at that exact moment that you see the achievement gap start to widen again." Hannah Jones explains "it is not that something magical happens when black kids sit in a classroom next to white kids. What integration does is it gets black kids in the same facilities as white kids, and therefore, it gets them access to the same things that those kids get: quality teachers and quality instruction." Summing

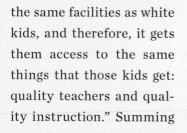

Gabrielle Douglas competes on the balance beam during the Senior Women's competition of the Visa Championships in St. Louis.

In the lead-up to Election Day 2012, supporters attend a speech by First Lady Michelle Obama in Miami.

demographic divide in the country, with Romney edging out Obama 59 to 39 percent among white voters, while Obama clinches a lopsided 93 percent of the black vote as well as a large majority of Hispanic (71 percent) and Asian (73 percent) voters. As in 2008, white support for Obama varies significantly by region and class. In seven states, all in the Deep South except for the Mormon Romney's stronghold of Utah, Obama wins less than 20 percent of the white vote, with the lowest registering at just 10 percent of Mississippi whites. In Washington, DC, and seven states, all in New England and the Northeast, except for his native Hawaii, Obama nets more than half of the white vote, including two thirds of Vermont's white voters. Although Obama's low support among older male working-class voters in Appalachia persists, his victory signals the growing importance of Hispanic, Asian, gay, and lesbian Americans and single white women, along with African Americans in the Democratic coalition. During his two election campaigns, Obama succeeds in building the "Rainbow Coalition" first promoted by Jesse Jackson in his historic 1984 and 1988 runs for the White House.[25]

up her findings, including reflecting on her own beneficial but "very hard" experiences as a student bused "two hours a day" to school in a "white," "wealthy community" in Iowa, where she grew up, Hannah-Jones says, "We want this to have been easy, and we gave up really fast.... There was really one generation of school desegregation."[24]

NOVEMBER 6, 2012 Making history once again, President Obama becomes the first African American elected to a second White House term when he defeats Republican Mitt Romney, the former governor of Massachusetts, by a margin of 51 to 47 percent. The results reflect a sharp

First Lady Michelle Obama greets students after performing *tai chi* with them at Chengdu No.7 High School in the SW province of Sichuan, China.

2013

JANUARY 21, 2013 Barack Obama is sworn in to a second term as president of the United States. "America's possibilities are limitless," he says in his inaugural address, "for we possess all the qualities that this world without boundaries demands: youth and drive; diversity and openness; an endless capacity for risk and a gift for reinvention." As President Obama retools his cabinet for the next four years, he retains Eric Holder as attorney general and appoints three African Americans to other top posts: Susan Rice as national security advisor, Anthony Foxx as secretary of transportation, and Jeh Johnson as secretary of homeland security.[26]

MARCH 13, 2013 A group of students at DePaul University releases a shareable interactive Web timeline tracking homicides in Chicago during January–February 2013, drawing attention to the problem of urban gun violence in America's major cities. In 2012, there were a devastating 506 homicides in the Windy City.[27]

Chicago police superintendent Garry McCarthy (right) offers the city's condolences to the family of Hadiya Pendleton, age fifteen, who performed in President Obama's inauguration festivities and later was killed in a Chicago park by a gunman not even aiming at her.

Four freed members of the Scottsboro Boys arrive in New York's Penn Station in 1937. It takes more than seventy-five years for the last of the Scottsboro Boys to be pardoned, posthumously.

APRIL 4, 2013 The Board of Alabama Pardons and Paroles votes unanimously to pardon, posthumously, Charles Weems, John Andy Wright, and Haywood Patterson, the last of the Scottsboro Boys, a group of nine black teenagers unjustly accused of raping two white women in 1931. Eight of the nine were convicted by all-white juries, while the case of the ninth ended in a mistrial. One official at the Board of Pardons says the case "remedied a wrongdoing of social and racial injustice," but others wonder why it has taken eighty-two years to clear the names of Weems, Wright, and Patterson.[28]

APRIL 29, 2013 In a *Sports Illustrated* cover story, NBA center Jason Collins becomes the first active male athlete in any of the four major American sports leagues to come out as gay. Public reaction is mostly, but not entirely, supportive. Collins, at age thirty-four and nearing the end of his career, will become the first openly gay

Jason Collins of the NBA "starts a conversation" on the cover of *Sports Illustrated*.

top: Representatives from the NAACP Legal Defense Fund stand in solidarity outside the US Supreme Court.
bottom: Protesters hold signs invoking the martyrs of Freedom Summer 1964 outside the US Supreme Court in advance of a hearing on voting rights.

athlete to play in a major American team event when the Nets sign him to a limited-term contract in February of the following year. "I didn't set out to be the first openly gay athlete playing in a major American team sport," Collins writes in a statement, echoing the WNBA's Sheryl Swoopes when she came out publicly in 2005. "But since I am, I'm happy to start the conversation."[29]

MAY 15, 2013 The late Jean-Michel Basquiat's painting *Dustheads* sells at a Christie's auction in New York for $48.8 million. Basquiat, who died in 1988 at age twenty-seven, began his career as a graffiti artist; this origin, as well as his frequent incorporation of controversial political messages about race and identity, made him a polarizing figure in the art world during his life, but his achievements as an artist are now widely recognized. "The everlasting power, relevance and integrity of his work have gradually identified him as the creative leader of his generation," says the critic Loic Gouzer in a Christie's press release. Gouzer goes on to declare Basquiat's *Dustheads,* which portrays two people high on PCP, as "perhaps the last great masterpiece to come to auction."[30]

JUNE 24, 2013 The US Supreme Court announces its decision in the case of *Fisher v. University of Texas,* in which white student Abigail Fisher was denied admission to the University of Texas at Austin under an admissions plan that considered race a factor. Fisher argued that UT's policies unfairly disadvantaged her in relation to black applicants in the pool. A district court and court of appeals sided with the university, and, in a 7–1 decision, the Supreme Court remands the case back to the lower courts, ruling that the appeals court failed to apply strict scrutiny to UT's policy. While the *Fisher* decision does not, as some supporters of affirmative action feared, end racial preferences at public universities, it does suggest a growing skepticism toward the form and scope of affirmative action programs.[31]

JUNE 25, 2013 The next day, in a 5–4 decision, the US Supreme Court strikes down part of the Voting Rights Act of 1965 in the case *Shelby County v. Holder*. The act required that state or local governments with a history of discriminatory voting practices obtain federal approval before making any changes to their election procedures. In the case before the Court, the government of Shelby County, Alabama, successfully argued that more recent data on voter participation by race did not support imposing additional scrutiny on the designated districts. Opponents of the decision, including the dissenting justices, worry that removing oversight will reverse the gains achieved under the 1965

act. The Justice Department, under Attorney General Eric Holder, expresses particular concern in light of ongoing attempts by a number of states to pass voter identification laws, which, in practice, will make it more difficult for disadvantaged citizens to cast ballots. Congressman and civil-rights-era veteran John Lewis, having been beaten on the Edmund Pettus Bridge in Selma in 1965, says of the *Shelby* decision: "The Supreme Court has struck a dagger in the heart of the Voting Rights Act, . . . the most powerful tool this nation has ever had to stop discriminatory voting practices from becoming law. Those justices were never beaten or jailed for trying to register to vote. They have no friends who gave their lives for the right to vote. I want to say to them, Come and walk in my shoes."[32]

JULY 11, 2013 The first season of Jenji Kohan's prison dramedy *Orange Is the New Black* pre-

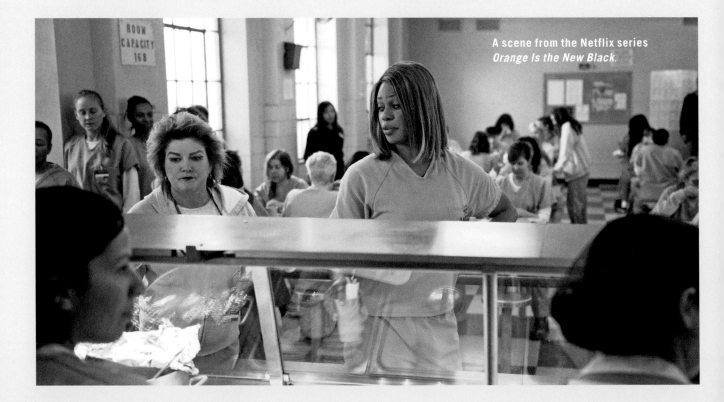

A scene from the Netflix series *Orange Is the New Black*.

mieres on the video streaming outlet Netflix. The critically acclaimed show, which mixes humor with a more serious examination of the criminal justice system, is also notable for turning public attention to the transgender African American actress Laverne Cox, who earns an Emmy nomination for her role on the show and becomes an activist for trans rights and awareness.[33]

JULY 26, 2013 *Fruitvale Station*, an independent film based on the last hours of Oscar Grant III, a twenty-two-year old unarmed black man shot by police at a BART rail station in Oakland, California, on New Year's Day 2009 (a tragedy captured in real time on witnesses' cell phones), premieres in theaters. The movie's director is African American filmmaker and Bay Area native Ryan Coogler, and it stars Michael B. Jordan as Grant, along with a strong supporting cast that includes Melonie Diaz and Academy Award winner Octavia Spencer. "The radicalism of 'Fruitvale Station' lies precisely . . . in its refusal to turn a man into a symbol," A.O. Scott writes in his review for the *New York Times*. "Nearly every black man, whether or not he is president, tends to be flattened out by popular culture and the psychopathology of everyday American life, rendered as an innocent victim, a noble warrior or a menace to society. There is a dehumanizing violence in this habit, a willed, toxic blindness that 'Fruitvale Station' at once exposes and resists." Among the numerous prizes *Fruitvale Station* receives are the Audience Award and Grand Jury Prize at the 2013 Sundance Film Festival.[34]

AUGUST 12, 2013 Attorney General Eric Holder announces the Justice Department's new Smart on Crime initiative, encouraging federal pros-

A man holds a banner honoring Oscar Grant in front of the Grand Lake Theater, Oakland, California. The film *Fruitvale Station*, showing inside, had sold out.

ecutors to use discretion in prosecuting drug offenses, especially in deciding whether to pursue charges that carry heavy mandatory minimum sentences. Holder maintains this will not only begin to rectify the problem of mass incarceration, especially in the black community, but that it will lead to more effective law enforcement. "By targeting the most serious offenses, prosecuting the most dangerous criminals, directing assistance to crime 'hot spots,' and pursuing new ways to promote public safety, deterrence, efficiency, and fairness," Holder affirms, "we can become both smarter and tougher on crime."[35]

SEPTEMBER 17, 2013 Glenn H. Hutchins, a Harvard alumnus and the founder of the private equity firm Silver Lake in New York, announces a $15 million gift to create the Hutchins Center for African & African American Research at Harvard University, with Professor Henry Louis Gates, Jr., as its inaugural director. It is believed to be the largest donation in history dedicated to the support of black studies in the United States, and will underwrite the formation of a center in Harvard Square that will

top: Oprah Winfrey receives the W. E. B. Du Bois Medal from Glenn H. Hutchins (left) and Professor Henry Louis Gates, Jr. (at the podium), with Harvard University president Drew Gilpin Faust (right) looking on, during a ceremony inside Memorial Hall, Cambridge, Massachusetts. bottom: Harvard professor Marcyliena Morgan teaches a class inside the Hutchins Center's Hiphop Archive and Research Institute, which she founded and oversees as executive director.

include an interconnected panoply of programs and initiatives, think tanks and art galleries, libraries and archives, teaching spots and conference rooms to advance understanding of the black world throughout the African diaspora. Among the center's anchors are the W. E. B. Du Bois Institute, the Cooper Gallery for African & African American Art (launched a year later), and the Hiphop Archive & Research Institute, which, on September 19, 2013, announces its new Nasir Jones Hiphop Fellowship, honoring one of the world's most dynamic songwriters, rappers, and actors. Hutchins, in discussing his

gift of the center in the *New York Times*, says that Professor Gates "is responsible for what I'll call the quattrocento of African American studies." Gates tells the *Times*, "As long as there's a Harvard, the study of people of African descent will have a place. . . . This is a perpetual part of Harvard. We have created something that has permanence."[36]

OCTOBER 8, 2013 The film *12 Years a Slave*, based on Solomon Northup's harrowing 1853 memoir recounting his kidnapping as a free black man in New York into bondage in Louisiana, pre-

top: A scene from *12 Years a Slave*, with Chiwetel Ejiofor as Solomon Northup kidnapped into bondage on a Louisiana plantation.

right: Director Steve McQueen holds up his Best Picture Oscar for *12 Years a Slave* with fellow producers Anthony Katagas, Jeremy Kleiner, Dede Gardner, and Brad Pitt.

mieres in theaters. The creation of the black British director Steve McQueen, its tactile, sensory realism represents a dramatic shift from Quentin Tarantino's postmodern spaghetti-western slave narrative from the previous year, *Django Unchained*, starring Jamie Foxx and Samuel L. Jackson. For many, *12 Years a Slave* is both a painful and cathartic theatergoing experience, with

the totality of slavery—from the confines of one man's perspective—depicted in the most vivid, often overwhelming way. The movie goes on to win Best Picture at the 2014 Academy Awards, the first time a film helmed by a black director receives the top prize. In addition, Lupita Nyong'o wins the award for Best Supporting Actress for her role as the sexually exploited plantation slave

Patsey, while the screenwriter John Ridley takes home honors for Best Adapted Screenplay. In her review for the *New York Times*, the critic Manohla Dargis applauds the movie for its refusal to sanitize the horrors of American slavery: "'12 Years a Slave' isn't the first movie about slavery in the United States," Dargis writes, "but it may be the one that finally makes it impossible for American cinema to continue to sell the ugly lies it's been hawking for more than a century."[37]

NOVEMBER 21, 2013 Musician and entrepreneur Pharrell Williams releases a twenty-four-hour music video of his catchy hit song "Happy," off the *Despicable Me 2* film soundtrack. The song soon becomes a global phenomenon, with fans paying creative homage to "Happy" on various social media sites. Williams goes on to win Producer of the Year at the 2014 Grammys, and in 2015, "Happy" is named Best Music Video and Best Pop Solo Performance.[38]

President Barack Obama prior to speaking at the memorial service for Nelson Mandela in South Africa.

DECEMBER 5, 2013 The revered anti-apartheid activist and former South African president Nelson Mandela dies in his home country at age ninety-five. President Obama, one of ninety-one world leaders to attend the memorial service in South Africa, delivers one of the eulogies at his funeral: "It took a man like [Mandela] to free not just the prisoner, but the jailer as well, to show that you must trust others so that they may trust you; to teach that reconciliation is not a matter of ignoring a cruel past, but a means of confronting it with inclusion and generosity and truth. He changed laws, but he also changed hearts." Observers point to the handshake between President Obama and Cuban leader Raúl Castro at the service as an important milestone in the thawing relationship between the two countries that culminates in the resumption of diplomactic relations in 2015.[39]

2014

FEBRUARY 27, 2014 At the White House, President Obama launches the My Brother's Keeper Initiative in response to the much-publicized crisis of too many young men of color following a school-to-prison pipeline. The five-year, $200 million program promises to provide young men with mentorships, jobs, and training in an effort to stem the tide of mass incarceration, but the efficacy of this effort remains to be seen, and it immediately attracts criticism for leaving out girls and women. Later in the year, on September 30, Obama follows up by announcing the similarly named My Brother's Keeper Community Initiative, in hopes of getting to a place where all children enter school emotionally, socially, and physically ready; that all children read at grade level by third grade; and that they graduate from high school, remain safe from violent crime, and go on to post-secondary education or, failing that, find employment. In his remarks at the White House on February 27, Obama recounts his encounter with the young men his new initiative is designed to help: "I could see myself in these young men. And the only difference is that I grew up in an environment that was a little bit more forgiving, so when I made a mistake the consequences were not as severe. I had people who encouraged me, not just my mom and grandparents, but wonderful teachers and community leaders, and they'd push me

President Obama introduces his *My Brother's Keeper Community Initiative* at the White House.

The Roots perform in New York's City Hall Park.

FEBRUARY 24, 2014 The Roots, a hip-hop band led by the acclaimed drummer and musical guru Questlove (born Ahmir Khalib Thompson in Philadelphia in 1971), becomes leader of the in-house band for *The Tonight Show* when comedian Jimmy Fallon takes over as host. The Roots have been with Fallon since he joined NBC's late-night lineup in 2009, but even with close to a thousand live shows under their belt, their nightly television performances catapult the band to a new level of visibility in American popular culture.

to work hard and study hard and make the most of myself. And if I didn't listen they said it again. And if I didn't listen they said it a third time. And they would give me second chances, and third chances. They never gave up on me, and so I didn't give up on myself. . . . I told these young men my story then, and I repeat it now because I firmly believe that every child deserves the same chances that I had."[40]

FEBRUARY 4, 2014 John W. Thompson, the sixty-three-year-old former CEO of Symantec Corporation, succeeds Bill Gates as chairman of Microsoft. "I don't know where you go after this," Charles King, an industry analyst, is quoted as saying on *TheRoot.com*. "He's a good man and a very able leader, and he should be exactly what Microsoft needs at this time."[41]

MARCH 9–JUNE 10 2014 Astrophysicist Neil deGrasse Tyson, director of the Hayden Planetarium in New York City, serves as presenter of the thirteen-episode documentary series *Cosmos: A Spacetime Odyssey* on the Fox network, a show intended to introduce sophisticated sci-

Award-winning physicist Neil deGrasse Tyson, host of the television series *Cosmos: A Spacetime Odyssey.*

entific concepts to a general audience. Tyson, who was inspired early in his career by a visit to Ithaca, New York, to meet Carl Sagan, the creator of the original 1980 *Cosmos,* is instrumental in bringing the series to television.[42]

APRIL 22, 2014 In *Schuette v. Coalition to Defend Affirmative Action,* the US Supreme Court rules 6–2 that the state of Michigan has the right to pass a constitutional amendment banning the use of race- or sex-based affirmative action in college admissions. The decision reverses a prior ruling by the Sixth US Court of Appeals. Justice Sonia Sotomayor pens a passionate dissent in the case, writing of the continuing significance of race in shaping the lives of individuals in America: "Race matters for reasons that really are only skin deep, that cannot be discussed any other way, and that cannot be wished away."[43]

APRIL 23, 2014 In its annual "50 Most Beautiful" issue, *People* magazine puts the Oscar winner Lupita Nyong'o at the top of the list, naming her the "Most Beautiful" of all. Though Nyong'o is not the first black woman to receive the honor, the choice is notable because unlike her predecessors, Halle Berry and Beyoncé, Nyong'o does not have the light complexion typically equated with beauty by both white and black Americans. Born to Kenyan parents in Mexico in 1983, Nyong'o speaks publicly about childhood self-image issues related to her dark skin: "I remember a time when I too felt unbeautiful. I put on the TV and only saw pale skin. I got teased and taunted about my night-shaded skin."[44]

APRIL 29, 2014 The NBA issues a lifetime ban on Los Angeles Clippers owner Donald Sterling after TMZ releases a recording in which Sterling is heard telling his mistress not to bring black guests to games. Two days earlier, Clippers players wore their uniforms inside-out during their pregame huddle as a protest against Sterling's comments. The ban effectively forces Sterling to sell the team, which Microsoft's CEO Steve Ballmer purchases for $2 billion in August.[45]

Protestors express their outrage over comments made by Los Angeles Clippers owner Donald Sterling.

MAY 8, 2014 Michael Sam, a former football player at the University of Missouri, becomes the first openly gay player to be drafted by the NFL when he is selected in the seventh round by the St. Louis Rams, leading to discussions about whether or not the NFL, with its heavily masculine culture, is ready to confront the weight of this change. Sam is ultimately cut from the Rams before regular-season play commences, but the conversation begun during his time on the team continues as Americans' increasing willingness to be open about their sexuality promises to bring more gay athletes into the spotlight.[46]

MAY 10, 2014 Kara Walker's art installation *A Subtlety, or the Marvelous Sugar Baby*, opens

A woman walks past an ad for Beats headphones outside an electronics store in Tokyo.

at the former site of the Domino sugar factory in Williamsburg, Brooklyn. Its centerpiece is a thirty-five-foot-tall sphinx figure coated in sugar and made in the image of a naked black

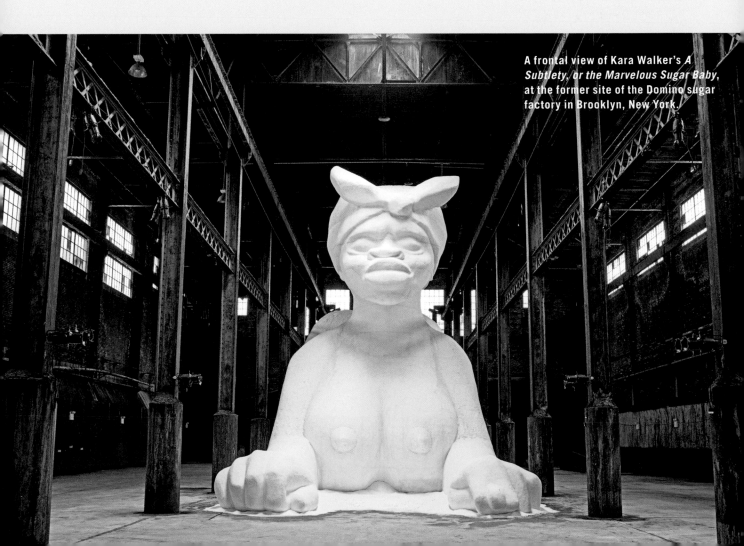

A frontal view of Kara Walker's *A Subtlety, or the Marvelous Sugar Baby*, at the former site of the Domino sugar factory in Brooklyn, New York.

"Mammy." Evoking the economic and sexual exploitation of black women, the exhibit attracts more than one hundred thousand visitors over the course of its two-month run.[47]

MAY 28, 2014 Dr. Dre and his business partner Jimmy Iovine sell Beats Electronics, maker of the popular "Beats by Dre" headphones, to Apple for $3 billion. The sale is the largest acquisition in Apple's history.[48]

JUNE 8, 2014 The theater star and acclaimed vocalist Audra McDonald becomes the first performer to win six Tony Awards for acting. In *Lady Day at Emerson's Bar and Grill*, the forty-three-year-old McDonald stars as the legendary blues singer Billie Holiday, who died in 1959 at

Maya Angelou smiles at the unveiling of her portrait at the National Portrait Gallery in Washington, DC, on April 5, 2014.

age forty-four. That summer, two black actors are cast in traditionally white Broadway leading roles: Norm Lewis as the Phantom of the Opera and Keke Palmer as the lead in Rodgers and Hammerstein's *Cinderella*. In accepting her statue, McDonald pays tribute to those who went before her: "I am standing on Lena Horne's shoulders. I am standing on Maya Angelou's shoulders. I am standing on Diahann Carroll and Ruby Dee and most of all, Billie Holiday."[49]

AUGUST 9, 2014 Michael Brown, an eighteen-year-old unarmed black man, is killed after a confrontation with white police officer Darren Wilson in Ferguson, Missouri. While witnesses claim Brown was retreating with his hands up when Wilson shot him, Wilson alleges he killed Brown in self-defense after Brown charged him. The shooting, one of several recent cases in which unarmed black men are killed by law enforcement, and a grand jury's failure to indict Wilson, inspires a massive protest movement in coming months. In the immediate aftermath of the killing, both peaceful protests and riots break out in Ferguson. Eventually, a state of emergency

Audra McDonald as Billie Holiday.

top: Norm Lewis and Sierra Boggess in Broadway's *The Phantom of the Opera*.
bottom: Legendary singer Valerie Simpson, of Ashford & Simpson, sings her hit song "I'm Every Woman" at the memorial service for Maya Angelou in New York's Riverside Church on September 12, 2014.

is declared and the National Guard is called in amid claims of excessive force and repression of peaceful protests by local police.[50]

AUGUST 25, 2014 Thirteen-year-old Mo'Ne Davis, the first female pitcher to earn a win in the Little League World Series, appears on the cover of *Sports Illustrated*. Davis, who is also the first girl to pitch a shutout in a Little League post-season game, is the first Little League player to appear on the magazine's cover.[51]

SEPTEMBER 30, 2014 *The African Americans: Many Rivers to Cross,* Henry Louis Gates's six-part, six-hour documentary film series tracing the full five-hundred-year sweep of African American history, wins the Emmy Award for Outstanding Historical Program, Long Form.

Tamika Staton leaves a personal message at a memorial to Michael Brown in Ferguson, Missouri.

Gates explains to The Root.com that the film, which aired on PBS in fall 2013, grew out of his desire "to show that black culture is inextricably intertwined with American culture" and "to provide a tool that teachers can use to enact the conversation about race every day in the classroom. Every day's gotta be Black History Month." In his review of *Many Rivers* for the *New Yorker,* Hilton Als writes, "What slave owners couldn't rip off or silence was the collective African-American voice, the stories people told not only to survive but so they could be remembered. Gates's magisterial series continues that tradition." It also wins the Peabody Award, the Alfred I. duPont-Columbia University Award, and an NAACP Image Award.[52]

NOVEMBER 4, 2014 Republicans win a significant victory in the midterm congressional elections, gaining sixteen seats in the House of Representatives and nine in the Senate, yielding them control of both houses of Congress. Two of the new Republicans are Mia Love of Utah, the first female black Republican to serve in Congress, and Tim Scott of South Carolina, who becomes the first African American senator from the South to be elected since Mississippi's Blanche K. Bruce left office in 1881. (In 1966 Edward Brooke, a Republican from Massachusetts, became the first African American elected to the US Senate since Blanche's term.) Exit polls suggest that the conservative Scott, a Tea Party favorite, secured just 10 percent of the African American vote and 88 percent of the white vote, with the vast majority of Palmetto State African Americans supporting Scott's black Democratic opponent. Also on Election Day, Proposition 47 passes in California, downgrading many felonies to misdemeanors in an attempt to relieve prison

Pitcher Mo'Ne Davis on the mound at the Little League World Series.

overcrowding and reduce rates of mass incarceration, particularly in minority communities.[53]

NOVEMBER 8, 2014 President Obama nominates Loretta Lynch, the U.S. attorney for New York's Eastern District, to succeed Eric Holder as attorney general, who announced his intention to resign his post in September. For months, Lynch's nomination is held up in the US Senate over Republication opposition to President Obama's executive action on immigration and legislative wrangling over an anti–human trafficking bill. Eventually, on April 23, 2015, Lynch, fifty-five, wins confirmation in a 56-43 vote, becoming the first African American woman to serve as the nation's top law enforcement official. At her swearing-in ceremony at the Justice

Mia Love, as mayor of Saratoga Springs, Utah, at the 2013 Conservative Political Action Conference.

Department on April 27, Lynch tells those gathered, "We are all just here for a time—whether in this building or even on this earth. But the values we hold dear will live on long after we have left this stage. Our responsibility, while we are here, is to breathe life into them; to imbue them with the strength of our convictions and the weight of our efforts. I know this can be done. Because I am here to tell you, if a little girl from North Carolina who used to tell her grandfather in the fields to lift her up on the back of his mule, so she could see 'way up high, Granddaddy,' can become the chief law enforcement officer of the United States of America, then we can do anything. We can imbue our criminal justice system with both strength and fairness, for the protection of both the needs of victims and the rights of all. We can restore trust and faith both in our laws and in those of us who enforce them. We can protect the most vulnerable among us from the scourge of modern-day slavery—so antithetical to the values forged in blood in this country. We can protect the growing cyber world. We can give those in our care both protection from terrorism and the security of their civil liberties. We will do this as we have accomplished all things both great and small—working together, moving forward, and using justice as our compass."[54]

A panel of former and current black US senators discuss their personal journeys and the nation's progress at a talk inside the Jefferson Building of the Library of Congress in Washington, DC: (from left to right) Rear Admiral Barry Black, the first African American to serve as senate chaplain; Carol Moseley Braun (Ill., 1993–2001), Roland Burris (Ill., 2009–2010), Tim Scott (S.C., 2013–present), William Cowan (Mass., 2013), and Cory Booker (N.J., 2013–present).

NOVEMBER 24–DECEMBER 20, 2014 Grand juries in Ferguson, Missouri, and Staten Island, New York, choose not to indict the police officers responsible for the deaths of, respectively, Michael Brown and Eric Garner, who died in July after being placed in what appears to have been an illegal chokehold during an arrest for selling untaxed cigarettes. In Ferguson, shops are burned and looted. Elsewhere, mostly peaceful protests are held over the next several days in more than 170 cities, including Toronto and London. Protests against police treatment of black men and women continue across America in 2015, organized under the rallying cry "Black Lives Matter," with networks of young activists leveraging an array of social media tools, from Twitter to Instagram, to communicate with one another and report directly from the front lines of the movement. Two of the most popular chants of the moment are "Hands Up Don't Shoot," a reference to the allegation that Brown had his hands up when Wilson shot him, and "We Can't Breathe," after Eric Garner's last words while being choked. While protesters continue to invoke the Brown and Garner cases, they increasingly shift their attention to wider goals involving the criminal justice system's treatment of minorities. In Brooklyn, New York, on December 20, events take a violent turn when a deranged gunman, vowing vengeance, travels up from Baltimore to assassinate two police offers while they are sitting, unaware, in their patrol car. The officers' identities—Wenjian Liu and Rafael Ramos—remind the country of the diversity of New York and further complicate the already tangled issue of police-community relations there. Addressing the situation in Ferguson back on November 24, President Obama offers these words: "We need to recognize that this is not just an issue for Ferguson; this is an issue for America. We have made enormous progress in race relations over the course of the past several decades. I've witnessed that in my own life. And to deny that progress I think is to deny America's capacity for change. . . . But what is also true is that there are still problems, and communities of color aren't just making these problems up. Separating that from this particular decision, there are issues in which the law too often feels as if it is being applied in discriminatory fashion. I don't think that's the norm. I don't think that's true for the majority of communities or the vast majority of law enforcement officials. But these are real issues. And we have to lift them up and not deny them or try to tamp them down. What we need to do is to understand them and figure out how do we make more progress. And that can be done." In a moving post in the *New Yorker* magazine that same night, "Chronic of a Riot Foretold," professor Jelani Cobb wonders what the Ferguson decision portends as the Obama presidency, just off a disappointing midterm election contest, moves toward its final quarter: "The man who once told us that there was no black America or white America but only the United States of America has become a President whose statements on unpunished racial injustices are a genre unto themselves. Perhaps it only seems contradictory that the deaths of Oscar Grant and Trayvon Martin, Ezell Ford and John Crawford and Michael Brown—all unarmed black men shot by men who faced no official sanction for their actions—came during the first black Presidency. Or perhaps the message here is that American democracy has reached the limits of its elasticity—that the symbolic empowerment of individuals, while the great many remain citizen-outsiders, is the best that we can hope for. The air last night, thick

Demonstrators call attention to the killing of Michael Brown outside the Greater St. Mark Family Church in St. Louis.

with smoke and gunfire, suggested something damning of the President." In March 2015, the U.S. Department of Justice, after conducting its own investigation of the events in Missouri, releases a 105-page report critical of the Ferguson Police Department, specifically that "Ferguson's law enforcement practices are shaped by the City's focus on revenue rather than by public safety needs. This emphasis on revenue," the Justice Department concludes, "has compromised the institutional character of Ferguson's police department, contributing to a pattern of unconstitutional policing, and has also shaped its municipal court, leading to procedures that raise due process concerns and inflict unnecessary harm on members of the Ferguson community." The report adds: "Further, Ferguson's police and municipal court practices both reflect and exacerbate existing racial bias, including racial stereotypes. Ferguson's own data establish clear racial disparities that adversely impact African Americans. The evidence shows that dis-

Marchers join hands in protesting the murder of Eric Garner in Staten Island, New York.

criminatory intent is part of the reason for these disparities. Over time," the report finds, "Ferguson's police and municipal court practices have sown deep mistrust between parts of the community and the police department, undermining law enforcement legitimacy among African Americans in particular." So far, the outcome of these and other incidents, including an expanding list of names of unarmed African Americans shot or killed by law enforcement, from Walter Scott in North Charleston, South Carolina, to Freddie Gray in Baltimore, Maryland, remains uncertain. What is clear is they have ignited an array of national and local reform movements as well as governmental actions demanding, among other solutions, increased accountability of police departments to their communities, stepped-up diversity hiring practices, police retraining and the implementation of body cameras, and greater—and more independent—oversight of cases involving the use of deadly force by police.[55]

DECEMBER 25, 2014 Against this backdrop, the film *Selma*, Ava DuVernay's account of the 1965 campaign led by Martin Luther King, Jr., to secure equal voting rights for African Americans, opens to widespread critical acclaim. At the film's premiere in New York City earlier in the month, the cast poses in "I Can't Breathe" T-shirts on the steps of the New York Public Library to show solidarity with the protests occurring throughout the city and country and, implicitly, to drive home the message that the work of the voting-rights campaign begun in Alabama a half century ago remains unfinished. Amid a flurry of

Movie poster, *Selma*.

film commentary, including debates over its portrayal of key players in the civil rights movement, especially the dynamic between King and President Johnson, *Selma* earns an Oscar nomination for best picture and for its signature song, "Glory," written and performed by Common and John Legend. In addition to the Oscar, *Selma* wins numerous other awards and is embraced as an anthem for the present moment and its connections to history.[56]

2015

JANUARY 7, 2015 The Fox network pilots *Empire,* a hip-hop-themed family drama that impresses critics and wins an instant audience, many of whom begin streaming and downloading original songs performed on the show. With its mix of new and established stars, including the Oscar-nominated actor Terrence Howard in the role of a record mogul seeking a successor within his family as he struggles with ALS, *Empire* is the creation of the black film director, Lee Daniels, who is quoted as saying in the *Washington Post*: "Right now we're seeing people enjoy the culture of America, the culture of the world. . . . We're showing real life now." One element of that real life is *Empire*'s exploration of homosexuality within black families, something Daniels, as a gay man, knows is critical. "Homophobia is rampant in the African American community, and men are on the DL [the so-called downlow]," Daniels points out. "So I wanted to blow the lid off more on homophobia in my community." After six weeks on air, *Empire* has nearly thirteen million viewers, with week-after-week growth among adults aged eighteen to forty-nine. "Don't have any new historical references for its post-premiere growth," a TV analyst tells *Entertainment Weekly*. "It has literally exceeded all Nielsen total viewer records to date."[57]

JANUARY 19, 2015 As President Obama faces the last two years of his historic White House administration, with encouraging signs that the economy is recovering from the recession that he encountered when he came into office, organizations involved in the Black Lives Matter movement issue calls to "reclaim MLK Day" by turning the commemoration into a time of nonviolent protest and civil disobedience in the tradition of the civil rights leader who, from Selma to Memphis and beyond, advanced the cause of human justice through radical, peaceful, nonviolent action. Resisting what these younger leaders call the "sanitizing" of Martin Luther King's legacy, armed with banners pairing King's eyes with those of the nation's recent black shooting victims, protesters vow, "From here on, MLK weekend will be known as a time of national resistance to injustice." Trying to make sense of the fifty years of history separating him from the slain leader he portrayed in the film *Selma,* the black British actor David Oyelowo says at a King Day celebration at King's Ebenezer Baptist

Church in Atlanta, "I only stepped into his shoes for a moment, but I asked myself, 'How did he do it?'" Part of the answer to the question, perhaps, can be found in the words King proclaimed at Brown's Chapel in Selma on January 2, 1965, the day he launched the historic voting-rights campaign that defined the decades cascading down from it: "If they refuse to register us . . . we will appeal to Governor Wallace. If he doesn't listen, we will appeal to the Legislature. If the Legislature doesn't listen, we will seek to arouse the Federal Government by marching by the thousands to the places of registration. We must be willing to go to jail by the thousands." Then, shifting his gaze to the future, King exhorted his listeners to believe: "When we get the right to vote . . . we will send to the State House not men who will stand in the doorways of universities to keep Negroes out but men who will uphold the cause of justice, and we will send to Congress men who will sign not a manifesto for segregation but a manifesto for justice."[58]

FEBRUARY 15, 2015 Journeying back to the Edmund Pettus Bridge in Selma, Alabama, fifty years on from the voting-rights campaign that left a permanent scar on his head, Representative John Lewis of Georgia, the former chair of the Student Nonviolent Coordinating Committee (SNCC), tells Bob Schieffer of CBS News, "I thought I was going to die on this bridge. I said to myself, 'This is the last protest for me.'" Then, putting the decades in between into perspective for younger audiences, Lewis adds, "I don't think as a group, we had any idea that our marching feet across that bridge would have such an impact 50 years later. If it hadn't been for that march across the Edmund Pettus Bridge on Bloody Sunday, there would be no Barack Obama as President of the United States of America."[59]

MARCH 7, 2015 On the fiftieth anniversary of "Bloody Sunday" in Selma, Alabama, President Obama addresses those who made the journey across time and space to return to the Edmund Pettus Bridge to chart the progress of a nation that, simultaneously, has worked hard to overcome racism while still being conflicted over race. With the fallout from Ferguson still weighing heavily on American minds (that same week, the US Justice Department released a report that sharply criticized the culture and practices of the Ferguson police department without bringing

President Barack Obama and Congressman John Lewis embrace on the fiftieth anniversary of the "Bloody Sunday" march in Selma, Alabama, on March 7, 2015.

federal charges against the officer responsible for the death of Michael Brown), the day offers the president an opportunity to address those who lived through—and courageously shaped—the history of the past fifty years as well as those in the rising generation who will determine how the next fifty years unfold.

"Because of campaigns like this, a Voting Rights Act was passed," he says, with John Lewis among those seated behind him on a stage fronting the Edmund Pettus Bridge. "Political and economic and social barriers came down. And the change these men and women wrought is visible here today in the presence of African Americans who run boardrooms, who sit on the bench, who serve in elected office from small towns to big cities; from the Congressional Black Caucus all the way to the Oval Office. . . . What a glorious thing, Dr. King might say. And what a solemn debt we owe. Which leads us to ask, just how might we repay that debt?

Turning to the present, President Obama shares these thoughts with the crowd. "First and foremost, we have to recognize that one day's commemoration, no matter how special, is not enough. If Selma taught us anything, it's that our work is never done. The American experiment in self-government gives work and purpose to each generation."

Implicit in his remarks is the Black Lives Matter campaign being waged in cities and towns across the country at that very hour. At the same time, President Obama urges those listening not to overlook—or forget—the progress that already has been by those who have gone before.

"We do a disservice to the cause of justice by intimating that bias and discrimination are immutable, that racial division is inherent to America. If you think nothing's changed in the past 50 years, ask somebody who lived through the Selma or Chicago or Los Angeles of the 1950s."

Then, balancing the record of progress at the Edmund Pettus Bridge against the difficult work that remains, the president makes clear, "Of course, a more common mistake is to suggest that Ferguson is an isolated incident; that racism is banished; that the work that drew men and women to Selma is now complete, and that whatever racial tensions remain are a consequence of those seeking to play the 'race card' for their own purposes. We don't need the Ferguson report to know that's not true. We just need to open our eyes, and our ears, and our hearts to know that this nation's racial history still casts its long shadow upon us."

The president concludes his remarks by looking to the future. "[E]verywhere in this country, there are first steps to be taken, there's new ground to cover, there are more bridges to be crossed. And it is you, the young and fearless at heart, the most diverse and educated generation in our history, who the nation is waiting to follow." It is both an invitation and a challenge that strikes at the heart of democracy itself. "Because Selma shows us that America is not the project of any one person. Because the single-most powerful word in our democracy is the word 'We.' 'We The People.' 'We Shall Overcome.' 'Yes We Can.' . . . That word is owned by no one. It belongs to everyone. . . . Fifty years from Bloody Sunday, our march is not yet finished, but we're getting closer."[60]

———————————

America's first black president and the nation he was twice elected to lead continue to confront the legacy of slavery and Jim Crow that led the civil rights generation to the Edmund Pettus Bridge in March 1965. And in the months that follow this anniversary celebration in Selma, violence against black bodies persists in unsettlingly frequent, and often horrifying, ways, from Baltimore, Maryland to North Charleston and Charleston, South Carolina, where, on a June evening, a twenty-one year-old white man, consumed with the anger and fear of white supremacy, guns down nine African Americans attending Bible study at the storied Emanuel A.M.E. Church, where, more than fifty years before, Dr. King came to preach on the importance of voting rights to the American Dream. Among those killed is the church's pastor, also a state senator, Clementa Pinckney, who, in a 2012 interview with Henry Louis Gates, Jr., cited the proverbial "Grandmother's Prayer" in discussing the imperative of black political participation: "Lord, let me be free. If not me, my children. If not my children, my children's children." The Charleston massacre, seen in part through the lens of contemporary debates on gun violence and the flying of the Confederate flag over the South Carolina capitol, also echoes the kind of terrorism visited on black churches throughout American history.[61]

What makes 2015 different, however, are the great strides the US, as a nation, and African Americans, as a people within that nation, have taken to strengthen citizenship, diversity, and equal opportunity as essential elements of our democracy, and of the broader human rights struggle. It is that history, as recounted in the preceding pages, that not only proves the lie of racism but provides truths and inspiration that this and all future generations will need to remain steadfast in overcoming the considerable challenges that remain.

———————

While this illustrated chronology ends where it began, in Selma, Alabama, fifty years after the voting-rights campaign opened up the road to the era that followed, the timeline of *Black America Since MLK* continues.

President Barack Obama delivers his inaugural address before a sea of witnesses at the US Capitol in Washington, DC, in 2009.

ENDNOTES

1965-1969

1. Martin Luther King, Jr., quoted in David J. Garrow, *Protest at Selma: Martin Luther King, Jr., and the Voting Rights Act of 1965* (New Haven: Yale University Press, 1980), 39; Diane Nash, "LBJ Doesn't Deserve Credit for Selma," *New Pittsburgh Courier*, February 9, 2015.

2. Morrie Turner's interview with the *San Francisco Chronicle* is quoted in his January 28, 2014, obituary in the *Washington Post.* For more on the significance of *Wee Pals*, see Jeff Chang, *Who We Be: The Colorization of America* (New York: St. Martin's Press, 2014), 17–34.

3. Roy Reed, "Alabama Victim Called a Martyr," *New York Times,* March 4, 1965.

4. Percy Sutton quoted in Peter Kihss, "Malcolm X Shot to Death at Rally Here," *New York Times*, February 22, 1965; King quoted in "Malcolm X Killed at N.Y. Meeting," *Chicago Daily Defender*, February 22, 1965; "Ossie Davis' Stirring Tribute to Malcolm X," *New York Amsterdam News*, March 6, 1965; Manning Marable, *Malcolm X: A Life of Reinvention* (New York: Penguin, 2011); Andy Newman and John Eligon, "Killer of Malcolm X is Granted Parole," *New York Times*, March 19, 2010; Geoff Bennett, "Questions Continue to Surround Death of Malcolm X," *NY1.com*, February 19, 2015.

5. Roy Reed, "Alabama Police Use Gas and Clubs to Rout Negroes," *New York Times*, March 7, 1965; Lyndon B. Johnson, "Speech before Congress on Voting Rights," March 15, 1965, online at the Miller Center at the University of Virginia: http://millercenter.org/president/speeches/speech-3386.

6. "Excerpts from Dr. King's Montgomery Address," *New York Times*, March 26, 1965.

7. The Moynihan Report, officially *The Negro Family: The Case for National Action,* by the US Department of Labor, Office of Policy Planning and Research (Washington: US Government Printing Office (1965); online at http://www.dol.gov/dol/aboutdol/history/webid meynihan.htm; "Daniel Patrick Moynihan Interview," *The First Measured Century,* with host/essayist Ben Wattenberg (PBS, 2000), online at www.pbs.org/fmc/interviews/moynihan.htm.

8. President Lyndon B. Johnson, "Commencement Address at Howard University: 'To Fulfill These Rights'," June 4, 1965, online at http://www.lbjlib.utexas.edu.

9. President Lyndon B. Johnson, "Remarks on the Signing of the Voting Rights Act (August 6, 1965)", online at http://millercenter.org/president/speeches/speech-4034; Jerry Cohen and William S. Murphy, *Burn, Baby, Burn!: The Los Angeles Race Riot, August 1965* (New York: Dutton, 1966); Art Peters, "Martin Luther King Jeered in L.A. as New Riots Threaten," *Philadelphia Tribune*, August 21, 1965.

10. Clive Barnes, "Dance: Nothing Less Than Superb," *New York Times*, December 18, 1965.

11. "'People Get Ready': Song Inspired by March on Washington Carries Enduring Message," National Public Radio, August 26, 2003, online at www.npr.org.

12. "Chicago Campaign (1966)", *Martin Luther King, Jr. and the Global Freedom Struggle* ("The King Encyclopedia"), Martin Luther King, Jr. Research and Education Institute at Stanford University, online at http://kingencyclopedia.stanford.edu/encyclopedia/encyclopedia_contents.html.

13. Felicia Ann Kornbluh, *The Battle for Welfare Rights: Politics and Poverty in Modern America* (Philadelphia: University of Pennsylvania Press, 2007), note 116 on p. 214; "Groups: National Welfare Rights Organization," *Eyes on the Prize: America's Civil Rights Movement 1954-1985* (PBS Online/WGBH, 1997-2006), online at http://www.pbs.org/wgbh/amex/eyesontheprize/profiles/47_nwro.html.

14. Clayborne Carson, *In Struggle: SNCC and the Black Awakening of the 1960s* (Cambridge, MA: Harvard University Press, 1981), 209–10.

15. "Fantastic Four Vol. 1 52," *Marvel Database*, at http://marvel.wikia.com/Fantastic_Four_Vol_1_52; Laura Bradley, "Everything You Need to Know about the Black Panther, Marvel's New Lead Superhero," *Slate.com*, October 31, 2014.

16. *Chicago Daily Defender*, August 30, 1966. For a profile of Jesse Jackson's early years in Chicago, see David Llorens, "Apostle of Economics," *Ebony*, August 1967, 78–80, 84–86.

17. Kathleen N. Cleaver, "Newton, Huey P.," in *African American National Biography*, ed. Henry Louis Gates, Jr., and Evelyn Brooks Higginbotham, Oxford African American Studies Center, online at http://www.oxfordaasc.com/article/opr/t0001/e0423.

18. Keith A. Mayes, *Kwanzaa: Black Power and the Making of the African-American Holiday Tradition* (New York: Routledge, 2009).

19. Amiri Baraka, "Black Art", in *The Norton Anthology of African American Literature,* eds. Henry Louis Gates, Jr., Nellie Y. McKay, et al. (New York and London: W. W. Norton & Company, 1997), p. 1883.

20. Larry Neal, "The Black Arts Movement," *Drama Review* 12 (Summer 1968): 29–39.

21. Carroll Kilpatrick, "White House Tribute Paid to First Medic to Win Medal of Honor in Vietnam," *Washington Post*, March 10, 1967; Meg Smith, "African American Men: Moments in History from Colonial Times to the Present," online at http://www.washingtonpost.com/wp-srv/metro/interactives/blackmen/chronologyblackmen.html; *Philadelphia Tribune*, "See Tan Casualties Even Higher," August 27, 1966.

22. Douglas Robinson, "Dr. King Proposes a Boycott of War," New York Times, April 5, 1967; Rev. Dr. Martin Luther King, Jr., "A Time to Break Silence (4 April 1967)." Oxford African American Studies Center, http://www.oxfordaasc.com/article/doc/ps-aasc-0291.

23. Robert Lipsyte, "Clay Refuses Army Oath; Stripped of a Boxing Crown," *New York Times*, April 29, 1967; Jackie Robinson, "Tragic Episode in Sports: The Ordeal of Muhammad Ali," *Philadelphia Tribune*, October 10, 1967.

24. Phyl Newbeck, *Virginia Hasn't Always Been for Lovers: Interracial Marriage Bans and the Case of Richard and Mildred Loving* (Carbondale, IL: Southern Illinois University Press, 2008), online at www.law.cornell.edu/supremecourt/text/388/1.

25. Sidney Fine, *Violence in the Model City: The Cavanagh Administration, Race Relations, and the Detroit Riot of 1967* (East Lansing: Michigan State University Press, 2007).

26. Rusty Restuccia, "The Pioneers: The Men," *A History of African-American New Car Dealers* (Ann Arbor, MI: Rustic Enterprise, 2008), online at http://www.aacardealers.com/men.html.

27. "King Calls for Massive Protests," *Washington Post*, August 16, 1967; Andrew Kopkind, "Soul Power," *New York Review of Books*, August 24, 1967.

28. Robert C. Albright, "Senate Confirms Marshall, 69–11, for High Court," *Washington Post*, August 31, 1967.

29. Stokely Carmichael and Charles V. Hamilton, *Black Power* (New York: Random House, 1967), 44; Fred Powledge, "A Slogan, a Chant, a Threat," *New York Times*, December 10, 1967.

30. "Singer Is Feared Dead in Air Crash," *New York Times,* December 11, 1967. Jann S. Wenner, "Otis Redding: The Crown Prince of Soul Is Dead," *Rolling Stone,* January 20, 1968.

31. Jack Bass and Jack Nelson, *The Orangeburg Massacre*, 2nd ed. (Macon, GA: Mercer University Press, 2002); http://www.orangeburgmassacre1968.com.

32. The full text of the Kerner Commission can be found online at http://historymatters.gmu.edu/d/6545.

33. Charlayne Hunter, "Mr. and Mrs. Yesterday," *New York Times*, March 24, 1968.

34. David Levering Lewis, *King: A Biography* (Urbana: University of Illinois Press, 2013); "Coretta King: Remarkable Woman," *New York Amsterdam News*, April 13, 1968.

35. Gregory Lewis, "Say It Loud, I'm Black and I'm Proud," *Sun Sentinel* (Fort Lauderdale, FL), August 10, 2008.

36. "Angela Davis Tribute to Charlene Mitchell," delivered at the Black Women and the Radical Tradition conference at the Graduate Center for Worker Education of Brooklyn College (2009), online at http://vimeo.com/10354190.

37. "A Museum Is Born in Harlem," *New York Amsterdam News*, September 21, 1968.

38. Met Opera Finals Held," *New York Amsterdam News*, November 23, 1968; *New York Amsterdam News*, "American Soprano Wins Competition in Munich," October 12, 1968; Paul Hume, "Postlude: Miss Norman Seems Headed for Distinguished Career," *Washington Post*, December 30, 1968; "Jessye Norman: Concert and Opera Singer," *Trustee Roster & Biographies,* Howard University Office of the Secretary, online at http://www.howard.edu/secretary/trustees/bios/norman.htm.

39. F. Erik Brooks, "Congressional Black Caucus," in Larry J. Sabato and Howard R. Ernst, *Encyclopedia of American Political Parties and Elections* (New York: Facts On File, Inc., 2006), *American History Online* (Facts On File, Inc.), online at http://www.fofweb.com/History/MainPrintPage.asp?iPin=EAPPE0077&DataType=AmericanHistory&WinType=Free.

40. Bob Pool, "Witness to 1969 UCLA Shooting Speaks at Rally," *Los Angeles Times,* January 18, 2008.

41. Alex Poinsctt, "The Quest for a Black Christ," *Ebony*, March 1969, 170–78.

42. James Barron, "Working to Revive a Movie House That Lived in a Palace," *New York Times*, June 21, 2013.

43. Tom Wicker, *A Time to Die: The Attica Prison Revolt* (Chicago: Haymarket Press, 2011).

44. "Retailing: Soul Stamps," *Time*, July 11, 1969.

45. *Billboard*, August 2, 1969; *New Journal and Guide*, December 20, 1969.

46. Gene Robertson, "Gordon Parks and His 'Learning Tree,'" *Sun-Reporter*, August 9, 1969.

47. John Murph, "Why We Should Celebrate Woodstock," *TheRoot.com*, August 14, 2009.

48. Ward Churchill and Jim Vander Wall, *The COINTELPRO Papers: Documents from the FBI's Secret Wars against Dissent in the United States* (Boston: South End Press, 2002).

49. "RS48: Miles Davis" (December 13, 1969), 1969 *Rolling Stone* Covers, online at http://www.rollingstone.com/music/pictures/1969-rolling-stone-covers-20040506/rs48-miles-davis-41660493; Langdon Winner, "Bitches Brew," *Rolling Stone* May 28, 1970; "95. Mile Davis, 'Bitches Brew,' *500 Greatest Albums of All Time, Rollingstone.com*, May 31, 2012, online at http://www.rollingstone.com/music/lists/500-greatest-albums-of-all-time-20120531/miles-davis-bitches-brew-20120524; Leonard Feather, "Miles Davis: Ahead or Rocking Back?," *Los Angeles Times* May 17, 1970; Paul Tingen, "Miles Davis and the Making of Bitches Brew: Sorcerer's Brew," *JazzTimes*, May 2001; "Miles Davis Biography," The Rock and Roll Hall of Fame and Museum, Inc. (2015), online at https://rockhall.com/inductees/miles-davis.

1970–1974

1. Hollie I. West, "The Author: Maya Angelou," *Washington Post*, April 3, 1970.

2. "The Black Mood: More Militant, More Hopeful, More Determined," *Time*, April 6, 1970.

3. Roland Forte, "If You're in New York You Must See 'Purlie,'" *Call and Post*, June 27, 1970.

4. "University Race-Sensitive Admissions Programs Are Not Helping Black Students Who Most Need Assistance," *The Journal of Blacks in Higher Education* (2007), online at http://www.jbhe.com/news_views/56_race_sensitive_not_helping.html; Paul Bass and Doug Rae, "The Panther and the Bulldog: The Story of May Day 1970," *Yale Alumni Magazine* (July/August 2006), online at http://archives.yale-alum nimagazine.com/issues/2006_07/panthers.html; Alex Harris, "May Day 1970: Yale on Strike" (Text and photo essay), *AlexHarris.com*, online at http://alex harris.com/photography/may-day-1970/1; Henry Louis Gates, Jr., and Cornel West, *The Future of the Race* (reprint) (New York: Vintage, 1997), 4.

5. "Black Women Are at Last Getting Break in Hollywood, Actress Says," *Philadelphia Tribune*, June 30, 1970.

6. Barbara Davis, "FBI Nabs Angela Davis," *Sun-Reporter*, October 17, 1970.

7. Albert Murray, *The Omni-Americans* (New York: Outerbridge and Dientsfrey, 1970).

8. Benjamin Chavis, "Prophetic Genius of Gil Scott Heron," *New Pittsburgh Courier*, June 1, 2011.

9. Agis Salpukas, "G.M. Elects First Negro as Member of Its Board," *New York Times*, January 5, 1971.

10. Dave Marsh, "Frazier Outpoints Ali and Keeps the Title," *New York Times*, March 9, 1971; Graham Houston, "Ten Historic Fights in Boxing History," *ESPN.com*, February 3, 2008.

11. The Associated Press, "Whitney Young Jr. Dies on Visit to Lagos," *New York Times*, March 12, 1971; The Associate Press, "Thousands Here Pay Tribute to Whitney Young Jr.," *New York Times*, March 16, 1971; "Vernon Jordan Named by Urban League as Young's Successor," *Chicago Daily Defender*, June 16, 1971; http://nul.iamempowered.com/who-we-are/mission-and-history

12. "Romare Bearden: The Prevalence of Ritual," Press Release No. 38 (March 25, 1971), The Museum of Modern Art, online at https://www.moma.org/moma.org/shared/pdfs/docs/press_archives/4609/releases/MOMA_1971_0046_38.pdf?2010; "Black Emergency Cultural Coalition Records, 1971-1984: Overview: Biographical/Historical Information," The New York Public Library: Archives & Manuscripts, online at http://archives.nypl.org/scm/20908.

13. Richard Kluger, *Simple Justice: The History of Brown v. Board of Education and Black America's Struggle for Equality* (New York: Vintage, 2011), 763.

14. Derrick Bell, *And We Are Not Saved: The Elusive Quest for Racial Justice* (New York: Basic Books, 1989), 172; "Palmer v. Thompson: Historic Case," Center for Constitutional Rights (2007), online at http://ccrjustice.org/ourcases/past-cases/palmer-v.-thompson.

15. Donald Bogle, *Toms, Coons, Mulattoes, Mammies, and Bucks: An Interpretive History of Blacks in American Film* (New York: Continuum, 1989), 238.

16. Tom Wicker, *A Time to Die* (New York: Quadrangle/New York Times Book Co., 1975); Gary Craig, Shawn Dowd, and Rich Kellman, "Attica Prison Riot: Memories Strong after 40 Years," *Democratandchronicle.com/WGRZ/com* (Rochester, NY), 2011, online at http://roc.democratandchronicle.com/section/attica.

17. "Lakers' Legendary Season Leads to Elusive Title," *NBA Encyclopedia: Playoff Edition, NBA.com* (2015), online at http://www.nba.com/history/finals/197 11972.html; "NBA All-Time Rebounds Leaders: Career Totals in the Regular Season," *LandofBasketball.com* (as of June 5, 2015), online at http://www.landofbasketball.com/all_time_leaders/rebounds_total_career_season.htm; Florence Mal, "Wilt Sets NBA Rebound Mark as Lakers Breeze," *Los Angeles Times* January 31, 1972.

18. Dave Heaton, "Country Music Ain't Black & White: 'Hidden in the Mix,'" *Popmatters.com,* June 30, 2013, online at http://www.popmatters.com/column/172627-country-music-aint-black-white-hidden-in-the-mix.

19. Andrew O'Hehir, "Shirley Chisholm, the Democrats' Forgotten Hero," *Salon.com,* September 9, 2012, online at http://www.salon.com/2012/09/09/shirley_chisholm_the_democrats_forgotten_hero./.

20. "Milestones: The National Black Political Convention (1972)," *Eyes on the Prize: America's Civil Rights Movement 1954-1985* (PBS Online/WGBH, 1997-2006), online at http://www.pbs.org/wgbh/amex/eyesontheprize/milestones/m13_nbpc.html.

21. "Equal Employment Opportunity Act of 1972" (March 24, 1972), *EEOC 35th Anniversary Website, EEOC.gov* (2000), online at http://www.eeoc.gov/eeoc/history/35th/thelaw/eeo_1972.html.

22. Alma Thomas quoted in Paul Richards, "First Solo Show at 77: A Joyful Colorist," *The Washington Post, Times Herald,* April 28, 1972.

23. President William J. Clinton, "Remarks by the President: In Apology for Study Done in Tuskegee," *The White House: Office of the Press Secretary,* May 16, 1997, online at http://clinton4.nara.gov/textonly/New/Remarks/Fri/19970516-898.html; James H. Jones, *Bad Blood: The Tuskegee Syphilis Experiment* (New York: Free Press, 1981); "The Tuskegee Timeline," Centers for Disease Control and Prevention, *CDC.gov* (September 24, 2013), online at http://www.cdc.gov/tuskegee/timeline.htm.

24. "Sammy Davis Jr. to Headline Expo Revue," *Chicago Daily Defender,* September 28, 1972.

25. John A. Jackson, *House on Fire: The Rise and Fall of Philadelphia Soul* (New York: Oxford University Press, 2004), ix; Mark Anthony Neal, "Who Owns the (Philadelphia) Soul of Black Music?", *TheRoot.com,* February 19, 2014, online at http://www.theroot.com/articles/culture/2014/02/black_owned_philadelphia_international_records_remaining_songs_sold.html.

26. "Excerpts from the Message by Governor Rockefeller on the State of the State," *New York Times,* January 4, 1973; Brian Mann, "The Drug Laws that Changed How We Punish," *North Country Public Radio,* February 14, 2013, online at http://www.npr.org/2013/02/14/171822608/the-drug-laws-that-changed-how-we-punish; Jon Fasman, "America's Prison Population: Who, What, Where and Why," *The Economist,* March 13, 2014, online at http://www.economist.com/blogs/democracyinamerica/2014/03/americas-prison-population.

27. Bill Kovachs, "New Unit to Fight for Child Rights," *New York Times,* May 23, 1973.

28. Jane Fritsch, "Tom Bradley, Mayor in Era of Los Angeles Growth, Dies," *New York Times*, September 30, 1998.

29. *The History Detectives,* "Birthplace of Hip Hop," originally airing on PBS on August 10, 2009; transcript online at http://www-tc.pbs.org/opb/historydetectives/static/media/transcripts/2011-05-21/611_hiphop.pdf; Angus Batey, "Grand Wizard Theodore Accidentally Invents Scratching (Or Does He?)," *The Guardian,* June 12, 2011, online at http://www.theguardian.com/music/2011/jun/13/grand-wizard-invents-scratching; Zack O'Malley Greenburg, "The Man Who Invented Hip-Hop," *Forbes.com,* July 9, 2009, online at http://www.forbes.com/2009/07/09/afrika-bambaataa-hip-hop-music-business-entertainment-cash-kings-bambaataa.html.

30. Drew Desilver, "Black Unemployment Rate Is Consistently Twice That of Whites," *FactTank: News in the Numbers,* Pew Research Center, August 21, 2013, online at at http://www.pewresearch.org/fact-tank/2013/08/21/through-good-times-and-bad-black-unemployment-is-consistently-double-that-of-whites/; "Spotlight on Statistics: African American History Month," US Department of Labor, Bureau of Labor Statistics, February 2010, online at http://www.bls.gov/spotlight/2010/african_american_history/data.htm#figure07_unemployment_rate.

31. "Atlanta Installs Black Mayor, 35," *New York Times,* January 8, 1974; Derek T. Dingle, "Maynard Jackson: The Ultimate Champion for Black Business," *Black Enterprise,* February 10, 2009.

32. Dave Anderson, "Ali Beats Frazier on Decision Here," *New York Times,* January 29, 1974.

33. Mike Connolly, director, *Killing Me Softly: The Roberta Flack Story* (Alleycats TV, 2014).

34. Ayana Byrd and Lori Tharps, *Hair Story: Untangling the Roots of Black Hair in America* (New York: St. Martin's Press), 64.

35. A.H. Weiler, "Pam Grier Typed as 'Foxy Brown,'" *New York Times,* April 6, 1974; Linda Gross, review of *Foxy Brown, Los Angeles Times,* April 15, 1974; Mary Murphy, "Pam's Stranglehold on Violent Roles," *Los Angeles Times,* January 4, 1976.

36. William Leggett, "A Tortured Road to 715," *Sports Illustrated,* May 28, 1973; Rick Perlstein, *The Invisible Bridge: The Fall of Nixon and the Rise of Reagan* (Simon & Schuster, 2014), 225–31.

37. Bart Landry, *The New Black Middle Class* (Berkeley: University of California Press, 1988).

38. *Milliken v. Bradley,* 418 U.S. 717 (1974).

39. Sam Goldpaper, "Robertson Ends Career," *New York*

Times, September 4, 1974; Michael Mink, "Basketball Teams Could Count on Oscar Robertson," *Investor's Business Daily*, February 24, 2010.

40. Vijay Prashad,. *Everybody Was Kung Fu Fighting:*

Afro-Asian Connections and the Myth of Cultural Purity (Boston: Beacon Press, 2001); Henry Edwards, "Disco Dancers Are Back, and the Kung Fu Has Got Them," *New York Times*, December 29, 1974.

1975–1979

1. William L. Van Deburg, ed., *Modern Black Nationalism: From Marcus Garvey to Louis Farrakhan* (New York: New York University Press, 1996).

2. Robert S. Lindsey, "A Cookie Transforms an Agent into a Star," *New York Times*, August 16, 1975.

3. Dena Kleiman, "The 'Hustle' Restores Old Touch to Dancing," *New York Times*, July 12, 1975.

4. Angela Davis, "Joan Little: The Dialectics of Rape" (1975), *Ms. Magazine,* Spring 2002, online at http://www.msmagazine.com/spring2002/davis.asp.

5. "Frazier Is Declared Unable to Continue: Ali's Shots Crumple 'Armored Division,'" *Washington Post,* October 1, 1975.

6. Andrew J. DeRoche, *Andrew Young: Civil Rights Ambassador* (Wilmington, DE: Scholarly Resources, 2003).

7. Lesli A. Maxwell, "U.S. Schools Become 'Majority-Minority'," *Education Week,* August 20, 2014, online at http://www.edweek.org/ew/articles/2014/08/20/01demographics.h34.html.

8. Eric Neel, "The Day the Dunk Was Born," *ESPN Page 2*, February 17, 2006.

9. "'Welfare Queen' Becomes Issue in Reagan Campaign," *New York Times*, February 15, 1976; Rick Perlstein, *The Invisible Bridge*, 603.

10. Ronald P. Formisano, *Boston against Busing: Race, Class, and Ethnicity in the 1960s and 1970s* (Chapel Hill: University of North Carolina Press, 2004).

11. Toni Morrison, "A Slow Walk of Trees (as Grandmother Would Say) Hopeless (as Grandfather Would Say)," *New York Times*, July 4, 1976.

12. Full text of speech delivered by Barbara Jordan at the Democratic National Convention (1976), online at http://www.oxfordaasc.com/article/doc/ps-aasc-0560. For the ranking of the speech, see http://gos.sbc.edu/top100.html.

13. Mel Gussow, "Stage: 'Colored Girls' Evolves," *New York Times,* September 16, 1976; "Ringgold, Faith (Elizabeth): Bibliography and Exhibitions," *African American Visual Artists Database,* online at http://aavad.com/artistbibliog.cfm?id=215.

14. "Jerry Lawson, Inventor of Modern Game Console, Dies at 70," *Wired,* April 11, 2011, online at http://www.wired.com/2011/04/jerry-lawson-dies/; *Fairchild Annual Report to Employees 1976,* Fairchild Camera and Instrument Corporation, April 1977, online at http://fndcollectables.com/CHANNEL_F_INFO/U_S_/TimeLine/fairannualreport76.pdf; "Biographical Note: Finding Aid to the Gerald A. ("Jerry") Lawson Papers, 1967-1994," *Brian Sutton-Smith Library and Archives of Play,* December 2013, online at www.museumofplay.org.

15. "United States Elections: How Groups Voted in 1976," Roper Center, University of Connecticut, online at http://www.ropercenter.uconn.edu/polls/us-elections/how-groups-voted/how-groups-voted-1976/.

16. J. Wynn Rousuck, "Pauli Murray: The First Episcopal Priest has Spent a Lifetime Doing What Others Got Around to Later," *The Sun*, April 24, 1977.

17. Wayne King, "Andrew Jackson Young, Jr.," *New York Times*, December 17, 1976; Clifford Alexander, "Colin Powell's Promotion: The Real Story," *New York Times,* December 23, 1997.

18. Joseph D. Whitaker, "Alex Haley Says 'Roots' Helped Dispel Myths," *Washington Post*, February 24, 1977. Luchina Fisher, "'Roots': Where Are They Now?" ABC News, November 7, 2013.

19. "Combahee River Collective Statement (1977)," *Oxford African American Studies Center*, online at http://www.oxfordaasc.com/article/doc/ps-aasc-0365; "Combahee River Collective" *Off Our Backs* 9 (June 30, 1979): 6; "Black, Feminist, Revolutionary Remembering the Combahee River Collective," *Ebony*, April 21, 2014.

20. Paul E. Masters, "Carter and the Rhodesian Problem," *International Social Science Review* 75, no. 3/4 (2000): 23–33.

21. Joseph Lelyveld, "Off Color," *New York Times*, November 6, 1977.

22. Bruce Bartlett, "How to End the Supreme Court Appointments Battle," *Forbes.com*, August 7, 2009.

23. "Reggie Candy Bar Makes Debut over a Week Late," *Wall Street Journal*, April 14, 1978.

24. Zack O'Malley Greenburg, "The Man Who Invented Hip-Hop," *Forbes.com,* July 9, 2009; Mark Caro, "Founding House Fathers to Reunite at the Riviera," *Chicago Tribune*, June 29, 1990; Greg Kot, "The Mixmaster," *Chicago Tribune*, October 10, 1991; Jody Rosen, "A Rolling Shout-Out to Hip-Hop History," *New York Times*, February 12, 2006.

25. Judy Klemesrud, "Planned Parenthood's New Head Takes a Fighting Stand," *New York Times*, February 3, 1978.

26. "Spinks Dethrones Ali," *Los Angeles Times,* February 16, 1978; Dave Brady, "Spinks Word on Ali: 'He's Still the Greatest,'" *Washington Post,* February 17, 1978; Alan Goldstein, "Champion Wins Title for Record 3rd Time," *The Sun,* September 16, 1978.

27. William Julius Wilson, "Poor Blacks' Future," *New*

York Times, February 28, 1978; William Julius Wilson, "*The Declining Significance of Race*: Revisited & Revised," *Daedalus* 140, no. 2 (2011): 55–69; William Julius Wilson, *The Declining Significance of Race: Blacks and Changing American Institutions,* 3rd ed. (Chicago: University of Chicago Press, 2012).

28. Allison Pond, "A Portrait of Mormons in the U.S.," *Pew Research Center's Forum on Religion & Public Life,* July 24, 2009, online at http://www.pewforum.org/2009/07/24/a-portrait-of-mormons-in-the-us/.

29. J. Harvie Wilkinson III, *From* Brown *to* Bakke*: The Supreme Court and School Integration, 1954–1978* (New York: Oxford University Press, 1981).

30. *Regents of the University of California v. Bakke* 435 U.S. 265 (1978), at 327–328.

31. Dhyana Ziegler, "Max Robinson, Jr.: Turbulent Life of a Media Prophet," *Journal of Black Studies* 20, no. 1 (September 1989): 97–112, at 100.

32. Andrew Brimmer, "The Humphrey-Hawkins Bill," *Black Enterprise,* March 1978, 55.

33. For the response to Wallace's *Black Macho,* see "The Black Sexism Debate," *Black Scholar* 10, no. 8/9 (May/June 1979).

34. Seth Davis, *When March Went Mad: The Game That Transformed Basketball* (New York: Times Books, 2009); Seth Davis, "Johnson Vs. Bird and the Dawn of March Madness," *NPR Books,* March 16, 2009, online at http://www.npr.org/templates/story/story.php?storyId=101967585.

35. "A Billion Dollar Baby," *Black Enterprise,* June 1979, 140–53.

36. "Jennie Patrick: Pioneering Chemical Engineer," *The History Makers,* April 10, 2013, online at http://www.thehistorymakers.com/news/jennie-patrick-pioneering-chemical-engineer; Patricia E. White, *Women and Minorities in Science and Engineering: An Update* (Washington, D.C.: National Science Foundation, 1992), NSF-92-303, online at www.eric.ed.gov.

37. David Yellin, "The Black English Controversy: Implications from the Ann Arbor Case," *Journal of Reading* 24, no. 2 (November 1980), 150–154.

38. Joe Lapointe, "The Night Disco Went Up in Smoke," *New York Times,* July 4, 2009.

39. Jim Fusilli, "How Jackson Did It," *Wall Street Journal,* July 1, 2009.

40. Kendall Wilson, "Hazel Johnson Is First Black Woman General," *Philadelphia Tribune,* June 8, 1971.

41. "Questlove's Top 50 Hip-Hop Songs of All Time," *RollingStone.com,* December 17, 2012, online at http://www.rollingstone.com/music/lists/questloves-top-50-hip-hop-songs-of-all-time-20121217.

42. V. P. Franklin, "Bethune Museum and Archives," *Black Women in America,* 2nd ed., ed. Darlene Clark Hine, Oxford African American Studies Center online at http://www.oxfordaasc.com/article/opr/t0003/e0027.

1980–1984

1. Peter Richmond, "Bob Johnson of BET/Standing at the Crossroads of Cable TV," *Washington Post,* December 7, 1980.

2. Matt Meltzer, "The Arthur McDuffie Riots of 1980," in *Miami: Local News, Miami Beach 411,* August 12, 2007, online at http://www.miamibeach411.com/news/mcduffie-riots.

3. William Raspberry, **"**Reagan's Race Legacy," *Washington Post,* June 14, 2004.

4. "Holmes Batters Ali Helpless in 11," *Hartford Courant,* October 3, 1980; George Vecsey, "Berbick Defeats Ali on Decision," *New York Times,* December 11, 1981; "Ali Retires with Laughs, a Few Tears," *The Sun,* December 13, 1981.

5. Andy Edelstein, "On TV at 19, He Leaves Them Laughing," *New York Times,* March 1, 1981.

6. Herbert H. Denton, "A Different Look at Old Problems," *Washington Post,* December 15, 1980.

7. "Blacks Disappointed with Reagan," *New Pittsburgh Courier,* September 19, 1981.

8. Greg Tate quoted in Franklin Sirmans, "*In the Cipher*: Basquiat and Hip-Hop Culture," in *Basquiat,* ed. Marc Mayer (London and New York: Merrell, 2005), 94; Clayton Perry, "Greg Tate: A Famed Journalist on Why Hip-Hop Will Never Die," *AllHipHop.com,* April 15, 2012.

9. Michael Hirsley, "21 Share $4 Million in MacArthur Awards," *Chicago Tribune,* May 19, 1981; Dick Davies, "Scholar's Windfall to Continue Projects," *New York Times,* June 7, 1981.

10. Frank Rich, "Stage: 'Dreamgirls,' Michael Bennett's New Musical, Opens," *New York Times,* December 21, 1981.

11. *Black Enterprise,* "25 Years of Black Economic Empowerment," June 1997, 90.

12. Jamie Gold, "Debbie Allen: The Plies of 'Fame'," *Washington Post,* February 21, 1982.

13. Guy Gugliotta, "Dwindling Black Farmers Fight Formidable Odds for Future," *Los Angeles Times,* December 30, 1990; US Department of Agriculture, "Agricultural Decisions," Vol. 70 (January–June 2011), Part One (General), Pages 1–416, online at http://www.dm.usda.gov/oaljdecisions/130320_YellowBook_Cover_To_Cover.pdf.

14. Derrick Z. Jackson, "The N-word and Richard Pryor," *New York Times,* December 15, 2005.

15. Megan Rosenfeld, "Profiles in Purple & Black," *Washington Post,* October 15, 1982.

16. Robert Hilburn, "Rap 'Message' Jumps Out in a Flash," *Los Angeles Times*, March 27, 1983.

17. Robert D. Bullard, "25th Anniversary of the Warren County PCB Landfill Protests," *Dissident Voice,* May 29, 2007, online at http://dissidentvoice.org/2007/05/25th-anniversary-of-the-warren-county-pcb-landfill-protests/; Bradford Mank, "Title VI and the Warren County Protests," *Faculty Articles and Other Publications,* 2007, paper 116, online at http://scholarship.law.uc.edu/fac_pubs/116.

18. Robert Hilburn, "The Renegade Prince," *Los Angeles Times*, November 21, 1982.

19. Blair Levin, "What Bradley Effect?," *New York Times*, October 19, 2008.

20. Leslie Bennetts, "An 1859 Black Literary Landmark Is Uncovered," *New York Times*, November 8, 1982.

21. David Axelrod, "Washington Elected," *Chicago Tribune*, April 13, 1983.

22. "List of Awards: Morton Dauwen Zabel Award," *American Academy of Arts and Letters,* online at http://www.artsandletters.org/awards2_all.php.

23. David Sargent, "People Are Talking About: Music: Michael Jackson—Growing Pains of a Boy Wonder," *Vogue*, March 1, 1983, 115; Robert Palmer, "Energy and Creativity Added Up to Exciting Pop," *New York Times*, December 25, 1983.

24. Mary Frances Berry, *And Justice for All: The United States Commission on Civil Rights and the Continuing Struggle for Freedom in America* (New York: Knopf, 2009).

25. Robert A. Jordan, "Jesse Jackson Announces He Will Run for President," *Boston Globe*, October 31, 1983; Watkins' memo quoted in George E. Curry, "Jesse Jackson," *Chicago Tribune*, June 3, 1984.

26. Helen Dewar, "Helms Stalls King's Day in Senate," *Washington Post*, October 4, 1983.

27. Chico C. Norwood, "Richard Pryor's Firing of Jim Brown Triggers Uproar in Black Community," *Los Angeles Sentinel*, December 22, 1983; Marina Zenovich, director, *Richard Pryor: Omit the Logic* (Showtime, 2013).

28. Drew Desilver, "Black Unemployment Rate Is Consistently Twice That of Whites," *FactTank: News in the Numbers,* Pew Research Center, August 21, 2013, online at http://www.pewresearch.org/fact-tank/2013/08/21/through-good-times-and-bad-black-unemployment-is-consistently-double-that-of-whites/; "25 Years of Black Economic Empowerment," *Black Enterprise*, June 1997, 90; Melvyn Dubofsky, "Organized Labor," *Encyclopedia of African American History, 1896 to the Present: From the Age of Segregation to the Twenty-first Century,* ed. Paul Finkelman, Oxford African American Studies Center, online at http://www.oxfordaasc.com/article/opr/t0005/e0934.

29. George E. Curry, "Jesse Jackson," *Chicago Tribune*, June 3, 1984.

30. Rev. Jesse Jackson, "1984 Democratic National Convention Address," San Francisco, CA, July 18, 1984, online at http://www.americanrhetoric.com/speeches/jessejackson1984dnc.htm; "Black Voter Registration Improves for Nation in '84," *Atlanta Daily World,* February 24, 1985.

31. "Olympians on Hill with Rights Torch," *Washington Post*, September 12, 1984.

32. Charles E. Rogers, "Cosby Show Opens White America's Eyes and Mind," *New York Amsterdam News*, October 13, 1984.

33. Frank Rich, "Wilson's 'Ma Rainey's' Opens," *New York Times*, October 12, 1984; Campbell Robertson, "Lloyd Richards, Theater Director and Cultivator of Playwrights, is Dead at 87," *New York Times*, July 1, 2006; Mike Downing, *The Life and Work of August Wilson,* slide show, English Department, Kutztown University of Pennsylvania, online at http://augustwilson.net/doc/The_Life_and_Work_of__August_Wilson_Slide_Show.pdf.

34. Jill Dupont, "Jordan, Michael," *Encyclopedia of African American History, 1896 to the Present,* ed. Paul Finkelman, online at http://www.oxfordaasc.com/article/opr/t0005/e0669; John Feinstein, "Tar Heels' Michael Jordan Reaches the Top of His Class," *Washington Post*, March 6, 1984; Bob Sakamoto, "A Bullish Beginning," *Chicago Tribune*, October 27, 1984; Bob Sakamoto, "Jordan Miracle Not Enough," *Chicago Tribune*, April 21, 1986.

35. "Def Jam Label Will Specialize in 'Real Street Music,'" *Billboard*, November 17, 1984.

36. Kenneth Bredemeier and Michel Marriott, "Fauntroy Arrested in Embassy," *Washington Post*, November 22, 1984.

37. "Celebrating the Life, Legacy and Values of Nelson Mandela/Chronology of the Free South Africa Movement," *TransAfrica.org,* online at http://transafrica.org/fsam-history/.

38. David E. Pitts, "Goetz Verdict Worries Black Leaders," *New York Times*, June 18, 1987.

39. "25 Years of Black Economic Empowerment," *Black Enterprise*, June 1997, 95.

40. Diahann Carroll told *JET* magazine, "I wanted to be the first Black bitch on nighttime television"; quoted in "Diahann Carroll and Joan Collins Add Intrigue to TV's Dynasty" *JET*, May 7, 1984.

1985–1989

1. Don Shewey, review of *Whitney Houston, Rolling Stone*, June 6, 1985.

2. Dennis McDougal, "'We Are the World' Charity Tops $50 Million Mark," *Los Angeles Times*, October 9,

1986; Jonathan Taylor and Gary Graff, *Chicago Tribune,* March 17, 1985.

3. Maureen Dowd, "'Sunday in the Park' Gains a Pulitzer Prize, and Lurie and Turkel Also Win," *New York Times*, April 25, 1985; The Pulitzer Prizes, 1985 Winners and Finalists, http://www.pulitzer.org/awards/1985.

4. "Gwendolyn Brooks Is Named Next Library Poetry Consultant," *Library of Congress Information Bulletin,* May 20, 1985, 106.

5. Marc Mazique, "MOVE," in *Africana: The Encyclopedia of the African and African American Experience*, 2nd ed., ed. Kwame Anthony Appiah and Henry Louis Gates, Jr., Oxford African American Studies Center, http://www.oxfordaasc.com/article/opr/t0002/e2755; Irv Randolph, "City on MOVE: 'We Made Tragic Mistake,'" *Philadelphia Tribune*, November 8, 1985.

6. Don Heckman, "Nina Simone Returns from Self-Imposed Exile," *Los Angeles Times*, July 30, 1985.

7. Jane Gross, "A New, Purified Form of Cocaine Causes Alarm as Abuse Increases," *New York Times*, November 29, 1985.

8. Roger Ebert, review of *The Color Purple*, December 20, 1985, online at http://www.rogerebert.com/reviews/the-color-purple-1985.

9. Maura Dolan, "Tutu Cheers Anti-Apartheid Protest at S. African Embassy," *Los Angeles Times*, January 9, 1986; *Afro-American*, "Freedom Letter Given Dr. Tutu," January 18, 1986.

10. Henry Louis Gates, Jr., "Nelson Mandela and the First MLK Day," *The Root*, January 20, 2014.

11. Jesse Helms, "The King Holiday and Its Meaning," *Congressional Record* 129, no. 130 (October 3, 1983), online at http://www.martinlutherking.org/helms.html; David Treadwell, "Urges Americans to Help in Fighting Apartheid: Tutu Pays Homage to King in Atlanta," *Los Angeles Times*, January 20, 1986.

12. Richard Harrington, "In Praise of the Rock Pioneers," *Washington Post,* January 24, 1986; Daniel Brogan, "An Old 'Stand by' Becomes a New Hit," *Chicago Tribune,* December 23, 1986.

13. Dudley Clendinen, "Ronald McNair," *New York Times*, February 9, 1986.

14. "Cover Story," *Washington Post*, March 16, 1986.

15. Rob Hoerburger, review of *Control*, by Janet Jackson, *Rolling Stone*, April 24, 1986.

16. Ann L. Trebbe, "The Len Bias Legacy," *Washington Post*, August 2, 1986.

17. "Behind the Scenes at Harpo Studios," *Oprah.com*, online at http://www.oprah.com/oprahshow/The-Oprah-Winfrey-Show-Trivia.

18. *Soul Man*, Internet Movie Database, online at http://www.imdb.com/title/tt0091991.

19. *Federal Elections 86: Election Results for the U.S. Senate and the U.S. House of Representatives* (Washington, DC: Federal Elections Commission, May 1987), 32, online at http://www.fec.gov/pubrec/fe1986/federalelections86.pdf.

20. Phil Bergers, "Tyson Wins W.B.C. Championship," *New York Times*, November 23, 1986 ; Avi Steinberg, "Mike Tyson's on Broadway," *The New Yorker,* August 9, 2012; Chuck Johnson, "Tyson Announces Retirement After Quitting vs. McBride," *USA Today,* June 11, 2005.

21. Ronald Smothers, "1,200 Protesters of Racial Attack March in Queens," *New York Times*, December 28, 1986.

22. "Murder, Manslaughter Charges Dropped in Howard Beach Attack," *Hartford Courant*, December 30, 1986.

23. "Forsyth County Civil Rights March, January 1987," *About North Georgia*, online at http://www.aboutnorthgeorgia.com/ang/Civil_Rights_March_January,_1987. "David Duke," Extremist Files, Southern Poverty Law Center web site, online at www.splcenter.org/get-informed/intelligence-files/profiles/david-duke.

24. Henry Hampton and Steve Fayer with Sarah Flynn, *Voices of Freedom: An Oral History of the Civil Rights Movement from the 1950s through the 1980s* (New York: Bantam, 1991 reissue), iii.

25. *Donald v. United Klans of America* Case Docket, Southern Poverty Law Center, online at http://www.splcenter.org/get-informed/case-docket/donald-v-united-klans-of-america.

26. John Voland, "Soul Train Awards Show Debuts," *Los Angeles Times*, March 25, 1987.

27. *Rolling Stone* 500 Greatest Songs of All Time, 446: 'Push It,'" online at http://www.rollingstone.com/music/lists/the-500-greatest-songs-of-all-time-20110407/salt-n-pepa-push-it-20110526.

28. Jonathan P. Hicks, "Beatrice Unit Brings $985 Million; International Food Is Sold to TLC Group," *New York Times*, August 10, 1987; Elliot D. Lee, "Wharton, Chief of $54 Billion Fund, Is Advocate of Social Responsibility," *Wall Street Journal*, February 13, 1987.

29. Margaret Atwood, "Jaunted by Their Nightmares," *New York Times*, September 13, 1987; "Nobel Prize for Literature 1993, Press Release," online at http://www.nobelprize.org/nobel_prizes/literature/laureates/1993/press.html.

30. Jane E. Brody, "Surgeons Hopeful as Saga of Siamese Twins Continues," *New York Times*, September 8, 1987; Thomas O. Edwards, "Carson, Ben," *African American National Biography*, ed. Henry Louis Gates, Jr., and Evelyn Brooks Higginbotham, online at http://www.oxfordaasc.com/article/opr/t0001/e0099; *The Sun*, March 30, 1987.

31. "James Baldwin: His Voice Remembered," *New York Times*, December 20, 1987; Baraka quoted in Benjamin Chavis, Jr., "James Baldwin Teacher, Friend, Freedom Fighter," *New Pittsburgh Courier*, January 9, 1988; Samuel F. Reynolds, "Dark Room Collective's

Literary Reading Was Provocative," *Philadelphia Tribune*, November 30, 1993.

32. Janet Maslin, review of *Eddie Murphy: Raw*, *New York Times*, December 19, 1987.

33. Roger Ebert, review of *School Daze*, February 12, 1988, online at http://www.rogerebert.com/reviews/school-daze-1988; Roger Ebert, review of *Malcolm X*, November 18, 1992, online at http://www.rogerebert.com/reviews/malcolm-x-1992.

34. George E. Curry, "Reagan Vetoes Civil Rights Bill, Wright Predicts a Speedy Override in House, Senate," *Chicago Tribune*, March 17, 1988; Wright quoted in Alison Shay, "On This Day: The Civil Rights Restoration Act," *Publishing the Long Civil Rights Movement*, online at https://lcrm.lib.unc.edu/blog/index.php/2012/03/22/on-this-day-the-civil-rights-restoration-act/; Helen Dewar, "Congress Overrides Civil Rights Law Veto," *Washington Post*, March 23, 1988.

35. Keith Love, "Jackson Wins by 2 to 1 in Michigan: He Also Leads Dukakis in Delegates in State; Gephardt Is Distant Third," *Los Angeles Times,* March 27, 1988; Rev. Jesse Jackson, "1988 Democratic National Convention Address," Atlanta, GA, July 19, 1988, online at http://www.americanrhetoric.com/speeches/jessejackson1988dnc.htm.

36. Numbers from Sue Heinemann, *Timeline of American Women's History* (New York: Penguin, 1996), 97.

37. Jon Pareles, "Public Enemy: Rap with a Fist in the Air," *New York Times*, July 24, 1988.

38. Ad's air date from Anthony Bennett, *The Race for the White House from Reagan to Clinton: Reforming Old Systems, Building New Coalitions* (New York: Palgrave Macmillan, 2013), 111; Clarence Page, "Cool Hand Duke's Last-Ditch Pitch," *Chicago Tribune*, October 16, 1988.

39. First statistic from Nikole Hannah-Jones, "Segregation Now," *ProPublica*, April 16, 2014, online at http://www.propublica.org/article/segregation-now-full-text; second statistic from Gary Orfield and Erica Frankenberg, with Jongyeon Ee and John Kuscera, "*Brown* at 60: Great Progress, a Long Retreat and an Uncertain Future," the Civil Rights Project, May 15, 2014, online at http://civilrightsproject.ucla.edu/research/k-12-education/integration-and-diversity/brown-at-60-great-progress-a-long-retreat-and-an-uncertain-future/Brown-at-60-051814.pdf.

40. Pamela Lee Gray, "Hall, Arsenio," *African American National Biography* and "Hall, Arsenio," *Africana*, both at Oxford African American Studies Center.

41. "*Richmond v. J.A. Croson Co.*," The Oyez Project at IIT Chicago-Kent College of Law, online at http://www.oyez.org/cases/1980-1989/1988/1988_87_998.

42. Douglas C. McGill, "Colgate to Rename a Toothpaste," *New York Times*, January 27, 1989; Janet Key, "At Age 100, A New Aunt Jemima," *Chicago Tribune*, April 28, 1989.

43. Abiola Sinclair, "*Newsweek* Raps Rap," *New York Amsterdam News*, April 14, 1990.

44. "Pepsi Cancels Madonna Ad," *New York Times*, April 5, 1989.

45. John J. O'Connor, "Review/Television; *Cops* Camera Shows the Real Thing," *New York Times*, January 7, 1989.

46. J. D. Harrison, "When We Were Small: FUBU," *Washington Post*, October 7, 2014.

47. PBS.com, "About the Central Park Five," online at http://www.pbs.org/kenburns/centralparkfive/about-central-park-five/; Lynette Holloway, "Judge Signs $41,000,000 Central Park 5 Settlement," *The Root*, September 6, 2014, online at http://www.theroot.com/articles/culture/2014/09/judge_signs_41_000_000_central_park_5_settlement.html; Dinitia Smith, "For the Child Who Rolls with the Punches," *New York Times*, July 2, 1996; Cyril Josh Baker, "Senate Passes Resolution for 'Central Park Five,'" *New York Amsterdam News*, June 17, 2010.

48. Frank J. Prial, "TV Film about Gay Black Men Is Under Attack," *New York Times*, June 25, 1991; Zan Dubin, "'Tongues Untied' Speaks to Moment," *Los Angeles Times*, May 7, 1992; "Marlon Riggs Dies," *New York Times*, April 6, 1994; David Mills, "Marlon Riggs, a Filmmaker Who Lives Controversy," *Washington Post*, June 15, 1992.

49. "The Second 100,000 Cases of Acquired Immunodeficiency Syndrome," *Mortality and Morbidity Report* 41, no. 2 (January 17, 1992), online at http://www.cdc.gov/mmwr/preview/mmwrhtml/00015924.htm; Timelines, Oxford African American Studies Center; Willie J. Pearson, Jr., "Mortality and Morbidity," *Encyclopedia of African-American Culture and History*, edited by Jack Salzman, David Lionel Smith, and Cornel West (New York: Macmillan, 1996), 4:1858.

50. Melissa Howell, "Colin Powell to Be Named Head of Joint Chiefs," *Los Angeles Times*, August 10, 1989; Melissa Howell, "Choice of Powell to Head Joint Chiefs of Staff Praised," *Los Angeles Times*, August 11, 1989; Juan Williams, "True Black Power—Colin Powell," *Washington Post*, January 15, 1989.

51. "Hasbro Unveils Urkel Toys Including 'Nerdy' Doll," *Philadelphia Tribune*, June 25, 1991; Joy Horowitz, "Snookums! Steve Urkel Is a Hit," *New York Times*, April 17, 1991.

52. Michael Janofsky, "Shell Is First Black Coach in N.F.L. Since 20's," *New York Times*, October 4, 1989.

53. Michael Brenson, "Critic's Notebook; Doors of Art Opening (Ignore the Squeaks)," *New York Times*, October 16, 1989; Roberta Smith, "Review/Art; 3 Museums Collaborate To Sum Up a Decade," *New York Times*, May 25, 1990.

54. Kim Foltz, "The Media Business; Campaign on Harmony Backfires for Benetton," *New York Times*, November 20, 1989; Kim Foltz, "The Media Business;

Benetton Changes Its Ads," *New York Times*, March 8, 1990; Carol Becker, *The Subversive Imagination: Artists, Society, and Social Responsibility* (New York: Routledge, 1994), 188.

55. Amy Duncan, "Latifah—The Queen of Rap," *Christian Science Monitor*, November 22, 1989; Rachelle Gold, "Queen Latifah," *Encyclopedia of African American History, 1896 to the Present*, ed. Paul Finkelman,

online at http://www.oxfordaasc.com/article/opr/t0005/e1005.

56. "Biographical Data: Frederick D. Gregory," National Aeronautics and Space Administration, online at http://www.jsc.nasa.gov/Bios/htmlbios/gregory-fd.html.

57. Vincent Canby, review of *Glory*, *New York Times*, December 14, 1989.

1990–1994

1. Dan Jacobson, "David Dinkins Inaugurated as NYC's First Black Mayor," *Atlanta Daily World*, January 4, 1990.

2. Fox Butterfield, "First Black Elected to Head Harvard's Law Review," *New York Times*, February 6, 1990; Fred A. Bernstein, "Derrick Bell, Law Professor and Rights Advocate, Dies at 80," *New York Times*, October 6, 2011; Jake Tapper, "Video Emerges of Obama in 1991 Rallying for Diversity at Harvard Law School," *ABC News.com*, May 7, 2012.

3. Steve Hochman, "Two Members of 2 Live Crew Arrested after X-Rated Show," *Los Angeles Times*, June 11, 1990; Henry Louis Gates, Jr., "2 Live Crew Decoded," *New York Times*, June 19, 1990; Leon E. Wynter, "NAACP Raps 2 Live Crew, Reflecting Division among Blacks over the Music," *Wall Street Journal*, June 21, 1990.

4. Michael Frisby, "First Fan's Club: President's Attention Makes Writer Soar," *Wall Street Journal*, January 2, 1997.

5. Jesse Greenspan, "Nelson Mandela Comes to America," *History in the Headlines*, online at http://www.history.com/news/nelson-mandela-comes-to-america; Joe Davidson, "Mandela Pledge Wins over U.S. Business Leaders," *Wall Street Journal*, June 25, 1990.

6. Jack Houston, "Operation PUSH Calls for National Boycott of Nike," *Chicago Tribune*, August 12, 1990; Eric Harrison and Bruce Horowitz, "Nike Feels Heat, Sets Minority Goals," *Los Angeles Times*, August 18, 1990.

7. "*Fresh Prince of Bel Air*," *Variety*, September 10, 1990.

8. Steven A. Holmes, "President Vetoes Bill on Job Rights; Showdown Is Set," *New York Times*, October 23, 1990.

9. Roger Cohen, "*Middle Passage* and *Morgan* Win," *New York Times*, November 29, 1990; David Streitfeld, "Fiction Prize to 'Passage's' Charles Johnson," *Washington Post*, November 28, 1990. ; Keneally quoted in John Williams, "Charles Johnson Discusses 'Middle Passage' at 25," New York Times, July 10, 2015.

10. "Powell, Colin Luther," *Africana*, ed. Kwame Anthony Appiah and Henry Louis Gates, Jr., online

at http://www.oxfordaasc.com/article/opr/t0002/e3196; Andy Pasztor and Gerald F. Seib, "Cool Commander," *Wall Street Journal*, October 15, 1990.

11. "Harvard Hires a Specialist in African-American Studies," *New York Times*, February 1, 1991; Adam Begley, "Black Studies' New Star," *New York Times*, April 1, 1990; Fox Butterfield, "Afro-American Studies Get New Life at Harvard," *New York Times*, June 3, 1992.

12. Steve "Flash" Juon, "M.C. Hammer," *RapReviews.com*, June 24, 2008; Gertrude Gipson, "It Was Grammy Night in the Big Apple," *Los Angeles Sentinel*, February 28, 1991.

13. Anthony Chase, "King, Rodney, case of," *The Oxford Companion to American Law*, ed. Kermit L. Hall, Oxford African American Studies Center, online at http://www.oxfordaasc.com/article/opr/t122/e0496; *Los Angeles Times*, "The Rodney King Affair," March 24, 1991.

14. Nina J. Easton, "'*Dances with Wolves*,' Irons, Bates Win Oscars," *Los Angeles Times*, March 26, 1991; Jube Shiver, Jr., "A Master of Sound, a Lesson in Color," *Los Angeles Times*, March 23, 1991.

15. Ross Newhan, "Rickey Is Heading into History," *Los Angeles Times*, May 2, 1991.

16. Andrew Rosenthal, "Marshall Retires from High Court; Blow to Liberals," *New York Times*, June 28, 1991; "Thomas, Clarence," *Africana*, ed. Kwame Anthony Appiah and Henry Louis Gates, Jr., online at http://www.oxfordaasc.com/article/opr/t0002/e3806; Wesley Borucki, "Thomas, Clarence," *Encyclopedia of African American History, 1896 to the Present*, ed. Paul Finkelman, online at http://www.oxfordaasc.com/article/opr/t0005/e1170; Miriam Bale, "Alone Then, Supported Today: 'Anita' Revisits the Clarence Thomas Hearings," *New York Times*, March 20, 2014.

17. Angela E. Chamblee, "Boyz n the Hood: A Welcome Relief," *Atlanta Daily World*, July 18, 1991.

18. Jesse J. Esparza, "Crown Heights Riot." *Encyclopedia of African American History, 1896 to the Present*, ed. Paul Finkelman, online at http://www.oxfordaasc.com/article/opr/t0005/e0316; John Kifner, "Youth Indicted in Fatal Stabbing in Crown Heights Racial

Rampage," *New York Times*, August 27, 1991; Alexis Okeowo, "Crown Heights, Twenty Years after the Riots," *The New Yorker*, August 19, 2011.

19. Lee May, "Pride, Pain Mix at Dedication of Rights Museum," *Los Angeles Times*, July 5, 1991; "The African Burial Ground," *Encyclopedia of African American History, 1896 to the Present*, ed. Paul Finkelman, online at http://www.oxfordaasc.com/article/opr/t0004/e0105; David W. Dunlap, "New York Dig Unearths Early Cemetery for Blacks," *New York Times*, October 9, 1991; *New York Amsterdam News*, "Sen. Paterson Concerned about Black Burial Ground in Lower NYC," December 21, 1991.

20. Richard W. Stevenson, "Basketball; Magic Johnson Ends His Career, Saying He Has AIDS Infection," *New York Times*, November 8, 1991; "Johnson, Magic," *Africana*, ed. Kwame Anthony Appiah and Henry Louis Gates, Jr., online at http://www.oxfordaasc.com/article/opr/t0002/e2104.

21. Chris Morris, "Quayle's 2Pac/Interscope Attack Puts New Heat on Time Warner," *Billboard*, October 3, 1992; Alvin Bianco, "Tupac Shakur Rejects 'Role-Model Label' in 1992," *MTV.com*, June 5, 2011; Shakur also quoted in Henry Louis Gates, Jr., and Marcyliena Morgan, "Broadway Was Made for Tupac," *The Daily Beast*, July 7, 2014.

22. *The Crisis* 99, no. 1 (January 1992), 24; Ronald Brownstein, "Edwards Defeats Duke in Louisiana Landslide," *Los Angeles Times*, November 17, 1991.

23. Jeremy Gerard, "Review: *Jelly's Last Jam*," *Variety*, April 27, 1992.

24. Jesse Katz, "Corrupting Power of Life on the Streets," *Los Angeles Times*, May 15, 1994; Angela Ford and Carla Rivera, "Hope Takes Hold as Bloods, Crips Say Truce Is for Real," *Los Angeles Times*, May 21, 1992.

25. Anthony Chase, "King, Rodney, case of," *The Oxford Companion to American Law*; "The Rodney King Affair," *Los Angeles Times*, March 24, 1991; "The LA Riots: 20 Years Later, 1992 Riots Timeline," *Los Angeles Times*, April 12, 2012, online at http://timelines.latimes.com/los-angeles-riots/; Ted Rohrlich and Rich Connell, "Police Pullout, Riot's Outbreak Reconstructed," *Los Angeles Times*, May 5, 1992; Walter Goodman, "Eyewitnesses to the Riots," *New York Times*, May 28, 1992.

26. Jeff Chang, *Can't Stop Won't Stop: A History of the Hip-Hop Generation* (New York: St. Martin's Press, 2005), 394–96.

27. *R.A.V. v. St. Paul*, online at http://www.oyez.org/cases/1990-1999/1991/1991_90_7675; and *Shaw v. Reno*, online at http://www.oyez.org/cases/1990-1999/1992/1992_92_357; both cases can be found online through *The Oyez Project at IIT Chicago-Kent College of Law*.

28. Robert Farrell, "Simmons, Russell," *Encyclopedia of African American History, 1896 to the Present*, ed. Paul

Finkelman, online at http://www.oxfordaasc.com/article/opr/t0005/e1095; Greg Braxton, "Laughz n the Hood," *Los Angeles Times*, August 6, 1992.

29. "1992 United States Men's Olympic Basketball," *Basketball Reference*, online at http://www.basketball-reference.com/olympics/teams/USA/1992; Michael Wilbon, "Perfect Match: Dream Team in a Dream World," *Washington Post*, July 22, 1992.

30. "First Black Woman Set to Go into Space," *New Pittsburgh Courier*, August 22, 1992.

31. "Press Release: The Nobel Prize in Literature 1992, Derek Walcott," October 8, 1992, online at http://www.nobelprize.org/nobel_prizes/literature/laureates/1992/press.html.

32. Isabel Wilkerson, "Milestone for Black Woman in Gaining U.S. Senate Seat," *New York Times*, November 4, 1992.

33. Gwen Ifill, "Clinton Appoints 2 to Oversee Change of Administration," *New York Times*, November 7, 1992; Bryant Gumbel is quoted in " 'First Friend' Vernon Jordan '57 Discusses President Clinton and Mentions DePauw on *Today*," DePauw University Web site, online at http://www.depauw.edu/news-media/latest-news/details/25696/.

34. *The Bodyguard (Original Motion Picture Soundtrack)*, AllMusic Guide, online at http://www.allmusic.com/album/the-bodyguard-original-motion-picture-soundtrack-mw0000180918; Arion Berger, *The Bodyguard: Original Soundtrack Album*, *Rolling Stone*, February 18, 1993; Leslie Richin, " 'The Bodyguard' Anniversary: Remembering the Soundtrack," *Billboard*, November 25, 2014.

35. "Dr. Dre, 'The Chronic' at 20: Classic Track-By-Track Review," *Billboard.com*, December 15, 2012; Chang, *Can't Stop Won't Stop*, 396–98.

36. Eileen Salmas, " 'Deep Space Nine' beyond Kirk, Picard, and to the Wormhole," *Washington Post*, January 3, 1993.

37. "M. Joycelyn Elders (1993-1994)," Office of the Surgeon General Web site, online at http://www.surgeongeneral.gov/about/previous/bioelders.html.

38. Jacqueline Trescott, "Maya Angelou's Pressure-Cooker Poem," *Washington Post*, January 16, 1993; John Hope Franklin and Evelyn Brooks Higginbotham, *From Slavery to Freedom: A History of African Americans*, 9th ed. (New York: McGraw Hill, 2011), 608; David Lauter and Sam Fulwood III, "Clinton Withdraws Guinier as Nominee for Civil Rights Job," *Los Angeles Times*, June 4, 1993; Patricia Washington, "Guinier, Lani," *Black Women in America*, ed. Darlene Clark Hine, online at http://www.oxfordaasc.com/article/opr/t0003/e0171; Douglas Jehl, "Surgeon General Forced to Resign by White House," *New York Times*, December 10, 1994.

39. "Arthur Ashe Statue Set Up in Richmond at Last," *New York Times*, July 5, 1996; "Arthur Ashe, Path-

breaker: From Richmond to Wimbledon, and Back," *New York Times*, July 4, 2014.

40. "Black Shows Headline Fox's Fall List," *New Journal and Guide*, August 18, 1993.

41. George L. Kelling and James Q. Wilson, "Broken Windows," *The Atlantic*, March 1982; Saki Knafo, "Bill Bratton, Stop-and-Frisk Architect, Takes over Nation's Biggest Police Force," *Huffington Post*, January 2, 2014.

42. Dan Kening, "Joyner Goes Nationwide with His Radio Program," *Chicago Tribune*, January 4, 1994; Tom Joyner, *I'm Just a DJ but . . . It Makes Sense to Me* (New York: Hachette Book Group, 2005); Jeffrey Yorke, "Joyner's Flight of Fancy," *Washington Post*, March 29, 1994.

43. David Stout, "Byron De La Beckwith Dies, Killer of Medgar Evers Was 80," *New York Times*, January 23, 2001; William Booth, "Beckwith Convicted of Murdering Evers," *Washington Post*, February 6, 1994; "NAACP History: Myrlie Evers-Williams," online at http://www.naacp.org/pages/naacp-history-Myrlie-Evers-Williams.

44. Linda M. Harrington, "On Capitol Hill, A Real Rap Session," *Chicago Tribune*, February 24, 1994.

45. Christopher Lehmann-Haupt, "Book of the Times; Colored to Negro to Black: A Journey," *New York Times*, May 16, 1994; Marian Aguiar, "West, Cornel," in *Africana*, ed. Kwame Anthony Appiah and Henry Louis Gates, Jr., online at http://www.oxfordaasc.com/article/opr/t0002/e4061.

46. Donald Roe, "Simpson, O.J., Trial of," in *Encyclopedia of African American History 1896 to the Present*, ed. Paul Finkelman, online at http://www.oxfordaasc.com/article/opr/t0005/e1098.

47. Henry Louis Gates, Jr., "Why Now?," in *The Bell Curve Wars: Race, Intelligence, and the Future of America*, ed. Steven Fraser (New York: Basic Books, 1995), 95–96.

48. Carrie Johnson, "20 Years Later, Parts of Major Crime Bill Viewed as Terrible Mistake," *NPR.org*, September 12, 2014, online at http://www.npr.org/2014/09/12/347736999/20-years-later-major-crime-bill-viewed-as-terrible-mistake; U.S. Department of Justice Fact Sheet, "Violent Crime Control and Law Enforcement Act of 1994," October 24, 1994, online at https://www.ncjrs.gov/txtfiles/billfs.txt; Peter Baker, "Bill Clinton Disavows His Crime Law as Jailing Too Many for Too Long," *New York Times*, July 15, 2015.

49. *The Source*, October 1994, reprinted at https://pressrewind.files.wordpress.com/2007/03/biggie_source1094.jpg; Kenneth Partridge, "TLC's 'CrazySexyCool' at 20: Classic Track-by-Track Album Review," *Billboard* online, November 15, 2004.

50. Pat Jordan, "How Samuel L. Jackson Became His Own Genre," *New York Times Magazine*, April 26, 2012; Henry Louis Gates, Jr., *Finding Your Roots: The Official Companion to the PBS Series* (University of North Carolina Press, 2014), 166.

51. Rachelle Gold, "Watts, J.C.," in *Encyclopedia of African American History, 1896 to the Present*, ed. Paul Finkelman, online at http://www.oxfordaasc.com/article/opr/t0005/e1239; Katharine Q. Seelye, "GOP, After Fumbling in '96, Turns to Orator for Response," *New York Times*, February 5, 1997.

52. Diane Haithman, "ART: As Defiant as Always, Thelma Golden, Curator of the L.A.-Bound 'Black Male,' Has Been Caught in a Firestorm of Criticism and Protest. It's OK; She Can Stand the Heat," *Los Angeles Times*, April 23, 1995; WGBH, "*Culture Shock*: The Art of Kara Walker," online at http://www.pbs.org/wgbh/cultureshock/provocations/kara/3.html.

1995–1999

1. Susan Kenney, "Shades of Difference," *New York Times*, February 12, 1995.

2. Gregory S. Bell, "Parsons, Richard Dean," in *African American National Biography*, ed. Henry Louis Gates, Jr., and Evelyn Brooks Higginbotham, online at http://www.oxfordaasc.com/article/opr/t0001/e0444; James Kates, "Parsons, Richard," *Encyclopedia of African American History, 1896 to the Present*, ed. Paul Finkelman, online at http://www.oxfordaasc.com/article/opr/t0005/e0949; Eben Shapiro, "Parsons Faces Ungainly Time Warner," *Wall Street Journal*, January 30, 1995.

3. Matthew L. Wald, "Outgoing N.R.C. Head Sees Nuclear Industry Revival: But Next Few Years Will Be Tough, He Says," *New York Times*, June 30, 1995; Sowandé Muskateem, "Jackson, Shirley Ann," in *Black Women in America*, ed. Darlene Clark Hine, online at http://www.oxfordaasc.com/article/opr/t0003/e0216.

4. *Adarand Constructors v. Pena*, The Oyez Project at IIT Chicago-Kent College of Law, online at http://www.oyez.org/cases/1990-1999/1994/1994_93_1841; Wesley Borucki, "Thomas, Clarence," in *Encyclopedia of African American History, 1896 to the Present*, ed. Paul Finkelman; John F. Harris, "Clinton Avows Support for Affirmative Action," *Washington Post*, July 20, 1995.

5. Steven J. Niven, "Obama, Barack," in *Encyclopedia of African American History, 1896 to the Present*, ed. Paul Finkelman, online at http://www.oxfordaasc.com/article/opr/t0005/e0922; review of *Dreams from My Father*, by Barack Obama, *Kirkus Reviews*, April 15, 1995; Paul Watkins, "A Promise of Redemption," *New York Times*, August 6, 1995; Todd Steven Burroughs,

"Abu-Jamal, Mumia," in *Encyclopedia of African American History, 1896 to the Present*, ed. Paul Finkelman, online at http://www.oxfordaasc.com/article/opr/t0005/e0027.

6. Zachery R. Williams, "Million Man March," in *Encyclopedia of African American History, 1896 to the Present*, ed. Paul Finkelman, online at http://www.oxfordaasc.com/article/opr/t0005/e0800.

7. History.com, "Colin Powell Declines Presidential Bid, and Related Media," online at http://www.history.com/speeches/colin-powell-declines-presidential-bid#colin-powell-declines-presidential-bid; Harry Amana, "Million Man March's Success: Media Misses the Real Story, Focuses on Controversy," *Black Issues in Higher Education*, November 2, 1995.

8. Melanie E.L. Bush, "McGruder, Aaron, and *Boondocks*," in *Encyclopedia of African American History from 1896 to the Present*, ed. Paul Finkelman, online at http://www.oxfordaasc.com/article/opr/t0005/e0757; Lonnae O'Neal Parker, "Strip Tease: U-Md. Senior Aaron McGruder's Edgy Hip-Hop Comic Gets Raves, but No Takers," *Washington Post*, August 20, 1997.

9. R. W. Apple, Jr., "Dole Ends the Race in Iowa as a Scalded Front Runner," *New York Times*, February 14, 1996; "1996 Presidential Republican Primary Election Results," *Dave Leip's Atlas of U.S. Presidential Elections*, online at http://uselectionatlas.org/RESULTS/national.php?f=0&year=1996&elect=2; "Buchanan and Keyes Press Social Issues," *New York Times*, February 3, 1996.

10. David Sprague, "Good Vibrations: The Fugees Score One for Positivity," *Rolling Stone*, March 7, 1996; "100 Best Albums of the Nineties," *Rolling Stone*, April 27, 2011, online at http://www.rollingstone.com/music/lists/100-best-albums-of-the-nineties-20110427.

11. Neil Strauss, "New Faces in Grammy Nominations," *New York Times*, January 5, 1996.

12. Marybeth Gasman, "Higher Education," in *Encyclopedia of African American History, 1896 to the Present*, ed. Paul Finkelman, online at http://www.oxfordaasc.com/article/opr/t0005/e0555; David Addams and Joseph Wilson, "Affirmative Action," in *Encyclopedia of African American History, 1896 to the Present*, ed. Paul Finkelman, online at http://www.oxfordaasc.com/article/opr/t0005/e0031; B. Drummond Ayers, Jr., "Fighting Affirmative Action, He Finds His Race an Issue: Fighting Affirmative Action, He Finds His Own Race an Issue," *New York Times*, April 18, 1996.

13. Ralph Blumenthal, "A Pulitzer Winner's Overnight Success of 60 Years," *New York Times*, April 11, 1996.

14. H. Nelson, "Upbeat Year for Rap, Despite Legal Matters." *Billboard*, December 28, 1996.

15. George Vecsey, "The Flame Still Burns," *New York Times*, July 19, 1996.

16. Francis X. Clines, "Clinton Signs Bill Cutting Welfare; States in New Role," *New York Times*, August 23, 1996; Bill Clinton, "How We Ended Welfare, Together," *New York Times*, August 22, 2006; Bryce Covert, "Clinton Touts Welfare Reform. Here's How it Failed," *The Nation*, September 6, 2012.

17. Robert Farrell, "Notorious B.I.G.," in *Encyclopedia of African American History, 1896 to the Present*, ed. Paul Finkelman, online at http://www.oxfordaasc.com/article/opr/t0005/e0920.

18. History.com, "This Day in History: Oprah Launches Influential Book Club," online at http://www.history.com/this-day-in-history/oprah-launches-influential-book-club.

19. "How Groups Voted in 1996," Roper Center, University of Connecticut, online at http://www.ropercenter.uconn.edu/polls/us-elections/how-groups-voted/how-groups-voted-1996/; "The Clinton Presidency: Building One America," *The Clinton-Gore Administration: A Record of Progress* (January 2001), online at http://clinton5.nara.gov/WH/Accomplishments/eightyears-11.html; Monique Morris, *Black Stats: African Americans by the Numbers in the Twenty-First Century* (New York: The New Press, 2014), 116; David E. Rosenbaum, "Clinton Fills Cabinet After Scramble to Diversify," *New York Times*, December 21, 1996; Lauren Victoria Burke, "Obama, Bush, or Clinton: Who Put More Blacks at the Top?" Politic365, April 26, 2012, online at http://politic365.com/2012/04/26/obama-bush-or-clinton-who-put-more-blacks-at-the-top/; "Bill Clinton Cabinet Members," *InsideGov.com*, online at http://cabinet-members.insidegov.com/d/a/Bill-Clinton.

20. Kurt Eichenwald, "Texaco to Make Record Payout in Bias Lawsuit," *New York Times*, November 16, 1996.

21. Virgie Murray, "Jakes Sets LA Confab," *Los Angeles Sentinel*, November 14, 1996; Shayna Lee, *T. D. Jakes: America's New Preacher* (New York: New York University Press, 2005), vii, 71–72; Virgie Murray, "Pulpit & Pew," *Los Angeles Sentinel*, November 13, 1997.

22. Peter Applebome, "School District Elevates Status of Black English," *New York Times*, December 20, 1996; Michael Adams, "Language," in *Encyclopedia of African American History, 1896 to the Present*, online at http://www.oxfordaasc.com/article/opr/t0005/e0010; John Baugh, "Ebonics Timeline," *Do You Speak American?*, online at http://www.pbs.org/speak/seatosea/americanvarieties/AAVE/timeline; "Jackson Criticizes Oakland Schools' 'Ebonics' Decision," *Los Angeles Times*, December 23, 1996; John F. Harris, "U.S. Bilingual Education Funds Ruled Out for Ebonics Speakers," *Washington Post*, December 25, 1996.

23. Karin L. Stanford, "Reverend Jesse Jackson and the Rainbow/PUSH Coalition: Institutionalizing Economic Opportunity," in *Black Political Organizations in the Post-Civil Rights Era*, ed. Ollie A. Johnson III and Karin L. Stanford (Piscataway, NJ: Rutgers University Press, 2002), 150, 165; Robert C.

Smith, "Jackson, Jesse L., Sr.," in *African American National Biography*, ed. Henry Louis Gates, Jr., and Evelyn Brooks Higginbotham, online at http://www.oxfordaasc.com/article/opr/t0001/e0288.

24. Shana L. Redmond, "Rock, Chris," in *African American National Biography*, ed. Henry Louis Gates, Jr., and Evelyn Brooks Higginbotham, online at http://www.oxfordaasc.com/article/opr/t0001/e1730; Cherry Bañez, "Chris Rock and Tommy Davidson Talk about the Business of Being Funny," *Philadelphia Tribune*, June 27, 1997.

25. Sharon Waxman, Robin Givhan, et al., "The 69th Annual Academy Awards," *Washington Post*, March 25, 1997.

26. "Strokes of Genius," *Sports Illustrated*, April 21, 1997, reprinted at http://www.golf.com/special-features/strokes-genius; Karen Crouse, "Treasure of Golf's Sad Past, Black Caddies Vanish in Era of Riches," *New York Times*, April 2, 2012; Alex Duval Smith, "'Cablinasian' Tiger Woods Sparks Multi-Racial Debate," *The Guardian*, April 24, 1997; Michael L. Krenn, "Woods, Tiger," in *Encyclopedia of African American History*, 1896 to the Present, ed. Paul Finkelman, online at http://www.oxfordaasc.com/article/opr/t0005/e1280; Sam Tanenhaus, "Tiger Woods and the Perils of Modern Celebrity," *New York Times*, December 12, 2009.

27. Ronald Blum, "Robinson Honored for Breaking Baseball Barrier," *Philadelphia Tribune*, April 1, 1997.

28. "For Immediate Release: Remarks by the President in Apology for Study Done in Tuskegee," online at http://clinton4.nara.gov/textonly/New/Remarks/Fri/19970516-898.html.

29. Sewell Chan, "The Abner Louima Case, 10 Years Later," *New York Times* City Room Blog, August 9, 2007, online at http://cityroom.blogs.nytimes.com/2007/08/09/the-abner-louima-case-10-years-later/; John Marzulli and Brian Kates, "The Abner Louima Case: 10 Years Later," *New York Daily News*, August 10, 1997.

30. Nancy Chambers, "Call to Action," *Management Review*, 86 no. 10 (November 1997), 40–41; Sophia Hollander, "Canada to Resign from Harlem's Children Zone," *Wall Street Journal*, February 10, 2014; Biography of Geoffrey Canada, Harlem Children's Zone Web site (2015), online at http://hcz.org/about-us/leadership/geoffrey-canada/.

31. Roger Ebert, review of *Amistad*, December 12, 1997, online at http://www.rogerebert.com/reviews/amistad-1997.

32. James Bennet, "Clinton in Africa: The Overview; In Uganda, Clinton Expresses Regret over Slavery in U.S.," *New York Times*, March 25, 1998; Toni Morrison, "Comment," *The New Yorker*, October 5, 1998.

33. Carol Marie Cropper, "Black Man Fatally Dragged in a Possible Racial Killing," *New York Times*, June 10, 1998; J. Zamgba Browne, "Black Man Dragged to Death in Racist Slaying," *New York Amsterdam News*, June 11, 1998; *Los Angeles Times*, "Texas Executes Man in 1998 Dragging Death," September 21, 2011; John Hope Franklin and Evelyn Brookers Higginbotham, *From Slavery to Freedom: A History of African Americans*, 9th ed. (New York: McGraw Hill, 2011), 598.

34. "Black Radical Congress [Mission]," March 16, 1998, archived online at http://www.hartford-hwp.com/archives/45a/524.html; Charles L. Lumpkins, "Black Radical Congress," in *Encyclopedia of African American History, 1896 to the Present*, ed. Paul Finkelman, online at http://www.oxfordaasc.com/article/opr/t0005/e0144; *People's Weekly World*, "Black Radical Congress Meet Draws 2000," June 27, 1998.

35. "International Business: L'Oreal to Acquire Soft Sheen Products," *New York Times*, July 2, 1998; Cliff Hocker and Sakina P. Spruell, "Bad Hair Days," *Black Enterprise* (November 2000), 144–50.

36. Georgia N. Alexakis, "Nelson Mandela to Receive Rare Harvard Honor," *Harvard Crimson*, September 8, 1998; Alvin Powell, "Mandela Thrills Thousands with Historic Visit," *Harvard University Gazette*, September 24, 1998.

37. Eugene A. Foster et al., "Jefferson Fathered Slave's Last Child," *Nature* 396 (November 5, 1998), 27–28; Thomas Jefferson Foundation, "Report of the Research Committee on Thomas Jefferson and Sally Hemings: Conclusions," January 2000, online at http://www.monticello.org/site/plantation-and-slavery/vi-conclusions; Brent Staples, "Jefferson and Sally Hemings, Together at Last?" *New York Times*, November 2, 1998.

38. "Arts and Humanities Awards Announced," *New York Times*, October 28, 1998.

39. Michel Marriott, "Planet Africa: A Global History: The Creation of Encarta Africana," *New York Times*, January 21, 1999; David D. Kirkpatrick, "Co-Founders of Africana.com Sell Venture to Time Warner," *New York Times*, September 7, 2000.

40. "Amadou Diallo," *New York Times* online at http://topics.nytimes.com/top/reference/timestopics/people/d/amadou_diallo/index.html; Jodi Wilgoren, "Cochran Promises Legal Team for Action in Diallo Death," *New York Times*, February 21, 1999; Jane Fritsch, "The Diallo Verdict," *New York Times*, February 26, 2000.

41. Neil Strauss, "5 Grammys to Lauryn Hill; 3 to Madonna," *New York Times*, February 25, 1999. Lee Hubbard, "Hip Hop Is Here to Stay America," *Los Angeles Sentinel*, March 4, 1999.

42. Lena Williams, "A Double Breakthrough: Winged Foot Award," *New York Times*, May 25, 1999.

43. "Entertainment Review 1999: Part 12," *AP Archive*, online at http://www.aparchive.com/metadata/Entertainment-Review-1999-Part-12/832f32ec9f9567d070dadd2b068c7f2d?searchfilter=Compilations%2FAP%2FEntertainment+Review+1999%2F19603; Marci Kenon, "Fashion Statements: Who, What, and Wear," *Billboard*, December 9, 2000.

44. David Zucchino, "Sowing Hope, Harvesting Bitterness," *Los Angeles Times*, March 23, 2012; Sharon LaFraniere, "U.S. Opens Spigot after Farmers Claim Discrimination," *New York Times*, April 25, 2013; Carmen V. Harris, "Agriculture and Agricultural Labor," in *Encyclopedia of African American History, 1896 to the Present*, ed. Paul Finkelman, online at http://www.oxfordaasc.com/article/opr/t0005/e0038.

45. Michiko Kakutani, "*Juneteenth* Executor Tidies Up Ellison's Unfinished Symphony," *New York Times*, May 25, 1999; Yvonne French, "*Juneteenth*: Ralph Ellison Editor Speaks at Library," Library of Congress website, online at http://www.loc.gov/loc/lcib/9908/juneteenth.html.

46. J. Zamgba Browne, "NAACP's Mfume Attacks Mainstream," *New York Amsterdam News*, July 15, 1999; "TV Networks Make Unequal Progress toward On-Screen Diversity," *Washington Post*, January 20, 2015.

47. "40 Important Women's Moments: 1999, Little Sister, Big Hit," USOpen.com, http://2013.usopen.org/en_US/news/articles/2013-09-01/20130901137804552061.html; Maureen M. Smith, "Williams, Serena, and Venus Williams," in *African American National Biography*, ed. Henry Louis Gates, Jr., and Evelyn Brooks Higginbotham, http://www.oxfordaasc.com/article/opr/t0001/e0611; Kenneth Miller, "U.S. Eyes Are Wide Open to Williams World," *Los Angeles Sentinel*, September 22, 1999; Matt Schiavenza, "The Astonishing Greatness of Serena Williams," *The Atlantic*, July 11, 2015, online at http://www.theatlantic.com/entertainment/archive/2015/07/the-astonishing-greatness-of-serena-williams/398339/.

2000–2004

1. "Harvard to Offer Black Studies Ph.D.," *Atlanta Daily World*, March 9, 2000.

2. David Firestone, "South Carolina Votes to Remove Confederate Flag from Dome," *New York Times*, May 19, 2000; David Slade and Jeff Hartsell, "Confederate Flag Controversy and NAACP Boycott Resurface Amid Talk of Football Bowl Game in Charleston," *Post and Courier*, August 10, 2013.

3. Steve Holsey, "The Original Kings of Comedy...Taking Movie Theaters by Storm," *Michigan Chronicle*, August 23, 2000.

4. Raymond Codrington, "Hip Hop," in *Encyclopedia of African American History, 1896 to the Present*, ed. Paul Finkelman, online at http://www.oxfordaasc.com/article/opr/t0005/e0560; Nathan Brackett, review of *Stankonia*, by Outkast, *Rolling Stone*, October 26, 2000.

5. Oxford African American Studies Center, "Voting Irregularities in the 2000 Presidential Election (2001)," online at http://www.oxfordaasc.com/article/doc/ps-aasc-0150; "How Groups Voted in 2000," Roper Center, University of Connecticut, online at http://www.ropercenter.uconn.edu/polls/us-elections/how-groups-voted/how-groups-voted-2000/.

6. Greg Winter, "Coca-Cola Settles Racial Bias Case," *New York Times*, November 17, 2000.

7. Alison Mitchell, "The 43rd President: The President-Elect; Powell to Head State Dept. as Bush's First Cabinet Pick," *New York Times*, December 17, 2000.

8. Geraldine Fabrikant, "BET Holdings to Be Bought by Viacom for $2.34 Billion," *New York Times*, November 4, 2000; *Los Angeles Times*, "Viacom Completes BET Acquisition," January 24, 2001.

9. Holland Cotter, "Art Review, A Full Studio Museum Show Starts with 28 Young Artists and a Shoehorn," *New York Times*, May 11, 2001.

10. Henry Louis Gates, Jr., "Who Killed Black Wall Street?," *The Root.com*, August 5, 2013; Lyle Denniston, "Judge Dismisses Riots Reparations Suit," *Boston Globe*, March 23, 2004; Donald Roe, "Tulsa Riot," in *Encyclopedia of African American History, 1896 to the Present*, ed. Paul Finkelman, online at http://www.oxfordaasc.com/article/opr/t0005/e1185; Ronald Roach, "Fighting the Good Fight," *Blacks in Higher Education*, November 8, 2001.

11. "What We Want," in *Let Nobody Turn Us Around: An African American Anthology*, ed. Manning Marable and Leith Mullings (Lanham, MD: Rowman and Littlefield, 2009), 603–04; "Hip-Hop Leaders Develop Initiatives at N.Y. Summit," *Billboard*, June 15, 2001.

12. "Pop Star Aaliyah Dead in Plane Crash," *ABC News*, August 27, 2001, online at http://abcnews.go.com/Entertainment/story?id=101199.

13. Larvester Gaither, "Racial Profiling," in *Encyclopedia of African American History, 1896 to the Present*, ed. Paul Finkelman, online at http://www.oxfordaasc.com/article/opr/t0005/e1007; Richard Prince, "No Blacks Pictured in 9/11 Commemorative," *The Root*, September 10, 2011, online at http://www.theroot.com/blogs/journalisms/2011/09/no_blacks_pictured_in_911_commemorative.html.

14. "Lawyer: Bonds Didn't Know He Used Steroids," *Washington Post*, March 23, 2011.

15. Brian Carovillano, "Ruth Simmons Inaugurated as Brown President," *New Pittsburgh Courier*, November 3, 2001; *Slavery and Justice, Report of the Brown University Steering Committee on Slavery and Justice*, 13, Brown University Web site, online at http://www.brown.edu/Research/Slavery_Justice; Paul Davis, "Former President Ruth Simmons Says Brown's New Slavery and Justice Center Should Not Be a Hub for Activism," *Providence Journal*, October 24, 2014;

Biography of Ruth J. Simmons, Brown University Web site, online at http://www.brown.edu/about/administration/president/simmons.

16. Shirley M. Geiger, "Mayors," in *Black Women in America*, ed. Darlene Clark Hine, online at http://www.oxfordaasc.com/article/opr/t0003/e0294.

17. "Cornel West: An Interview, Academic Speaks Out on Conflict with Harvard's New President," NPR, January 7, 2002, online at http://www.npr.org/programs/tavis/features/2002/jan/020107.west.html; Felicia R. Lee, "A Popular Black Host Is to Leave NPR," *New York Times*, December 1, 2004; Todd Steven Burroughs, "Smiley, Tavis," in *Encyclopedia of African American History, 1896 to the Present*, ed. Paul Finkelman, online at http://www.oxfordaasc.com/article/opr/t0005/e1106; Felicia Lee, "Media Man on a Mission: The Whirl of Tavis Smiley," *New York Times*, October 10, 2006.

18. Yvette Walker, "No Child Left Behind," in *Encyclopedia of African American History, 1896 to the Present*, ed. Paul Finkelman, online at http://www.oxfordaasc.com/article/opr/t0005/e0914.

19. Rick Lyman, "'Beautiful Mind' Wins; Best Actress Goes to Halle Berry," *New York Times*, March 25, 2002. Excerpts from the acceptance speeches of Berry, Poitier, and Washington can be found in the Academy Awards Acceptance Speech Database, at http://aaspeechesdb.oscars.org/.

20. Ian P. Campbell, "Gates Publishes Unique 19th Century Slave Manuscript," *Harvard Crimson*, April 15, 2002; Julie Bosman, "Professor Says He Has Solved a Mystery over a Slave's Novel," *New York Times*, September 18, 2013.

21. "Winners of the 2002 Pulitzer Prizes," *New York Times*, April 9, 2002.

22. Hal Hinson, "Revisiting Baltimore's Embattled Streets," *New York Times*, June 2, 2002; Matt Ehlers, "It's Not HBO, It's College: 'The Wire' as Textbook," *McClatchy-Tribune Business News*, April 11, 2010.

23. Joe Lago, "Lakes Sweep Aside Nets, Make History," *Espn.com*, June 13, 2002, online at http://scores.espn.go.com/nba/recap/_/id/220612017/gameId/220612017/la-lakers-lakers-vs-new-jersey-nets.

24. Michael Katz, "Boxing, Laila Ali Stops Prison Guard and Adds Two More Titles," *New York Times*, November 9, 2002.

25. Carl Hulse, "Lott's Praise for Thurmond Echoed His Words of 1980," *New York Times*, December 11, 2002; Carl Hulse, "Lott Fails to Quell Furor and Quits Top Senate Post," *New York Times*, December 20, 2002; Jeffrey Gettleman, "Final Word: 'My Father's Name Was James Strom Thurmond,'" *New York Times*, December 18, 2003.

26. Mark D. Cunningham, "Chappelle, Dave," in *African American National Biography*, ed. Henry Louis Gates, Jr., and Evelyn Brooks Higginbotham, online at http://www.oxfordaasc.com/article/opr/t0001/

e2221; Kam Williams, "Dave's World," *New Pittsburgh Courier*, March 5, 2003.

27. Christian Hoard, Review of *Get Rich or Die Tryin'*, by 50 Cent, *Rolling Stone*, February 11, 2003.

28. "Oprah Winfrey Joins Forbes Billionaires List," *Los Angeles Times*, February 28, 2003; "Oprah Winfrey's Official Biography: Philanthropy," Oprah.com, online at http://www.oprah.com/pressroom/Oprah-Winfreys-Official-Biography; Moira Forbes, "Oprah Winfrey Talks Philanthropy, Failure and What Every Guest—Including Beyoncé—Asks Her," *Forbes* online, September 18, 2012; Lonnae O'Neal Parker, "Oprah Winfrey Donates $12 Million to Smithsonian," *Washington Post*, June 11, 2013.

29. Cliff Hocker, "NAACP Brokers Export Deal: Black Farmers to Sell Goods to Cuban Government," *Black Enterprise*, March 1, 2003.

30. "Transcript: Obama's Speech against the War," (October 2, 2002) NPR, January 20, 2009, online at http://www.npr.org/templates/story/story.php?storyId=99591469; *The Guardian*, "Full Text of Colin Powell's Speech," February 5, 2003; Joseph Carroll, "Iraq Support Split along Race Lines," *Gallup*, September 14, 2004, online at http://www.gallup.com/poll/13012/iraq-support-split-along-racial-lines.aspx; Anthony Aiello, "Iraq War," in *Encyclopedia of African American History, 1896 to the Present*, ed. Paul Finkelman, online at http://www.oxfordaasc.com/article/opr/t0005/e0617.

31. Scott Sheidlower, "Beyoncé," *Encyclopedia of African American History from 1896 to the Present*, online at http://www.oxfordaasc.com/article/opr/t0005/e0124; Kia Makarechi, "Obama Says 'Beyoncé Could Not Be a Better Role Model for My Girls' as Event with Jay-Z Nets $4 Million," *Huffington Post*, September 19, 2012.

32. *Gratz v. Bollinger*, The Oyez Project at IIT Chicago-Kent College of Law, online at http://www.oyez.org/cases/2000-2009/2002/2002_02_516; Franklin and Higginbotham, *From Slavery to Freedom*, 615; *Grutter v. Bollinger*, The Oyez Project at IIT Chicago-Kent College of Law, online at https://supreme.justia.com/cases/federal/us/539/306.

33. LeBron James, as told to Lee Jenkins, "LeBron: I'm Coming Back to Cleveland," *Sports Illustrated*, July 1, 2014.

34. Toure, "Kanye West: Head of the Class," *Rolling Stone*, April 29, 2004.

35. Andrew Dansby, "Usher Tops One Million," *Rolling Stone*, March 21, 2004.

36. Ta-Nehisi Coates, "This Is How We Lost to the White Man: The Audacity of Bill Cosby's Black Conservatism," *The Atlantic*, May 1, 2008; Ta-Nehisi Coates, "Ebonics! Weird Names! $500 Shoes!" *Village Voice*, May 18, 2004; Andrew R. Chow, "Spelman College Terminates Professorship Endowed by Bill Cosby," New York Times, July 26, 2015.

37. Tammy La Gorce, "A Political Convention, with

Beats," *New York Times*, June 27, 2004; Raymond Codrington, "Hip Hop," in *Encyclopedia of African American History, 1896 to the Present*, ed. Paul Finkelman, online at http://www.oxfordaasc.com/article/opr/t0005/e0560.

38. "Transcript: Illinois Senate Candidate Barack Obama," *Washington Post*, July 27, 2004; WGBH online, "Barack Obama's 2004 DNC Speech," online at http://www.pbs.org/weta/washingtonweek/web-video/barack-obamas-2004-dnc-speech.

39. Ben Ratliff, "The Making of a Jazz Statesman," *New York Times*, October 18, 2004; Phil Schaap, "Jazz," *Encyclopedia of African American History, 1896 to the Present*, ed. Paul Finkelman, online at http://www.oxfordaasc.com/article/opr/t0005/e0638.

40. Ari Berman, "Ohio Early Voting Cutbacks Disenfranchise Minority Voters," *The Nation*, August 8, 2012; Abby Goodnough and Christopher Drew, "Bush Holds Comfortable Lead as Voting Problems of 2000 Do Not Reappear," *New York Times*, November 3, 2004; "How Groups Voted in 2004," Roper Center, University of Connecticut, online at http://www.ropercenter.uconn.edu/polls/us-elections/how-groups-voted/how-groups-voted-2004/.

2005–2009

1. Ewen MacAskill, Stephen Bates, and Agencies, "Rice Gave Early Approval for CIA Waterboarding, Senate Report Reveals," *The Guardian*, April 23, 2009; "Confirmation Hearing of Condoleezza Rice" (transcript), *New York Times*, January 18, 2005.

2. David Halbfinger, "'Million Dollar Baby' Dominates Oscars," *New York Times*, February 28, 2005.

3. Ellen Barry, "Killen Gets Sixty Years in '64 Killings," *Los Angeles Times*, June 24, 2005.

4. John L. Beven II, et al, "Annual Summary: Atlantic Hurricane Season 2005," *Tropical Prediction Center, National Oceanic and Atmospheric Administration and National Weather Service*, April 30, 2007, online at http://www.aoml.noaa.gov/general/lib/lib1/nhclib/mwreviews/2005.pdf.

5. "State and County Quick Facts, New Orleans, Louisiana," United States Census Bureau, December 4, 2014.

6. LZ Granderson, "Three-time MVP 'tired of having to hide my feelings,'" *ESPN The Magazine*, October 27, 2005.

7. CNN Transcripts, "Rosa Parks' Funeral Underway in Detroit," November 2, 2005, http://transcripts.cnn.com/TRANSCRIPTS/0511/02/se.01.html; Shaila Dewan and Elizabeth Bumiller, "At Mrs. King's Funeral, a Mix of Elegy and Politics," New York Times, February 8, 2006; James Comey, "Hard Truths," transcript of remarks delivered at Georgetown University on February 12, 2015, Federal Bureau of Investigations (FBI) Web site, online at https://www.fbi.gov/news/speeches/hard-truths-law-enforcement-and-race.

8. Damien Cave, "On 2nd Try, Booker Glides in as Newark Mayor," *New York Times*, May 10, 2006.

9. Jeffrey Felshman, "Up Everest, Quietly," *Chicago Reader*, July 13, 2006.

10. William H. Frey, "Diversity Spreads South: Metropolitan Shifts in Hispanic, Asian, and Black Populations since 2000," the Brookings Institution, March 2006, 6–11, online at http://www.brookings.edu/~/media/research/files/reports/2006/3/demograph-ics%20frey/20060307_frey.pdf; Mike King, "Racial Shifts Speak Volumes; And Metro Atlanta Will Have to Listen," *Atlanta Journal-Constitution*, March 6, 2006.

11. Richard G. Jones, "Louisiana Protest Echoes the Civil Rights Era," *New York Times*, September 21, 2006.

12. Patrick K. Thornton, "The Increased Opportunity for Minorities in the NFL Coaching Ranks," *Willamette Sports Law Journal* 6, no. 1 (2009): 45–56.

13. "Text: Obama's 'Announcement for President,'" *Time*, February 10, 2007.

14. Steve Holsey, "2007 Academy Awards: Great Night for Black Nominees, but Show Was Too Long," *Michigan Chronicle*, February 28, 2007.

15. "Text: Comments of Rutgers Coach," *New York Times*, April 10, 2007.

16. "*Parents Involved in Community Schools v. Seattle School District No. 1*," the Oyez Project at IIT Chicago-Kent College of Law, online at http://www.oyez.org/cases/2000-2009/2006/2006_05_908.

17. NAACP, "The 'N-Word' is Laid to Rest by the NAACP," July 9, 2007, online at http://www.naacp.org/press/entry/the—n--word-is-laid-to-rest-by-the-naacp.

18. Elizabeth Day, "Americanah by Chimamanda Ngozi—Review," *The Guardian*, April 15, 2003.

19. Tricia Rose, *The Hip-Hop Wars: What We Talk About When We Talk About Hip-Hop*, (Philadelphia: Basic, 2006), 160.

20. Rakesh Kochhar and Richard Fry, "Wealth Inequality Has Widened along Racial, Ethnic Lines since End of Great Recession," Pew Research Center Fact Tank, December 12, 2014, online at http://www.pewresearch.org/fact-tank/2014/12/12/racial-wealth-gaps-great-recession.

21. *Kimbrough v. United States* (2007), online at www.law.cornell.edu/supct/html/06-6330.ZS.html; Gilbert Price, "State Senator Hails Federal Cocaine Sentencing Ruling," *Call & Post*, December 19, 2007.

22. Kristen Mascia, "Misty Copeland on Love, Life, and Leaps of Faith," *Elle*, May 29, 2014, online at http://

www.elle.com/culture/career-politics/interviews/ a17/misty-copeland-interview; Michael Cooper, "Misty Copeland Is Promoted to Principal Dancer at American Ballet Theater," *New York Times,* June 30, 2015; "Company History," American Ballet Theatre website, online at http://www.abt.org/insideabt/history.asp.

23. Niven, Steven J. *Barack Obama: A Pocket Biography of Our 44th President* (New York: Oxford University Press, 2009); Kenneth B. Vogel and Jeanne Cummings, "January Yields Debt for HRC, Cash for Obama," *Politico,* February 20, 2008, online at http://www.politico.com/news/stories/0208/8613.html.

24. Richard Perez-Pena, "Washington Post Starts an Online Magazine for Blacks," *New York Times,* January 28, 2008; Maeve Duggan and Joanna Brenner, "The Demographics of Social Media Users—2012," *Pew Research Center,* February 14, 2013, online at online at http://www.pewinternet.org/files/old-media//Files/Reports/2013/PIP_SocialMediaUsers.pdf; Apryl Williams and Doris Domoszlai, "#BlackTwitter: A Networked Cultural Identiy," *The Ripple Effect,* Harmony Institute, August 6, 2013, online at http://harmony-institute.org/therippleeffect/2013/08/06/blacktwitter-a-networked-cultural-identity/.

25. Brian Ross and Rehab El-Buri, "Obama's Pastor," *ABCNews.com,* March 13, 2008; the full text of Obama's "A More Perfect Union" speech can be found in Steven J. Niven, *Barack Obama: A Pocket Biography of Our 44th President* (Oxford University Press, 2009)

26. Touré, "Jay-Z's 'Glory' for Blue: One of Hip-Hop's Greatest Love Songs," *Time,* January 10, 2010.

27. "Alan Keyes Stokes Obama Birth Certificate Controversy," *Los Angeles Times*, February 21, 2009.

28. Theodore R. Johnson III, "Africans Have Apologized for Slavery, So Why Not the U.S.?" The Root, June 17, 2004, online at http://www.theroot.com/articles/history/2014/06/why_won_t_the_united_states_apologize_for_slavery.2.html; Ta-Nehisi Coates, "The Case for Reparations," *The Atlantic,* June 2014, online at http://www.theatlantic.com/features/archive/2014/05/the-case-for-reparations/361631/.

29. Brian Naylor, "Obama's Acceptance Pledge: Fix Broken Promises," *NPR,* August 29, 2008, online at http://www.npr.org/templates/story/story.php?storyId=94110630.

30. Lawrence D. Bobo, Camille Z. Charles, Maria Krysan, and Alicia Simmons, "The *Real* Record on Racial Attitudes," in *Social Trends in American Life: Findings from the General Social Survey Since 1972,* ed. Peter J. Marsden (Princeton: Princeton University Press, 2012) 38–93.

31. Cathy Cohen, "'My President Is Black': Barack Obama and the Post-Racial Illusion," in *Democracy Remixed, Black Youth and the Future of American Politics* (New York: Oxford University Press, 2012), 201–34.

32. Macon Phillips, "President Barrack Obama's Inaugural Address" (transcript), *The White House Blog,* January 21, 2009, online at https://www.whitehouse.gov/blog/inaugural-address.

33. M.J. Stephey, "Embattled Michael Steele: A Profile," *Time*, February 2, 2009.

34. Terry Freidan, "Holder: U.S. a 'Nation of Cowards' on Race Discussions," CNN News, February 19, 2009, online at http://www.cnn.com/2009/POLITICS/02/18/holder.race.relations.

35. Jerry Markon and Krissah Thompson, "Dispute over New Black Panthers Case Causes Deep Divisions," *Washington Post*, October 22, 2010.

36. "Civil Rights History Project National Survey of Collections," The American Folklife Center of the US Library of Congress, online at http://www.loc.gov/folklife/civilrights/.

37. Charles Isherwood, "Playwrights Bring Uncommon Bond to Broadway," *New York Times*, September 15, 2011.

38. *Anderson Cooper: 360 Degrees,* "A Recap of the Michael Jackson Memorial Service at the Staples Center in Los Angeles," July 7, 2009, online at http://transcripts.cnn.com/TRANSCRIPTS/0907/07/acd.02.html.

39. *Ricci v. DeStefano* (2009), The Oyez Project at IT Chicago-Kent College of Law online at http://www.oyez.org/cases/2000-2009/2008/2008_07_1428.

40. Michele McPhee and Sara Just, "Obama: Police Acted 'Stupidly' in Gates Case," *ABC News,* July 22, 2009; President Barack H. Obama, "Statement from the President Following His Conversation with the Vice President, Professor Gates and Sergeant Crowley," The White House: Office of the Press Secretary, July 30, 2009, online at http://www.whitehouse.gov/the-press-office/statement-president-following-his-conversation-with-vice-president-professor-gates-.

41. Bruce Weber, "E. Lynn Harris, Who Wrote of Gay Black Men's Lives, Dies at 54," *New York Times,* July 24, 2009.

42. Patricia Sellers, "Xerox CEO's Career Advice? Listen to Your Mom," *Fortune*, August 16, 2011.

43. Steven Erlanger and Sheryl Gay Stolberg, "Surprise Nobel for Obama Stirs Praise and Doubts," *New York Times*, October 9, 2009.

44. Ben Sisario, "Alicia Keys Finds Her Own 'Empire State of Mind," *New York Times Arts Beat Blog,* November 19, 2009, online at http://artsbeat.blogs.nytimes.com/2009/11/19/alicia-keys-finds-her-own-empire-state-of-mind/; Sophie Harris, "'Empire State of Mind' by Jay-Z with Alicia Keys (Video)", *Time Out New York,* March 7, 2012, online at http://www.timeout.com/newyork/music/empire-state-of-mind-by-jay-z-with-alicia-keys-video.

45. President Barack H. Obama, "Remarks by the President at Reception Commemorating the Enactment of the Matthew Shepard and James Byrd, Jr. Hate Crimes Prevention Act," The White House: Office of the Press Secretary, October 28, 2009, online at https://www.whitehouse.gov/the-press-office/re marks-president-reception-commemorating-enact ment-matthew-shepard-and-james-byrd-.

46. Breeanna Hare, "Parents: Disney's 'Princess' Is a Hop toward Progress," CNN, February 1, 2010, online at http://www.cnn.com/2009/SHOWBIZ/Movies/12 /11/princess.frog.parents.

2010–2015

1. *Haiti One Year Later: The Progress to Date and the Path Forward: A Report from the Interim Haiti Recovery Commission,* January 12, 2011, online at http://www. state.gov/documents/organization/154802.pdf; Deborah Sontag, "Earthquake Relief Where Haiti Wasn't Broken," *New York Times,* July 5, 2012; "Haiti Earthquake Fast Facts," CNN Library, January 6, 2015, online at http://www.cnn.com/2013/12/12/world/ haiti-earthquake-fast-facts/index.html; Randal C. Archibold, "As Beyoncé Visits Haiti, Facebook Users Show Skepticism," *New York Times,* May 18, 2015.

2. Michelle Alexander, *The New Jim Crow: Mass Incarceration in the Age of Colorblindness* (New York: The New Press, 2010).

3. "Mo'Nique Wins Best Supporting Actress Oscar," *Miami Times,* March 20, 2010; Kate Harding, "In Defense of Mo'Nique's Oscar Speech," *Salon.com,* March 8, 2010.

4. Dan Mangan, "Obamacare Signups Hit 9.5 Million, Strong Pace as Deadline Looms," MSNBC, January 27, 2015, online at http://www.cnbc.com/id/102373371; Jenna Levy, "In U.S, Uninsured Rate Sinks to 12.9%," *Gallup,* January 7, 2015, http://www.gallup.com/poll /180425/uninsured-rate-sinks.aspx.

5. Ben Brantley, "It's No More Mr. Nice Guy for This Everyman," *New York Times,* April 27, 2010.

6. Jesse Lee, "President Obama Signs the Fair Sentencing Act," *The White House Blog,* August 3, 2010, online at https://www.whitehouse.gov/blog/2010/08/03/ president-obama-signs-fair-sentencing-act.

7. Jeevan Vasagar and Allegra Stratton, "Geoffrey Canada Warns Michael Gove Unions 'Kill' Innovation," *The Guardian,* October 5, 2010; Anya Kamenetz, "Charters Schools, Money and Test Scores," *NPR Ed,* July 22, 2014, online at http://www.npr.org/sections/ ed/2014/07/22/334049393/charters-money-and- test-scores; "The Opinion Pages: Are Charter Schools Cherry-Picking Students," *New York Times,* December 10, 2014, online at http://www.nytimes.com/ roomfordebate/2014/12/10/are-charter-schools- cherry-picking-students; Elizabeth Harris, "As Common Core Testing Is Ushered in, Parents and Students Opt Out," *New York Times,* March 1, 2015.

8. Kevin Arceneaux and Stephen P. Nicholson, "Who Wants to Have a Tea Party? The Who, What and Why of the Tea Party Movement," *PS: Political Science and Politics* 45 no. 4 (2012): 700–10.

9. Cynthia Greenlee-Donnell, "Rhiannon Giddens," *African American National Biography,* ed. Henry Louis Gates, Jr., and Evelyn Brooks Higginbotham, online at http://www.oxfordaasc.com/article/opr/ t0001/e2282?hi=0&highlight=1&from=quick&pos=1

10. Kevin Fallon, "Oprah's Last Show: A Recap in Quotes," *The Atlantic,* May 25, 2011.

11. Daniel Kreps, "Jay Z, Macklemore, Kendrick Lamar Dominate 2014 Grammy Nominations," *RollingStone. com,* December 6, 2013; Lizzy Goodman, "Kendrick Lamar, Hip-Hop's Newest Old-School Star," *New York Times Magazine,* June 25, 2014; Adam Fleischer, "Kendrick Lamar Already Set a Record with *To Pimp a Butterfly,*" *MTV.com,* March 18, 2015; August Brown, "Kendrick Lamar Commended at California State Senate," *Los Angeles Times,* May 12, 2015.

12. Dorothy Pomerantz, "The Highest-Paid Men in Entertainment," Forbes.com, September 12, 2011, online at http://www.forbes.com/sites/dorothypomerantz /2011/09/12/the-highest-paid-men-in-entertain ment.

13. Stacey Patton, "Why Blacks Aren't Embracing Occupy Wall Street," *Washington Post,* November 25, 2011.

14. Nikki Sutton, "President Obama at the Martin Luther King Jr. Memorial Dedication: 'We Will Overcome,'" *The White House Blog,* October 16, 2011, online at http://www.whitehouse.gov/blog/2011/10/16/pre sident-obama-martin-luther-king-jr-memorial- dedication-we-will-overcome.

15. *Key and Peele* Comedy Central Web site, online at online at http://www.cc.com/shows/key-and-peele.

16. Wendy Wang, "The Rise of Intermarriage," *Pew Research Social and Demographic Trends,* February 16, 2012, online at http://www.pewsocialtrends .org/2012/02/16/the-rise-of-intermarriage.

17. President Barack H. Obama, "Remarks by the President on Trayvon Martin," The White House: Office of the Press Secretary, July 19, 2013, online at https:// www.whitehouse.gov/the-press-office/2013/07/19/ remarks-president-trayvon-martin.

18. Lynn Elber, "Octavia Spencer Wins Best Supporting Actress Oscar," *Charlotte Post,* March 1, 2012.

19. "Transcript: Robin Roberts ABC News Interview With President Obama," *ABCNews.com,* May 9, 2012, online at http://abcnews.go.com/Politics/transcript- robin-roberts-abc-news-interview-president- obama/story?id=16316043. Adam Liptak, "Supreme

Court Ruling Makes Same-Sex Marriage a Right Nationwide," *New York Times,* June 26, 2015.

20. Sabrina Tavernise, "Whites Account for Under Half of New Births in US," *New York Times,* May 17, 2012.

21. Karen L. Willoughby, "Historic: Fred Luter Elected SBC President," *Baptist Press,* June 19, 2012, online at http://www.bpnews.net/38081.

22. Melissa Harris, "New McDonald's CEO Stays True to His Roots," *Chicago Tribune,* March 23, 2012.

23. Trymaine Lee, "On the Road with the Dream Defenders," MSNBC, August 24, 2013, online at http://www.msnbc.com/msnbc/the-road-the-dream-defenders.

24. Gary Orfield, John Kucsera, and Genevieve Siegel-Hawley, "E Pluribus . . . Separation: Deepening Double Separation for more Students," *The Civil Rights Project at UCLA,* 2012, http://civilrightsproject.ucla.edu/research/k-12-education/integration-and-diversity/mlk-national/e-pluribus . . . separation-deepening-double-segregation-for-more-students; Nikole Hannah-Jones quoted in "The Problem We All Live With," *This American Life from WBEZ,* National Public Radio, July 31, 2015, online at http://www.thisamericanlife.org/radio-archives/episode/562/the-problem-we-all-live-with; Nikole Hannah-Jones "Segregation Now," *ProPublica,* April 16, 2014, online at http://www.propublica.org/article/segregation-now-full-text; Gary Orfield and Erica Frankenberg, with Jongyeon Ee and John Kuscera, "*Brown* at 60: Great Progress, a Long Retreat and an Uncertain Future," the Civil Rights Project, May 15, 2014, online at http://civilrightsproject.ucla.edu/research/k-12-education/integration-and-diversity/brown-at-60-great-progress-a-long-retreat-and-an-uncertain-future/Brown-at-60-051814.pdf; Paul E. Barton and Richard J. Coley, *Policy Information Report: The Black-White Achievement Gap: When Progress Stopped,*" (Princeton, NJ: Educational Testing Service, 2010).

25. "Percent of White Vote Won by 2012, by State," *Daily Kos,* November 10, 2012, online at http://www.dailykos.com/story/2012/11/10/1159759/-Percent-of-White-vote-won-by-Obama-2012-by-state.

26. "Inaugural Address of President Barack Obama," The White House: Office of the Press Secretary, January 21, 2013, online at https://www.whitehouse.gov/the-press-office/2013/01/21/inaugural-address-president-barack-obama.

27. "Chicago Gun Violence Time Line and Graphic," *The Red Line Project,* March 6, 2013, online at http://redlineproject.org/2013chicagogundeaths.php.

28. Tom Watkins and Marlena Baldacci, "Posthumous Pardons in 1931 Scottsboro Boys Rape Cases," CNN, November 21, 2013, online at http://www.cnn.com/2013/11/21/justice/alabama-scottsboro-pardons.

29. "Jason Collins Says He's Gay," *ESPN.com,* April 30, 2013, online at http://espn.go.com/nba/story/_/id/9223657/jason-collins-first-openly-gay-active-player.

30. "Jean-Michel Basquiat (1960-1988): *Dustheads,*" Sale 2785 (May 15, 2013), Christies Web site, online at http://www.christies.com/lotfinder/paintings/jean-michel-basquiat-dustheads-5684046-details.aspx.

31. "*Fisher v. University of Texas* (June 24, 2013)," The Oyez Project at IIT Chicago-Kent College of Law, online at http://www.oyez.org/cases/2010-2019/2012/2012_11_345.

32. "John Lewis and Others React to the Supreme Court's Voting Rights Act Ruling," *Washington Post,* June 25, 2013.

33. "*Orange is the New Black,*" *Internet Movie Database,* online at http://www.imdb.com/title/tt2372162/.

34. A.O. Scott, "A New Year, and a Last Day Alive," *New York Times,* July 11, 2013.

35. "The Attorney General's Smart on Crime Initiative," U.S. Department of Justice, online at http://www.justice.gov/ag/attorney-generals-smart-crime-initiative.

36. Michael J. De La Merced, "Inspired by Professor, Investor Makes Big Gift for Black Studies," *New York Times,* September 17, 2013.

37. Manohla Dargis, "The Blood and Tears, Not the Magnolias," *New York Times,* October 17, 2013.

38. Kory Grow, "Pharrell Williams Creates First 24-Hour Music Video," *RollingStone.com,* November 21, 2013.

39. Office of the White House Press Secretary, "Remarks by President Obama at Memorial Service for Former South African President Nelson Mandela," December 10, 2013, online at http://www.whitehouse.gov/the-press-office/2013/12/10/remarks-president-obama-memorial-service-former-south-african-president-. The Associated Press, "Historic Encounter with Cuba's Castro Awits Obama in Panama," *New York Times,* April 9, 2015; Michael D. Shear, "Obama Reaches Out to Cuba's Leader, But the Meaning May Elude Grasp," *New York Times,* December 10, 2013.

40. The White House, "My Brother's Keeper," online at http://www.whitehouse.gov/my-brothers-keeper.

41. Breanna Edwards, "John W. Thompson to Become 1st Black Chairman of Microsoft," *TheRoot.com,* February 6, 2014, online at http://www.theroot.com/articles/culture/2014/02/john_w_thompson_to_be_first_black_chairman_of_microsoft.html.

42. "Cosmos: A Spacetime Odyssey (2014)," *Internet Movie Database,* online at http://www.imdb.com/title/tt2395695/.

43. *Schuette v. Coalition.* 572 US 12 (2014).

44. "Lupita Nyong'o Delivers Moving Black Women Hollywood Acceptance Speech," *Essence,* February 28, 2014.

45. "Steve Ballmer Completes Purchase of Los Angeles Clippers (Press Release)," *NBA.com,* August 12, 2014, online at http://www.nba.com/clippers/steve-ballmer-completes-purchase-los-angeles-clippers.

46. Ethan Westbrooks, "Michael Sam on Draft: Longest 3 Days," *ESPN.com,* December 28, 2014, online at http://espn.go.com/nfl/story/_/id/12084681/michael-sam-says-coming-was-right-thing-do.

47. Blake Gopnik, "Fleeting Artworks, Melting Like Sugar," *The New York Times*, July 11, 2014.

48. Brian Solomon, "It's Official: Apple Adds Dr. Dre With $3 Billion Beats Deal," *Forbes.com,* May 28, 2014, online at http://www.forbes.com/sites/briansolomon/2014/05/28/apple-brings-dr-dre-on-board-with-official-3-billion-beats-deal/.

49. Ryan McPhee, "Tony Poll Top Three: Audra McDonald Wins Fans' Hearts (On Top of a Sixth Tony) with Heartfelt Acceptance Speech," *Broadway.com,* June 9, 2014, online at http://www.broadway.com/buzz/176294/tony-poll-top-three-audra-mcdonald-wins-fans-hearts-on-top-of-a-sixth-tony-with-heartfelt-acceptance-speech/.

50. "Q&A: What Happened in Ferguson?", *New York Times,* Updated on November 25, 2014, online at http:// online at www.nytimes.com/interactive/2014/08/13/us/ferguson-missouri-town-under-siege-after-police-shooting.html.

51. Scooby Axson, "Mo'ne Davis on This Week's National Sports Illustrated Cover," *SI.com,* August 19-20, 2014, online at http://www.si.com/more-sports/2014/08/19/mone-davis-little-league-world-series-sports-illustrated-cover.

52. Jenée Desmond-Harris, "Skip Gates' 'Many Rivers' Premieres," *TheRoot.com,* October 22, 2013; Hilton Als, "A Magisterial Slave Documentary," *New Yorker,* September 11, 2014.

53. Jamelle Bouie, "Tim Scott Will Rise Again," *Slate.com,* November 10, 2014, online at http://www.slate.com/articles/news_and_politics/politics/2014/11/tim_scott_won_south_carolina_s_senate_seat_the_first_black_republican_senator.html.

54. Russell Berman, "Loretta Lynch, America's Next Attorney General," *TheAtlantic.com,* April 23, 2015; "Attorney General Loretta E. Lynch Delivers Remarks at Swearing-In by Vice President Joe Biden," *Justice News,* The United States Department of Justice, April 27, 2015, at online at http://www.justice.gov/opa/speech/attorney-general-loretta-e-lynch-delivers-remarks-swearing-vice-president-joe-biden.

55. Jay Caspian Kang, "Our Demand Is Simple: Stop Killing Us," *New York Times Magazine,* May 4, 2015; Lindsay Holst, "President Obama Delivers a Statement on the Ferguson Grand Jury's Decision," *The White House Blog,* November 24, 2014, online at http://www.whitehouse.gov/blog/2014/11/24/president-obama-delivers-statement-ferguson-grand-jurys-decision; Jelani Cobb, "Chronicle of a Riot Foretold," *The New Yorker,* November 25, 2014, online at http://www.newyorker.com/news/daily-comment/chronicle-ferguson-riot-michael-brown; United States Department of Justice-Civil Rights Division, "Investigation of the Ferguson Police Department," March 4, 2015, 2.

56. Catherine Shoard, "Selma Cast and Crew Wear 'I Can't Breathe' T-shirts to New York Premiere," *The Guardian,* December 15, 2014, online at http://www.theguardian.com/film/2014/dec/15/selma-cast-wear-i-cant-breathe-t-shirts-new-york-premiere-martin-luther-king.

57. Justin Moyer, "The Tragedy behind Fox's 'Empire': Lee Daniels's Father Beat Him for Being Gay," *Washington Post*, January 22, 2015; James Hibberd, "*Empire* Ratings: Guess What Just Happened," *EW.com,* February 19, 2015.

58. "This MLK Day, We Will #ReclaimMLK," *Ferguson Action* Web site, January 15-19, 2015, online at http://fergusonaction.com/reclaim-mlk; "Commemorating King's Legacy and Invoking Change," *New York Times,* January 19, 2015, online at http://www.nytimes.com/2015/01/20/us/martin-luther-king-day.html; King quoted in John Herbers, "Alabama Vote Drive Opened by Dr. King," *New York Times,* January 3, 1965.

59. Rebecca Kaplan, "John Lewis Reflects on Selma Marches," CBSNews.com, February 15, 2015.

60. President Barack H. Obama, "Remarks by the President at the 50th Anniversary of the Selma to Montgomery Marches," The White House: Office of the Press Secretary, March 7, 2015, online at https://www.whitehouse.gov/the-press-office/2015/03/07/remarks-president-50th-anniversary-selma-montgomery-marches.

61. Sarah Kaplan, "For Charleston's Emanuel AME Church, Shooting Is Another Painful Chapter in Rich History," *Washington Post*, June 18, 2015. Henry Louis Gates, Jr., "Henry Louis Gates: If Clementa Pinckney Had Lived," *New York Times*, June 18, 2015

ACKNOWLEDGMENTS

Without the support of a talented, unfailingly dedicated team, this illustrated chronology would "still" be a dream, unable to "rise." The authors would especially like to thank their colleague, Dr. Sheldon Cheek, Senior Curatorial Associate at the Hutchins Center for African and African American Research at Harvard University, for his creativity and help in identifying images for this book and securing the appropriate permissions for their use. Sheldon's artistic eye and attention to detail have been crucial at every stage. Also critical were the contributions of the project's historical researchers, Dr. Steven Niven, Dr. Robert Heinrich, and Dr. Carra Glatt, who worked with the authors at an extraordinary pace last winter to assess and compile the raw materials of the book, with an expansive view of what has comprised the African American experience across fields, time, and space, from politics to religion to business, entertainment, the high arts, science, social justice, and beyond. Special thanks, too, are owed to Julie Wolf, who copyedited the manuscript at a critical early stage, and to graphic designer Chris Welch, who helped to translate the initial concept of this illustrated chronology into various sample layouts.

Along the way, *And Still I Rise* benefited from the wisdom of the brilliant production team working on Professor Gates's companion PBS series, *And Still I Rise,* beginning with senior producers Leslie Asako Gladsjo, Sabin Streeter, and Rachel Dretzin, and extending to the remarkable staff they have assembled at Ark Media, including series producers Talleah Bridges McMahon and Leah Williams. Also vital, as ever, has been Professor Gates's production partner, Dyllan McGee of McGee Media, a driving force on all of Professor Gates's documentary films. Bill Gardner, Vice President of Programming and Development at PBS, was indispensable as well, especially in thinking through the audience for the film and, by extension, this book.

For his decisiveness and vision in championing the publication of *And Still I Rise,* the authors are indebted to Daniel Halpern, Ecco's cofounder and impresario at HarperCollins. Collaborating with Dan and his dedicated team has been a joy. Bridget Read, in particular, deserves thanks for her efforts in shepherding the text and image files through the production process. The same must be said of the literary agent who brought this book to market, Paul Lucas.

And Still I Rise has had countless other shepherds along the way. The authors are deeply grateful to all those who not only believed but let their inspiration to this project. Nothing means more, or is more valuable, than the constancy of friends, colleagues, and family, especially: Marial Iglesias Utset, Abby Wolf, Amy Gosdanian, Anna Barranca-Burke, and Sharon and Brian Burke. To quote that illustrious maestro of the Black Power era, Sly Stone, "It's a Family Affair."

A certain humility comes with studying history year-by-year, almost month-to-month, as we have done in this book, accompanied by a profound sense of wonder at the ways individuals, families, even entire communities, manage to rise, despite so many setbacks and disappointments, not least the often overwhelming uncertainty of a future of race relations in the United States informed by the long duree of slavery and Jim Crow racism, legacies of both of which still contribute to the structural causes of anti-black racism that continue to plague our society today. Nevertheless, the spirit of hope, determination, sacrifice, commitment, and triumph embodied in the plethora of remarkable stories of astonishing black achievement over the last half century that we have compiled in this book, argues strongly for the continued progress of our country toward fulfilling Martin Luther King's dream of a bias-free nation over the next half century. What a tribute to the centenary of Dr. King's martyrdom that would be! Towards that goal, and for the history that marks our rising from coordinates deep, deep in the past, the authors dedicate this wonderful project.

INDEX

ABOUT THE AUTHORS

HENRY LOUIS GATES, JR., is the Alphonse Fletcher University Professor and Director of the Hutchins Center for African & African American Research at Harvard University. An Emmy Award–winning filmmaker, literary scholar, journalist, cultural critic, and institution builder, Professor Gates has authored or co-authored twenty books and created fourteen documentary films, including *Wonders of the African World*, *African American Lives*, *Black in Latin America*, and *Finding Your Roots*, series three of which is currently in production. His six-part PBS documentary series, *The African Americans: Many Rivers to Cross* (2013), which he wrote, executive produced, and hosted, earned the Emmy Award for Outstanding Historical Program: Long Form, as well as the Peabody Award, Alfred I. duPont–Columbia University Award, and NAACP Image Award. Having written for such leading publications as the *New Yorker*, the *New York Times*, and *Time*, Professor Gates now serves as chairman of *TheRoot.com*, a daily online magazine he co-founded in 2008, while overseeing the Oxford African American Studies Center, the first comprehensive scholarly online resource in the field. In 2012, *The Henry Louis Gates, Jr. Reader*, a collection on his writings, was published.

The recipient of fifty-five honorary degrees and numerous prizes, Professor Gates was a member of the first class awarded "Genius Grants" by the MacArthur Foundation in 1981, and in 1998, he became the first African American scholar to be awarded the National Humanities Medal. He was named to *Time*'s 25 Most Influential Americans list in 1997, to *Ebony*'s Power 150 list in 2009, and to *Ebony*'s Power 100 list in 2010 and 2012. He earned his BA in English Language and Literature, summa cum laude, from Yale University in 1973, and his MA and PhD in English Literature from Clare College at the University of Cambridge in 1979. Professor Gates has directed the W. E. B. Du Bois Institute for African and African American Research—now the Hutchins Center—since arriving at Harvard in 1991, and during his first fifteen years on campus, he chaired the Department of Afro-American Studies as it expanded into the Department of African and African American Studies with a full-fledged doctoral program. He also is a member of the American Academy of Arts and Letters and serves on a wide array of boards, including the New York Public Library, the NAACP Legal Defense Fund, the Aspen Institute, Jazz at Lincoln Center, the Whitney Museum of American Art, Library of America, and the Brookings Institution.

KEVIN M. BURKE is the Director of Research at the Hutchins Center for African & African American Research at Harvard University, and serves as president of the Downing Film Center, an award-winning nonprofit independent movie theater he helped launch in Newburgh, New York, in 2006.

Dr. Burke graduated magna cum laude from Harvard College in 1998 and cum laude from Harvard Law School in 2003. He also received his master's degree in History and his PhD in the History of American Civilization from Harvard in 2004 and 2006, respectively.

A member of the New York State Bar, Dr. Burke is currently serving as a Senior Historical Advisor to Professor Gates's documentary film series *Finding Your Roots 3* and *And Still I Rise: Black America After MLK*. He and his wife, Anna Barranca-Burke, reside in Brooklyn, New York.